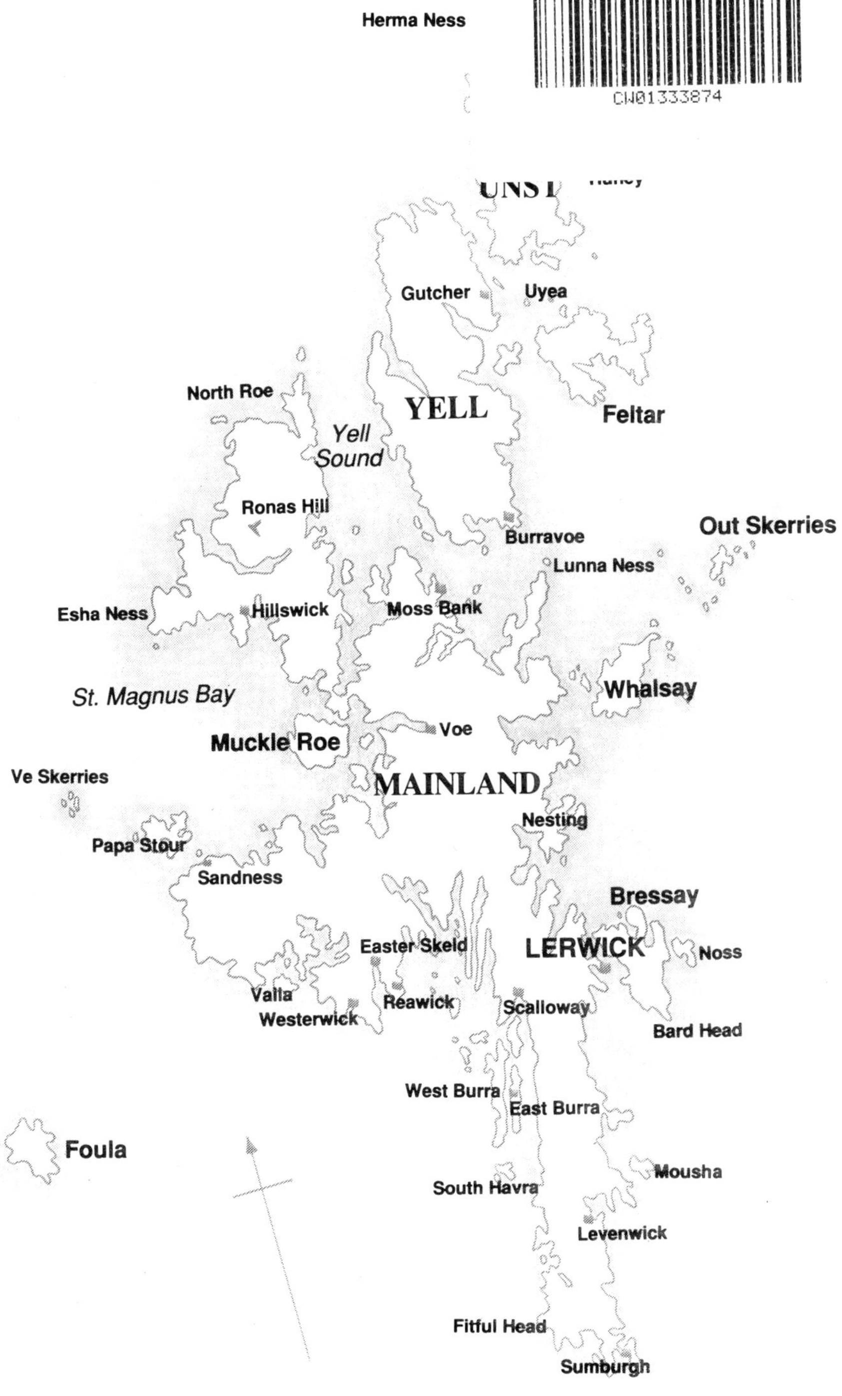

Herma Ness

UNST

Gutcher Uyea

North Roe

YELL Feltar

Yell Sound

Ronas Hill

Burravoe Out Skerries
Lunna Ness

Esha Ness Hillswick Moss Bank

St. Magnus Bay Whalsay

Muckle Roe Voe

Ve Skerries

MAINLAND

Nesting

Papa Stour

Sandness

Bressay

Easter Skeld LERWICK Noss

Valla Reawick Scalloway
Westerwick Bard Head

West Burra
East Burra

Foula

Mousha

South Havra

Levenwick

Fitful Head

Sumburgh

Jan Moody - 'at home with some of her friends'

SHETLAND SHEEPDOGS
— The Sheltie

by Jan Moody

Published by
Bredicot Publications
The Old Rectory, Bredicot,
Spetchley, Worcester WR7 4QA

© Jan Moody

All rights reserved. No part of this publication may be reproduced, stored in any retrieval system, or transmitted, in any form or by any means, without prior permission, in writing, of the publisher.

First published 1990

ISBN 0-9516812-0-6

Jacket front: Janetstown Jorrocks
Jacket back: Felthorn Our Kate and Jack Point of Janetstown

Phototypeset in 10 on $11^{1}/_{2}$ point New Century Schoolbook and
Printed and Bound by: Elgar Printing Limited,
Unit 7, Barrs Court Trading Estate, Hereford, England.
Design & Publishing Consultants: Rivers Media Services,
30 Haydock Avenue, Hereford, England.

Contents

Foreword	vii
Acknowledgements	viii
Introducing the Shetland Sheepdog	ix
Origins of the Breed	1
Development of the Breed	7
Post-War Development	11
Influential Dogs and Bitches - Lines and Families	15
The Breed Standards 1908 - 1986	49
The current Breed Standard, 1986	57
Buying the Sheltie Puppy	77
Bringing up the Sheltie Puppy	81
Responsible Dog Ownership	89
Feeding	92
Grooming	97
Breeding	115
The Bitch	119
The Stud Dog	124
Whelping and Rearing	127
Bringing up the Show Puppy	145
Showing	157
Judging	168
Training	181
General Health	200
Useful Addresses	222
General Index	223

To the memory of my father - John Godrich
who schemed with me to find my first Sheltie
and would have so enjoyed seeing this book
in print.

Foreword

Jan Moody is a person of varied talents and interests. Although the men in her life have been known to murmur whimsically about the trials of living in a household where her son is called Toby and dogs answer to William, George and Henry, they have to admit that her pre-occupation with four legs has not submerged a compensating interest in both two and four wheels. Jan met her husband John in competitive motor sport where she won awards at Silverstone and Shelsley Walsh, whilst Toby's choice of a speed machine ensures that family holidays take in some of the more scenic stretches of the Tour de France.

Jan acquired her first Shetland Sheepdog, whom she worked in Obedience, in 1957. After showing at Camborne Show in Cornwall in 1958 Jan met the knowledgeable Cornish breeder Mr. C. V. Smale and she decided that her Sheltie did not look a bit like the rest. She is however a quick learner and soon acquired a granddaughter of the great Helensdale Ace whom she mated to an Ace grandson to produce Ch. Janetstown Jacqualine in 1961. Since then she has made up three more Champions and another couple of Janetstowns are currently on their way to their titles.

She has judged the breed throughout Scandinavia and has been invited to judge at Crufts Jubilee Show in 1991.

Having had previous interests in rabbits, show ponies and pedigree sheep Jan also ran a Poodle grooming business. She now maintains a small, specialised boarding kennel for Shelties.

This combination of activities contributes to her reputation as a successful breeder with a wide knowledge of the general care of dogs, and as a perfectionist in show-ring presentation.

A hard working and enthusiastic member of the English Shetland Sheepdog Club's Committee, she is currently its Vice Chairman.

It would be difficult to think of a person better qualified to write a really practical, factual book on the Sheltie. The beginner will find a great deal of sound advice, whilst many experienced exhibitors will be only too keen to pick her brains.

Mary Davis
September, 1990

Acknowledgements

Writing this book has been one of the most exacting tasks I have ever undertaken, if I had realised quite what was involved I may never have even started! However, without the encouragement, patience and help given by my husband John and son Toby none of it could have happened.

Particular thanks go to Mary Roslin-Williams for her guidance and encouragement, Anne Roslin-Williams for her advice and the majority of the excellent photographs and Ken Barber M.R.C.V.S. Dip.Opthal. for his advice on veterinary matters.

Grateful thanks also to Professor Stanley Bowie, Margaret Collett, Mary Davis, Margaret Dobson, Judy Entwistle, June Johns, Mavis Mills and Carol Wood and acknowledgements for help from The Kennel Club, The English Shetland Sheepdog Club, Pedigree Petfoods Limited and The Shetland Library for the use of their material. Additionally to all those who have supplied photographs.

I hope that the book will answer some of the everyday questions I am frequently asked about Shelties. So many things are taken for granted by the experienced breeder and one tends to forget that there are those who may never have owned a dog before. Not everything can be covered but I have hopefully glanced on those aspects that are significant to the breed.

Photographs by:
Anne Roslin-Williams, Diane Pearce, Cooke, Mike Davis, J. Doherty, John Francis, Gerwyn Gibbs, David Hawkins, Anne Helenius, Marc Henrie, Esmee Jones, John Moody, Toby Moody, Graham Russell, David Sharp, Colin Swift, David Terry, Bill Tingley, Betrand Unne, Anna Uthorn.

Diagrams:
Jan Moody and Toby Moody.

Grateful thanks for support from Croft Engineering, Phillips Yeast Products Limited, Shaws Pet Products Limited and Vetbed (Animal Care) Limited.

Introducing the Shetland Sheepdog

THE SHETLAND SHEEPDOG, or Sheltie is a most delightful and attractive breed of dog. They resemble the Rough Collie in miniature, the ideal size being $14\frac{1}{2}$ inches (37 cms) at the shoulder for a dog and 14 inches (35.5 cms) for a bitch. Their advantages are their size, their lovely temperament, devotion and willingness to please. They are relatively light in build under their double coat, weighing around 16 - 18 pounds (7.26 kg - 8.17 kg). I often say that they have the ideal type of coat as they do have 'clothes' but have clean faces, legs and feet.

They will keep themselves remarkably clean, licking their legs and paws like a cat when wet. The coat is as easy as any to care for and even when they shed their coat the hair is easily removed from your carpet or clothes. Regular weekly grooming keeps the coat tidy and the occasional bath when moulting helps remove the dead hair and keeps them sweet smelling.

Shelties make an excellent family dog and are very good with children of all ages. They are very sociable and will mix politely with other dogs but may display an initial characteristic reserve towards strangers. They need to be with their owners the majority of the time and will travel happily in the car. Two Shelties create great interest when out together.

They expect their regular walks and will enjoy going anywhere at whatever time and for however long.

Being extremely intelligent the breed is very popular for working in obedience and with their great jumping ability show great proficiency at agility.

As a breed they can be exceedingly vocal, this can sometimes be an advantage as they make excellent burglar alarms, nobody is allowed within their territory without an announcement.

Once having had a Sheltie few people would want any other breed.

They will laugh with you and cry with you, be sympathetic to your moods and be a great companion for many years.

Origins of the Breed

WHEN asked by a totally non-doggy person to describe the appearance of a Shetland Sheepdog I will very often say they resemble a 'miniature Lassie Collie'. This statement brings instant recognition to the layman but sends shudders down the backs of many a purist Sheltie person. I remember being castigated by a well known breeder for having advertised my first litter as "Shetland Sheepdogs (miniature Lassies)" and although she was correct in saying they are not a miniaturised Rough Collie there is undoubtedly a good deal of Collie blood in the breed as there were deliberate crossings done after the first World War. This was done quite openly at the time although not always approved of by the purists.

There seem to be many conflicting ideas as to the original purpose of the little dogs with so many stories and myths told over the years regarding the history of the Shetland Sheepdog. Some could be true, most is conjecture and the rest could be complete fabrication. However, all stories get better with the telling and in my research into the breed history I naturally turned to breed books. Apart from one book a good deal has been written but with widespread variations. I had presumed that everything there was to know had already been said.

I spoke to Professor Stanley Bowie, a Shetlander at present living in

Lithograph by John Irvine, 1830

<u>*Something out of the ordinary*</u>

SHETLAND SHEEP-DOGS

The Original Type
of these
**Miniature
Delightful Working Collies**

(<u>Not</u> Miniature Show Collies)

☐

Apply to

Dr. J. C. Bowie
PARK HALL
BIXTER, SHETLAND, SCOTLAND

☐

See illustration in this work

Dr. Bowie advertised his dogs in the 1920's as the original type - for keeping stray animals off the arable land.

Devon. His father, Dr. J. C. Bowie, was born in Lerwick in 1867. He and his father before him, bred the dogs that were advertised as the Shetland Sheep-dog. I am led to believe that the name 'Sheltie' is purely a mainland term and has never been used by the Islanders.

Dr. Bowie thought that the most authentic early picture of the Shetland breed was the lithograph by John Irvine (1830).

This dog was probably around 14 inches high and as the head can scarcely be seen little comment can be made about the type.

What we do know is that our breed is based on a variety of breeds and has on more than one occasion been described as a mongrel, a very apt description when one sees such a variety of types that still exist, even today.

The Shetland Islands belonged to Norway until 1469 and it is thought that Shetland Sheepdogs originally came from that country with the Vikings about 700-800 A.D. The same pioneers settled in the Faeroes, Iceland and Greenland so it is no wonder that there is a resemblance to the Spitz and Yakki dogs due to the undoubted movement between these countries. The small sheep, ponies and cattle of the islands have a separate evolutionary history due to their isolation.

One can imagine from the situation of the Shetland Isles, standing some fifty miles off the north coast of Scotland, that it was a very convenient place for trading and fishing boats from places such as Norway and Iceland, as well as the mainland, to shelter from the elements. The story goes that many of these boats carried a companion

Miss Hunter's Shetland Collie at the County Show, August 9th 1905.

dog on board who obviously enjoyed their stay, meeting other canines and adding their influence to the already mixed population. Sailors would take the resulting attractive, fluffy puppies back home as pets which helped to spread their popularity.

On the Islands, as the story continues, a small dog was selected as it was cheap to feed and did not take up too much room in the small crofts or toons as the farms or smallholdings were called. Hence the name Toonie dog.

Many people have been under the misapprehension that the Shelties' purpose in life was to be a herder and one conjures up visions of them working in a similar way to the Border Collie. This never has been the case. It is a myth that the early dogs were sent off for miles across the islands to gather the sheep. In fact if you talk to the Islanders they do not know the Sheltie as we know it as a breed. It was just a dog around the toon.

There were 'Shetland Sheepdog Trials' but these were not for our breed but for the true working sheepdogs brought onto the Islands specifically for the purpose of herding the sheep. These larger breeds of collie were introduced around 1840-1850 when the commercial sheep farmers from Scotland cleared the heather from many of the crofts to make way for easier grazing.

The working sheepdogs were crossed with the Toonie dogs which gave them a degree of herding ability which would no doubt have proved useful when the sheep were being tended around the crofts. There is no way that the Sheltie would have been sent off to gather the sheep, as seen in sheepdog trials, as they would have been unable to cope with the heather which dominated the Islands, it being at least nine to eighteen inches high. The Sheltie at that time was only 12" high.

The Sheltie came into its own around the croft, driving the sheep away, as opposed to herding, and guarding the farmers' cultivated unfenced ground from any stray sheep trying to gain an easy meal from his crops.

One can only assume that in temperament, little has changed. Today's Shelties are notoriously vocal and retain their guarding instinct and nobody, but nobody, is allowed within their territory without that excited chorus; a characteristic which was obviously inherited from his predecessors although, I am told by some, that they were not quite as noisy as they are these days.

The original *Toonie* dog is sometimes called the *Peerie* dog. The term Peerie dog comes from the Shetland word *piri* which is of old Norse origin and means small. Small is a word associated with fairies hence the term *Fairy* dog.

The Sheltie has no doubt evolved from several breeds, which can clearly be seen from some of the early photographs, with one resembling

Shetland Collie at the County Show 1905 - a marked resemblance to a King Charles Spaniel

a King Charles Spaniel!

The Yakki Dog from Iceland is reputed to be responsible for the smutty muzzles still occasionally seen.

The Norwegian Buhund gave us the wheaten sable and the Pomeranian could well be there somewhere. He could well have been the one to have left us with a legacy of small prick ears, round eyes and apple skulls. We use the expression Pommy as a description today for Shelties displaying these characteristics.

The little dogs were regularly exhibited on the Islands and it was around 1905 that the occasional Sheltie appeared at shows on the mainland.

The deliberate introduction of the Working Collie, for better working ability stamped more of a type on this 12" dog but also raised his size, with the effect that when the Shetland Collie Club was formed in 1908 there were two Stud books, one being the "A" list for dogs under 12 inches high and the other "B" list for dogs over 12 inches. The records of the "A" list are, to say the least, a little sparse on any direct parentage. There were no records at all from the "B" list and it died out. So there was very little documented history prior to that time.

The Scottish Shetland Collie Club was formed in 1909 and the breed's popularity spread south. It was in 1913 that the breed was supposedly recognised by the Kennel Club.

My research revealed that they were first listed as Shetland Sheepdogs by the Kennel Club in the October 1909 issue of the Kennel Gazette, contrary to the popular belief that they were known as Shetland Collies until 1914. Previous to 1909 they were listed in the Kennel Gazette as 'Shetland Collies' in the section for 'Foreign and Rare breeds'.

In April 1914 a notice appeared in the Kennel Gazette. It was an application to the Kennel Club to form the English Shetland Sheepdog

Club. This was published as granted in the June 1914 issue.

Previous stories say that the application was made as 'The English Shetland *Collie* Club'. This title may have been talked about but the breed must have been recognised as 'The Shetland Sheepdog' as it was catalogued as such by the Kennel Club in the Kennel Gazette issue of October 1909.

Therefore the Shetland Sheepdog as we know it today is a relatively new breed and although their origins remain in the Shetlands it is a breed which has evolved on the Scottish mainland and further south, in England, where the majority of breeding took place after the 1914-18 War.

The English Shetland Sheepdog Club which has always been regarded as 'the Mother Club' of the breed has maintained a continuity that has assured the future of the breed. There cannot be many clubs that have had only six secretaries in 75 years.

Miss Shove, the club's first secretary, cannot have had an easy task, trying to steer a new breed off the ground literally days before the outbreak of the First World War.

In 1918 Miss Grey took the office until 1928 when Miss Clara Bowring took over until 1948.

Miss Day Currie continued until 1962 and Mrs. Win Thatcher held office for 20 years until Dick Thornley became secretary in 1982 when she became Chairman.

The Larkbeare Kennels - Mrs. Lumsden and Miss Clara Bowring with some of their old favourites

Development of the Breed

IN 1917 dog shows ceased and breeding was dramatically reduced. In 1918 only three Shelties were registered at the Kennel Club and a total of 152 during the period 1914-18. Type was varied and there were relatively few dogs to draw from at that time.

At the end of the war the idea of introducing a Rough Collie cross was put into action. This was not relished by the purists who wished to make haste more slowly. They could foresee many problems such as size and the over-long foreface, problems we are still faced with today. At the time all the breed clubs' Standards mentioned in their paragraph on General Appearance, that the breed should resemble a show Collie in miniature, so it did not sound unreasonable to help it along by carrying out those Collie crosses.

Miss Humphries of the 'Mountfort' affix was the first to take the plunge when she bought a small Collie bitch called Teena, who was interestingly out of a sable bitch but by a blue merle dog (blue merles were unheard of in the original Shetland Collie). She was mated to Wallace, a son of Butcher Boy who was to lend his name to the BB Line, one of the two male tail Lines active in the breed today. The Wallace to

Ch. Eltham Park Eureka

Teena mating produced War Baby of Mountfort. A son of War Baby, Rufus of Mountfort, was then mated to another Teena daughter thereby doubling up on the Collie and stamping more type. The result was Ch. Specks of Mountfort who was then mated to a granddaughter of Teena which produced Peter Pan of Mountfort. He changed hands several times before being acquired by Mr. E. C. Pierce who changed his name to Eltham Park Eureka. He was one of the greatest winners of the time and a significant stud dog in the breed's history. Not only was he in-bred to Teena, the Collie, but he was also in-bred to Wallace. Regrettably he was sold to America, where the majority of Mr. Pierce's dogs went, but fortunately not before his influence had been established. His descendents, through the BB Line, maintain the most prolific and continuous line down to present day Shelties. Teena was later sold to Mr. J. G. Saunders of the Helensdale Affix.

Pedigree of **Ch Eltham Park Eureka** (formerly Peter Pan of Mountfort) born 1925

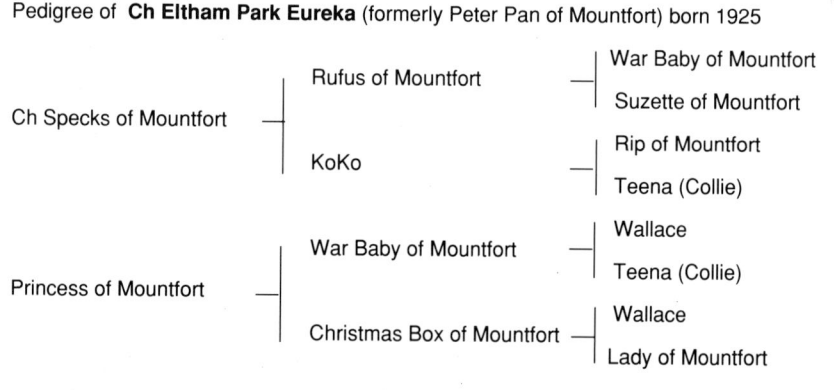

The export of the Shetland Sheepdog to America was big business particularly through Mr. E. C. Pierce who seemed to purchase good dogs, campaign them to their titles then sell them, often changing their names in the process. Many excellent dogs were sold when their influence could well have been used to greater advantage in this country. Whereas the Collie crossing was accepted to a point, difficulties in obtaining registrations for these American dogs compounded the situation and the export market diminished.

When I first came into the breed in 1959 I was quietly assured that there were still some Collie crossings being done (unofficially, of course) which may account for the great variations in size still being encountered today.

In 1923 the height was raised to between 12 and 15 inches, the ideal being $13^1/_2$ inches, where it remained for many years. With all the Collie influence the increase in size was somewhat inevitable. There was also great controversy with regard to the head type. Some favoured the longer Collie head and others wished to keep the original Shetland type that was in existence when the breed was first recognised. At a later date Miss Clara Bowring verbally disapproved of the Collie type.

The early Kennels

Of the early affixes, 'Kilravock' was registered by Miss Thynne in 1914 as was Miss Grey and Miss Hill's 'Greyhill'. The 'Mountforts' were registered in 1915 and in 1917 Miss Day Currie formed her famous 'Bonheur' kennel. In 1921 it was the 'Larkbeares' of Miss Clara Bowring as well as Mr. Pierce's 'Eltham Park'.

Shelties being judged c.1923 - Left to right: Miss Hill with Hurley Burley, Mrs. Lowes with Kep and Sandy, Miss Currie with Tarn, Miss Grey with Comfrey and Miss Humphries with Fifinella. Golliwog of Mountfort is seen in the foreground

In 1925 Mrs. Baker formed the very famous 'Houghton Hill' kennel at the same time as the name that is synonymous with Shelties, Mr. J. G. Saunders' 'Helensdale'. The following year Mr. and Mrs. Campbell's 'Tilford', Dr. Todd's 'Clerwood' and Mrs. Rae Fraser's 'Fetlar' affixes were registered. 1926 also saw the 'Cameliards' of Mrs. Allen and her daughter Mrs. Nicholson. In 1927 Mrs. Baker's daughter, Mrs. Geddes, registered her own 'Exford' affix. Mrs. Geddes was later to become Mrs. Constance Sangster.

Mr. Bob Taylor's 'Wyndoras' were beginning to make their mark at that time.

In the 1930's Mr. Hendry's famous 'Aberlours' were founded followed by Miss Bootle Wilbraham's 'Wansdykes' and Miss Wright's 'Michelmere'.

It was in 1932 that the world renowned Riverhill affix was registered by the Misses Patience and Felicity Rogers. A true landmark in the history of the Shetland Sheepdog as their extremely clever breeding, over a span of 50 years, had such a tremendous influence on the breed as a whole. The Riverhill line is greatly revered throughout the world and many of the present day kennels are based on these bloodlines. The Rogers were true stock people and recognised good conformation whether it was horses or dogs. Their knowledge and experience was so willingly imparted and their records, so religiously kept, are a marvellous legacy for the breed.

To continue on into the 1930's, in 1935 Mr. E. Watts' 'Dryfesdales' came about, in 1936 Miss Singles' 'Tibbets' and Miss Margaret Osborne's 'Shiel'. Miss Osborne initiated the charts for the English Shetland Sheepdog Club (E.S.S.C.) Handbooks which are an ongoing record of the breed, documenting the pedigree of every Champion and C.C. winner in the breed and allows one to be able to trace the origins of one's own dog's pedigree. Miss Osborne was a formidable character with very individual but definitive ideas whilst being very forthright.

1936 and Mr. Alf Broughton's 'Fydell' and Miss Olwen Gwynne-Jones 'Callart' were first registered. There are many Callarts behind the dogs of today, particularly through Ch Orpheus of Callart.

Immediately prior to the Second World War in 1938 came Mrs. Fishpool's 'Ellington's' and in 1939 Miss Charley's 'Foula'.

Fortunately for the breed, during the period between the Wars there were a healthy number of kennels established that were to become the backbone of the breed, and the true foundation of the Sheltie, as we know it today, was moulded then.

During the Second World War there were no Championship shows but there were still one or two Open shows, which did help to maintain the interest. Breeding ticked over and gradually increased towards the end of the War. In 1941 registrations dropped to their lowest total of 78; there having been 476 in 1938, 329 in 1939 and 100 in 1940. By 1946 they had reached a total of 417 for the year.

There were a few influential kennels formed during the war, notably Mrs. Charlton's 'Melvaig' and Mr. and Mrs. George Bellas-Simpsons' 'Hallinwood's'. It was after the war that such names as Mr. E. J. Allsop's 'Merrion' and Mrs. Aileen Greig's 'Lydwell' came into being. Aileen Greig was one of those rare characters who in the early '60s passed on a few pearls of wisdom which have stayed with me over the years and have proved extremely useful.

Post-War Development

BOTH pre and post Second World War the Helensdale kennel of Mr. Jim Saunders from Aberdeen were a strong force consistently producing leading and influential dogs. Ch. Helensdale Bhan created history by jumping the fence and mating his own mother Helensdale Gentle Lady. The result was Ch. Helensdale Ace who was a striking golden sable with an uneven blaze. Everyone who saw him could not help but be impressed and he became the first Sheltie to win best dog of the day, overall, this was at Birmingham City Championship Show in 1951. He won 11 C.C.s in total, a record for the breed.

Probably his most famous son was Ch. Alasdair of Tintobank, bred by Mr. W. E. Guthrie of Sutton Coldfield who based his 'Tintobank' kennel on Helensdale stock.

In 1951 two very forthright sisters from Yorkshire, Miss Beryl and Miss Joan Herbert bought a bitch from the Misses Rogers, namely

J. G. Saunders showing Ch. Helendale Ace

Kath Jeffries with Ch. Heathlow Luciana, and Alan Jeffries with Jefsfire By Achievement

Riverhill Royal Flush. She became a Champion and with Riverhill Rosalie were the foundation of the famous 'Shelert' kennel. The always approachable sisters have a tremendously dominant line and have bred 26 British Champions with 17 others having won C.C.s. Over the years they have exported to 13 different countries where so many gained their titles.

The 1950's also saw the rise of the 'Dilhornes' of Mrs. Cynthia Charlesworth when a dog that she had bred and was actually working as a sheepdog, became a Champion. He was Ch. Dilhorne Norseman of Melvaig. He sired Ch. Dilhorne Blackcap who was to become such a prominent sire.

A young couple who were interested in Shelties and were very successful with their Jefsfire Rough Collies were Alan and Kath Jeffries. They bought a bitch puppy by Ch. Francis of Merrion from Mrs. Heather Lowe of the Heathlows' she was Heathlow Luciana. They campaigned her to her title and she then produced that amazing sire Ch. Jefsfire Freelancer.

During the 1950's Shelties had become increasingly popular and even more so during the 1960's, reaching seventh most popular breed in the

Kennel Club registration charts. Fortunately numbers levelled out and they have remained around twelfth or below ever since.

Not being the easiest or most prolific of breeders has had a self levelling effect with regard to the numbers of puppies available.

We are lucky that there is always a nucleus of dedicated breeders who assure the breed's continuity. There is always a vast turnover of enthusiasts who come in with a great flourish only to fall by the wayside when they find their initial flush of success, in both breeding and in the show ring, difficult to follow.

Present day successful established kennels, which will hopefully assure the breed's future are Mrs. Jean Angell's 'Rockaround', the Beaden sisters' 'Myriehewe', Mrs. Rosalind Crossley's 'Willow Tarn', Miss Mary Gatheral's 'Herds', Mrs. Rosemary Marshall's 'Forestland', Mrs. Margaret Norman's Francehill', Mr. Derek Rigby's 'Lythwood' and Dick and Barbara Thornley's 'Felthorn'. These kennels have been mentioned as they have all bred consistently for several generations and have a strong and influential male and, or, female lines that are benefitting the new breeders.

Already in the history books, but still making their mark, are Miss Diana Blount's 'Rhinog' and Miss Mary Davis' 'Monkswood' and, on a smaller scale than during the '50s, Miss Olwen Gwynne-Jones' 'Callart' and of course Alan and Kath Jeffries' 'Jefsfire'.

Col. Sangster exercising Exfords in the New Forest with helper Hugh Russell

When I first started there were a number of large kennels having in excess of fifty dogs at any one time. I remember visiting the Sangster's Exford kennel in the heart of the New Forest during the early 1960s and saw mostly tricolours with the occasional blue merle and sable. I was fascinated at the time as the Sangsters used to fill an old van with half of the dogs, drive across the road then let them all out. They would then go back and collect the rest of them and do the same thing. They would return with the van to the same spot two hours later when the dogs would be waiting to go home! They told me that they had only ever lost one, although I gather that Ch Exford Piskiegye Taw was killed on the road whilst pursuing a stag. He was only four years old.

Today there are very few kennels that have more than twenty dogs. Most smaller 'kennels' have a small number of dogs that are kept in the house and are very much a part of the family.

Left to right: Ch. Riverhill Rather Dark, Ch. Riverhill Rogue, Ch. Riverhill Raider, Ch. Riverhill Richman, Ch. Riverhill Rash Promise and Ch. Riverhill Ratafia

Post-War Influential Lines and Families

THE study of pedigrees and bloodlines can be the most absorbing occupation and anyone who is interested in the breed, and in breeding, cannot fail to spend a considerable amount of time pouring over the family tree of their own dogs. Those who are considering breeding should study the pedigrees of possible stud dogs as well as their own bitch line to see whether there is a link. Club Handbooks provide in-depth information and are a must for any serious breeder.

The English Shetland Sheepdog Club produce and update The Charts with the Handbook every five years. This invaluable and fascinating record originated by the late Miss Margaret Osborne and the late Miss Felicity Rogers of the Riverhills, has become so much a part of the Sheltie breeder's bible and is now in the capable hands of Mrs. Marion Marriage. People who are in the serious business of breeding better Shelties should have all the Charts as reference.

The Charts are the family tree of every dog or bitch that is a Champion or has won a Challenge Certificate in the breed, tracing back to their origins. These are referred to as Lines and Families. The Line, or male tail line, is the top line of the pedigree on the sire's side. The Family, or female tail line, is the bottom line of the pedigree on the bitch side.

The early history and influential pre-war dogs have been written about many times before. Therefore I prefer to concentrate on those dogs and bitches whose influence has continued since the Second War. One cannot try to mention every winning offspring so the emphasis is on those that have bred on and perpetuated the breed.

It is fascinating to see how certain lines have merged successfully in different generations and where outcrossings have paid off. It is also interesting to note how the influence of a particular dog or dogs is not felt until after they are dead. Some may have had a limited stud career but what they produced was of such quality as to have had a great impact on the breed.

Although we often talk only about the tail lines one must not forget the all important sires of dams. The middles of pedigrees are equally important. Some sires appear to be better producers of bitches than others. Ch. Alasdair of Tintobank, who featured so prominently in the Charts as a sire during the 1960s, only appears on the male tail Line significantly through Ch. Trumpeter of Tooneytown, yet he and

Trumpeter sired many bitches who have bred on. Alasdair was the sire of Ch. Riverhill Rare Gold, (Family 9) that amazing bitch to whom the breed owes so much and whose descendents are endless. Ch. Trumpeter of Tooneytown sired the C.C. winner Stormane Sherry who proved her worth as a brood bitch.

A grandson of Trumpeter, Ch. Midnitesun Justin Time sired four bitch Champions but only one dog Champion, Ch. Shemaur Noel Edmunds. Bitches, not featured in the Charts, by Justin Time have bred on well.

Riverhill Rolling Home was the sire of five bitch Champions.

Ch. Jefsfire Freelancer is another dog who, at the same time as producing Champions and C.C. winners of both sexes sired a number of bitches who proved their worth in their own right.

Monkswood Marauder, litter brother to Ch. Monkswood Moss Trooper, sired a number of bitches who have bred on.

Ch. Haytimer of Hanburyhill at Hartmere, having been used extensively during the eighties, produced many Champion and winning bitches as well as siring bitches that have produced Champions and winners. For some years his progeny and grandchildren dominated the show scene as did Ch. Jefsfire Freelancer's during the seventies.

There are other dogs who may not feature in the Charts as C.C. winners or Champions but have made their contribution to winning Lines and Families. A study of pedigrees as a whole will reveal these facts as well as those more famous names who have influenced the dogs in the middle of pedigrees.

The Lines

The Male Tail Line

There are only two male tail Lines in existence and have been for many years. The most influential and dominant male tail Line is the BB line, so named after Butcher Boy, with the CHE, Chestnut Rainbow, line being the other. All the Shelties of today are descended from those two dogs.

Line BB (Butcher Boy)

The post-war dogs who had the most significant bearing on the present day Shetland Sheepdog were all descended from the BB line and Ch. Eltham Park Eureka (born 1925) who was a great-great-great grandson of Butcher Boy. Ch. Helensdale Ace (born 1949) came from one branch of the family. The other branch, through Harvey, was responsible for another two branches via Ch. Orpheus of Callart (born 1948) and Ch. Midas of Shelert (born 1955). Interestingly two of the branches rejoined to produce Ch. Midas of Shelert; Ch. Helensdale Ace was the sire of

Midas' dam Ch. Riverhill Royal Flush. Naturally, all are linked together many many times in the present day dogs.

Ch. Helensdale Bhan

Ch. Helensdale Bhan (born 1947).
by: Fydell Startler.
ex: Helensdale Gentle Lady

Bhan's fame as a stud dog became somewhat overshadowed by the success of one of his sons, Ch. Helensdale Ace. However, he did sire three Champions as well as five C.C. winners. Another son, Helensdale Frolic, was purchased by Miss Margaret Bagot (later to become Mrs Searle and now Mrs Norman). Being resident in the south-east of England meant that Frolic was so situated that a number of breeders had the opportunity of using him. Even so, he was used by Mrs Rosemary Morewood, who lived in Cumbria and produced Ch. Sumburgh Sirius who sired the influential bitch Ch. Star Princess of Callart and Jaylea Chestnut Ripple who had such an influence on Mrs Rosemary Marshall's Forestlands, as well as so many of the Sumburghs. My own first Sheltie was by Helensdale Frolic.

Ch. Helensdale Ace (born 1949)
by: Ch. Helensdale Bhan
ex: Helensdale Gentle Lady

Ch. Helensdale Ace's influence was very considerable producing ten Champions and ten C.C. winners and was directly responsible for much

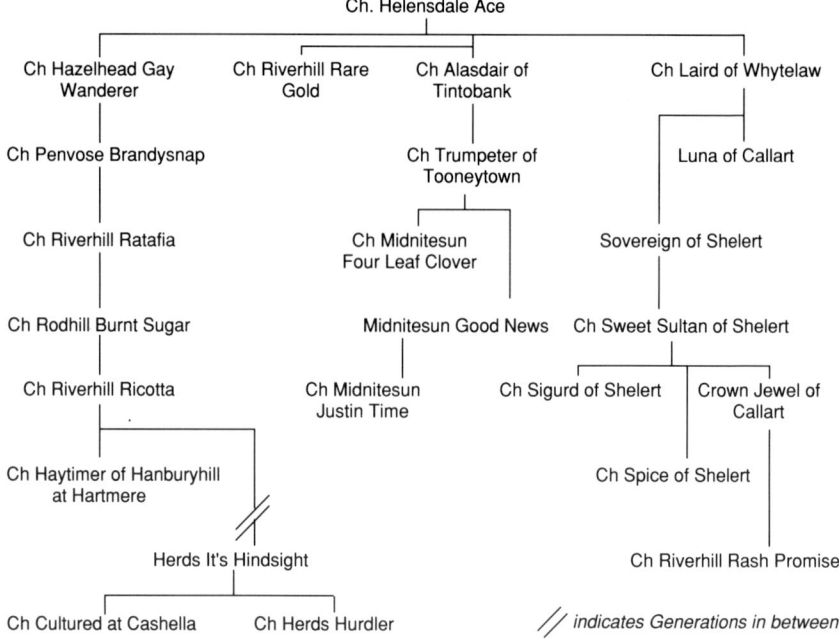

```
                              Ch. Helensdale Ace
          ┌──────────────────────┬──────────────┬──────────────────────┐
  Ch Hazelhead Gay        Ch Riverhill Rare   Ch Alasdair of      Ch Laird of Whytelaw
    Wanderer                    Gold            Tintobank
        │                                          │                    │
  Ch Penvose Brandysnap                      Ch Trumpeter of       Luna of Callart
                                               Tooneytown
        │                                          │                    │
  Ch Riverhill Ratafia                       Ch Midnitesun         Sovereign of Shelert
                                            Four Leaf Clover
        │                                          │                    │
  Ch Rodhill Burnt Sugar                    Midnitesun Good News   Ch Sweet Sultan of Shelert
        │                                          │              ┌─────┴─────────┐
  Ch Riverhill Ricotta                       Ch Midnitesun   Ch Sigurd of Shelert  Crown Jewel of
        │                                      Justin Time                           Callart
  ┌─────┴──────┐                                                                     │
  Ch Haytimer of Hanburyhill                                              Ch Spice of Shelert
    at Hartmere
             //                                                                      │
        Herds It's Hindsight                                              Ch Riverhill Rash Promise
      ┌──────┴──────┐
  Ch Cultured at Cashella    Ch Herds Hurdler          // indicates Generations in between
```

Ch. Helensdale Ace

Ch. Alasdair of Tintobank

of the success of the Hallinwood, Penvose, Shelert and Tintobank kennels of the 1950s, and the continued success of the Riverhills.

On studying the E.S.S.C. Charts 1915-1979, Ace influenced other kennels which are behind present day pedigrees, such as Durnovaria, Heathlow, Janetstown, Lydwell, Midnitesun, Rodhill, Sumburgh and Tooneytown.

He has continued the direct male tail lines to present day dogs through Ch. Alasdair of Tintobank but appears more significantly in the middle of so many pedigrees, as does Ch. Laird of Whytelaw (born 1951) although Laird does not feature now in the male tail Line of the 1990 Charts.

In relation to present day pedigrees Ace is only in direct male tail line, through Ch. Rodhill Burnt Sugar, to the Herds kennel of Mary Gatheral also to that prolific sire, Ch. Haytimer of Hanburyhill at Hartmere.

18

The breed owes a very great deal to Ace, that golden dog with the big, uneven white blaze. Everyone who saw him has said that the dog had a certain charisma and presence that stood him apart from so many others. His life was cut short when at the age of six he was accidentally poisoned. He had visited the neighbour's garden, which he did everytime he went for a walk, the neighbour had put weed-killer down and not shut the gate. On his return Ace sat and licked his paws, in the way that Shelties do, thus ingesting the poison.

Ch. Orpheus of Callart (born 1948)
by: Hector Of Aberlour
ex: Heatherbell of Callart

Ch. Orpheus of Callart, a clear golden sable with full collie markings, was a key sire being in direct line to so many contemporary and prominent stud dogs.

Left: Ch. Orpheus of Callart

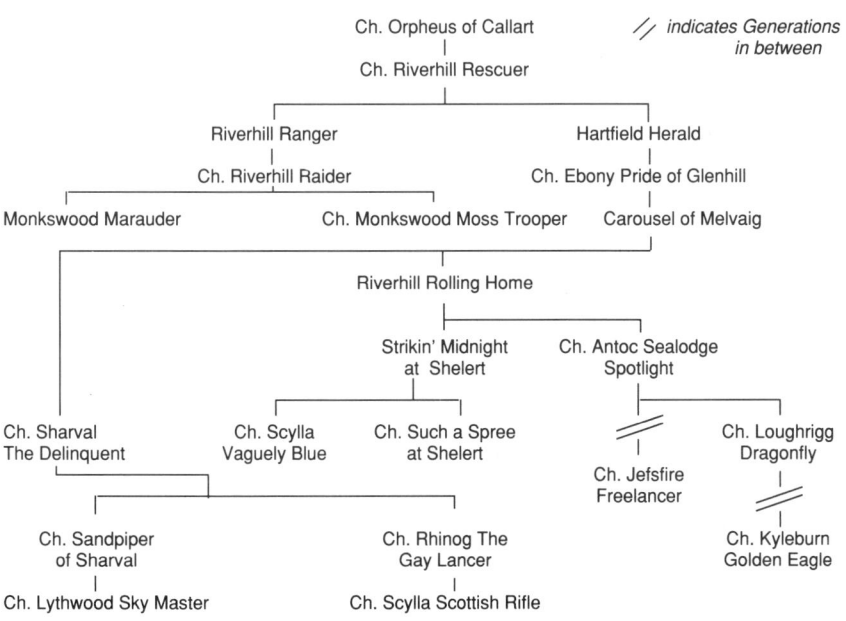

19

Leeds 1958 - Granthorpe Carla, Miss F. M. Rogers (Judge),
Ch. Ebony Pride of Glenhill

Ch. Sharval The Delinquent at 10 months old

Ch. Ebony Pride of Glenhill (born 1956)
By: Hartfield Herald
ex: Una of Tintobank

This influential tricolour was very much a product of the Helensdales as he was out of a daughter of Ch Alasdair of Tintobank (by Ch. Helensdale Ace) and Fiona of Tintobank, who was pure Helensdale.

Ch. Sharval The Delinquent (born 1968)
By: Carousel of Melvaig
ex: Sharval Cilla Black

This dark tricolour was campaigned extensively throughout the U.K. but may have had more stud work had he lived in England rather than Scotland. However, he did sire Ch. Rhinog The Gay Lancer and Ch. Sandpiper of Sharval who have ensured his male tail Line. He became a record holder for the breed winning 15 C.C.s. His combination of Riverhill, Helensdale, Exford and Melvaig lines was obviously a winning formula which has successfully bred on to modern day bloodlines through:

Ch. Rhinog The Gay Lancer (born 1972)
By: Ch. Sharval the Delinquent
ex: Ch. Rhinog Waltzing Matilda

Sired: **Ch. Scylla Scottish Rifle** and the Line has continued through Janetstown Jorrocks, Ch. Jazzman of Janetstown and Colmae Jazz Juke of Janetstown. Another son of Ch. Rhinog The Gay Lancer was Ch. Shetlo The Gay Piper, out of the charming little bitch Ch. Shetlo Sheraleigh.

Ch. Sandpiper of Sharval (born 1976)
By: Ch. Sharval The Delinquent
ex: Chamwood Gay Girl

A very shapely dog who was always presented immaculately and shown to perfection he won 14 C.C.s and 3 Groups as well as being the only Sheltie to achieve Best in Show status at an all-breed Championship show.
Ch. Sandpiper sired Ch. Lythwood Sky Master who features well in modern pedigrees, having sired three Champions; Ch Marnham The Joker, Ch. Lythwood Spaceman and Ch. Marnham Melady at Arcot.
Another branch from Carousel of Melvaig produced Riverhill Rolling Home.

Riverhill Rolling Home

Riverhill Rolling Home (born 1959)
by: Carousel of Melvaig
ex: Ch. Riverhill Rare Gold

Roly had two famous sisters in Ch. Riverhill Rather Rich and Ch. Riverhill Rarity of Glenmist. He was a dog I greatly admired as a newcomer to the breed. His showmanship and presence stood out at the time. He always used his very natural well placed ears, a rarity at the time, which gave him such a lovely expression. To me he was a model of showmanship so ably handled by his owner Miss Mary Davis. Both were an example to follow. Regrettably my own plans to use him were thwarted.

He sired seven Champions: Ch. Antoc Sealodge Spotlight, Ch. Deloraine Dilys of Monkswood, Ch. Monkswood Meridian, Ch. Tumblebays Topaz of Monkswood, Ch. Tumblebays Amethyst, Ch. Riverhill Ring the Bell and Ch. Sharval Small Dark 'n' Handsome, who went abroad, and the amazing tricolour stud dog Strikin' Midnight at Shelert, who is behind so many present day lines of all colours.

Ch. Antoc Sealodge Spotlight (born: 1962)
by: Riverhill Rolling Home
ex: Sealodge Single

As with his sire, Riverhill Rolling Home, I had a very soft spot for

Left to right: Mrs. Aileen Speding and Ch. Antoc Sealodge Spotlight, Judge: Miss Olwen Gwynne-Jones, Mrs. Peggy Nichols and Ch. Bramble of Wytchfields. WELKS 1964.

Left: Ch. Samantha of Shelert, right: Strikin' Midnight at Shelert

'Copper'. His glorious expression won him many friends. A very well balanced dog with a superb outline and proud headcarriage. He always showed to perfection, ably handled by his owner Mrs Aileen Speding. His temperament and showmanship were similar to his father.

He sired three Champions: two bitches, the tricolour Ch. Samantha of Shelert and Ch. Loughrigg Day Festivity of Lysebourne, and one dog, Ch. Loughrigg Dragonfly who was a basis for the Loughrigg and Kyleburn kennels. Another son, Glenmist Golden Falcon influenced the kennels of Lysebourne, Shelridge and Tyneford as well as being the grandsire, through Golden Falcon of the famous Ch. Jefsfire Freelancer who made such a bearing on the sable lines of today.

Strikin' Midnight at Shelert (born: 1962)
 By: Riverhill Rolling Home
 ex: Ch. Slipper Satin of Shelert

Strikin' Midnight was a very prolific sire as well as being useful in that he was able to be bred to all colours, being a tricolour of sable breeding. When mated to blue merles he had a great influence on the size of the blue merle ears, the somewhat large and ugly ears of blues of the past became neater and tidier. He sired eleven Champions of all colours. The most notable being:

Ch. Scylla Vaguely Blue (born: 1968)

Ch. Such A Spree at Shelert pictured left with son and daughter Ch. Such a Frolic at Shelert and Ch. She's My Fancy at Shelert

Ch. Such A Spree at Shelert (born: 1968)
Both Ch. Scylla Vaguely Blue and Ch. Such A Spree at Shelert are significantly behind the present day blue merle lines and have a great bearing on the successful blue merle kennels of today, namely Felthorn, Rockaround and Ruscombe. The glorious coloured blue merle, Ch. Ruscombe Silver Lining can be classed as the most successful blue merle stud dog of the present day.

The breed record holder for the number of C.C.s won by a Sheltie (21 C.C.s - 1990) is presently held by the blue merle Ch. Pepperhill Blue Fizz who is descended through direct tail male Line from Strikin' Midnight.

Blue Fizz and his half brother, Ch. Pepperhill Naughty But Nice (they had the same dam) and are descended, via the tail male Line from, Ch. Such A Spree at Shelert. Naughty But Nice sired Ch. Rosdyke Moonlight Shadow, Ch. Reubicia Orion and Felthorn Cornflower.

The successful Felthorn blue merle bitches, namely, Ch. Felthorn Button Moon, Ch. Felthorn Lady and Felthorn Star Appeal, the dam of Ch. Reubicia Orion, are line bred to Strikin' Midnight at Shelert and incorporate so many of the lines already mentioned. They exemplify classic line breeding without close in-breeding.

The influence of Strikin' Midnight on the Rockaround kennel can be seen through the female lines, via Ch. Scylla Vaguely Blue and Scylla Mr Valentino, who produced Ch. Rockaround Crystal Sky who subsequently produced so many winning blue merle offspring.

Ch. Ruscombe Silver Lining must be one of the most successful blue merle stud dogs of today and is descended from Strikin' Midnight and Ch. Such A Spree at Shelert.

Ch. Jefsfire Freelancer (born: 1970)
by: Glenmist Golden Falcon
ex: Ch. Heathlow Luciana

Ch. Jefsfire Freelancer winning his second C.C. at 11 months old

A dominant sable with an excellent temperament, Freelancer sired twelve Champions and two C.C. winners. He greatly influenced the Allanvail, Dippersmoor, Forestland, Harribrae, Janetstown, Lythwood, Monkreddan, Myriehewe, Snabswood, Sonymer, WillowTarn and, of course, the Jefsfire kennels.

His most significant sons were: Ch. Francehill Persimon, Ch. Ferdinando of Myriehewe, Ch. Scarabrae Sinjon, Ch. Scarabrae Statesman, Ch. Sumburgh Tesoro Zhivago and Int. Ch. Jefsfire Allanvail Gold Spark. All have bred on.

Ch. Francehill Persimon (born: 1974) has a very strong bearing on contemporary kennels, having become a Key sire. Persimon's son, Ch. Francehill Andy Pandy sired Ch. Glaysdale Buccaneer whose son, Ch. Francehill Goodwill sired Ch. Francehill Florentine, and Bonny Rogers' always immaculate C'urC'in Fun Bug as well as the Mottram's Ch. Francehill Dollar Bid of Lochkaren.

Ch. Francehill Persimon

Left to right: Ch. Ferdinando of Myriehewe with daughters Ch. Myriehewe Fantasia and Ch. Monkreddan Sunray

Ch. Ferdinando of Myriehewe features heavily in Scotland in the successful Monkreddan kennel owned by the late Madge Caldwell, and continued, albeit in a small way, by her daughter with whom Ch. Monkreddan Royal Blend, was able to continue at stud.

Other Ferdinando offspring influence the present day kennels of Orean and Crisanbee as well as the continuence of the Myriehewes.

Ch. Scarabrae Sinjon's progeny influenced the present day Scottish Kennels of Harribrae and Orean as well as the Monkreddans.

Ch. Scarabrae Statesman's most notable son was Ch. Marksman of Ellendale who features in the pedigrees of Arcot, Forestland, Greenscrees, Rinsey, Sonymer, Milesend, Snabswood and WillowTarn.

Another son, Ch. Shezlynn Brown Velvet was short lived but sired the C.C. winning Allanvail Gold Degree who subsequently bred on through Dippersmoor and Arowmist.

Ch Sumburgh Tesoro Zhivago was to continue the Freelancer male tail Line by being behind Tirrick, Bridgedale and Shelabane.

Freelancer's most significant daughter was the lovely Ch. Jefsfire Rich Reward who was a one time breed bitch record holder with eight C.C.s. Another daughter, Ch. Drannoc Susiley Spacegirl appears in many modern day pedigrees.

Pictured left to right: Ch. Spark of Shelert, Ch. Spice of Shelert, Ch. Sweet Sultan of Shelert, Ch. Sea Urchin of Shelert, Ch. Midas of Shelert and Ch. Shantung of Shelert

Ch. Midas of Shelert (born 1955).

Ch. Midas of Shelert has bred on through his most famous son, Ch. Sea Urchin of Shelert (born: 1961) who directly influenced the early Joywil and Loughrigg kennels.

Great grandsons of Midas are: Ch. Riverhill Richman and Ch. Strict Tempo of Shelert.

Through those two dogs many prominent present day kennels owe their most influential bloodlines, notably, Beckwith, Blenmerrow, Felthorn, Francehill, Milesend, Monkswood, Nitelife.

Midas' daughter Ch. Riverhill Rather Rich (Family 9, part ll) was the dam of four Champions: Ch. Riverhill Raider, Ch Riverhill Rather Dark, Ch. Riverhill Rather Nice and Ch. Riverhill Richman, who have all bred on.

Midas' granddaughter Ch. Slipper Satin of Shelert was mated to Riverhill Rolling Home and produced that great tricolour sire Strikin' Midnight at Shelert whose offspring are now so widespread.

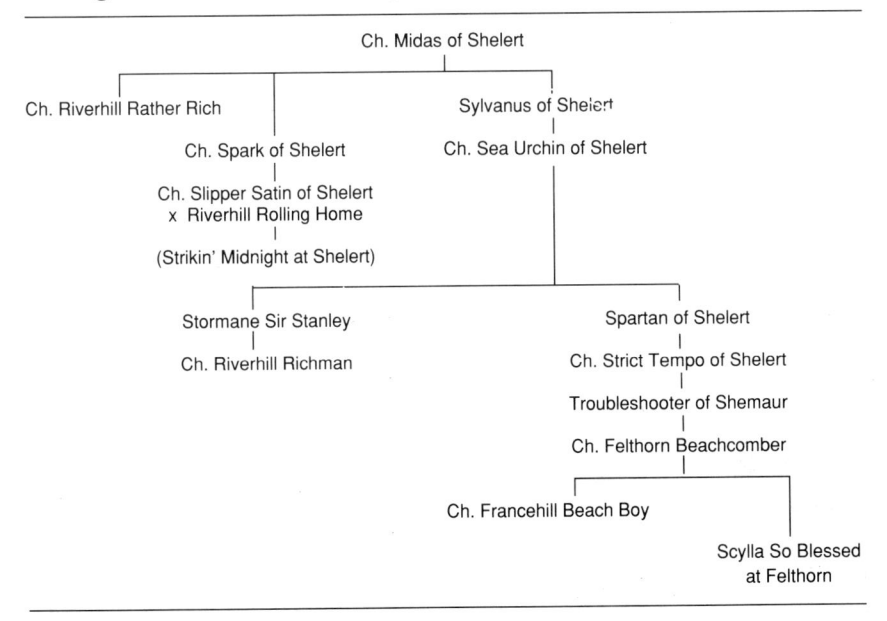

```
                          Ch. Midas of Shelert
                                  |
        ┌─────────────────────────┴─────────────────┐
Ch. Riverhill Rather Rich                    Sylvanus of Shelert
            |                                        |
     Ch. Spark of Shelert                   Ch. Sea Urchin of Shelert
            |
     Ch. Slipper Satin of Shelert
     x  Riverhill Rolling Home
            |
     (Strikin' Midnight at Shelert)
            |
      ┌─────┴──────────────────────────────┐
 Stormane Sir Stanley              Spartan of Shelert
         |                                   |
  Ch. Riverhill Richman          Ch. Strict Tempo of Shelert
                                             |
                                  Troubleshooter of Shemaur
                                             |
                                  Ch. Felthorn Beachcomber
                                 ┌───────────┴───────────┐
                         Ch. Francehill Beach Boy
                                                 Scylla So Blessed
                                                    at Felthorn
```

Ch. Riverhill Richman (born: 1967)
by: Stormane Sir Stanley
ex: Ch. Riverhill Rather Rich

It can be seen from the family tree how Richman was line bred to Ch. Midas of Shelert. His dam Ch. Riverhill Rather Rich was a daughter of Midas and Richman was also a great-great grandson through Ch. Sea Urchin and Stormane Sir Stanley.

He is in direct line to present day kennels such as Monkswood Beckwith, Bridgedale, and the blue merle Lythwoods.

Ch. Riverhill Richman

Ch. Francehill Beachboy

Ch. Strict Tempo of Shelert (born: 1965)
Strict Tempo's male tail Line is dominated through his son Troubleshooter of Shemaur who sired:

Ch. Felthorn Beachcomber (born: 1972)
by: Troubleshooter of Shemaur
ex: Felthorn April Dancer

His sire, Troubleshooter of Shemaur, was all Shelert breeding, being line bred to Ch. Midas but a total outcross to his dam who was from the Francehill blue merle line which came down from the Exfords.

The influence of Beachcomber is now being felt on the present day dogs through sable, tricolour and blue merle lines but particularly through his blue merle granddaughter, Felthorn Marionette who produced so many excellent blue merle and tricolour bitches as well as dogs. Beachcomber's proving litter contained Ch. Francehill Beachboy and his last litter, Scylla So Blessed at Felthorn.

Ch Francehill Beachboy (born: 1974) won seven C.C.s. He sired Ch. Glaysdale Boy Wonder and that delightful bitch Ch. Shelert Sands of Delight, whom I had the pleasure of awarding her second C.C., she was a particular favourite at Shelert.

Scylla So Blessed at Felthorn (born: 1970) who is assuring the male tail Line and has proved particularly useful in that he is one of the few dogs that is genetically clear of Collie Eye Anomaly. He is the sire of Ch. Forestland Farmers Boy and the C.C. winner Jack Point of Janetstown.

CHE Line (Cheshunt Rainbow)

The present day active CHE line comes down from Ch. Uam Var of Houghton Hill to two branches, the main one of which is to Ch. Riverhill Rufus, he being a Key sire and from whom most of the CHE lines now stem, whether they be on the male tail Line or as sires of dams. Both Ch. Viking of Melvaig and Ch. Exford Piskiegye Taw have their branches. The male tail line to Piskiegye Taw does not feature in present day Charts but is nonetheless in the middle of many pedigrees. Others who are descended from Rufus are the two Ch. Viking of Melvaig sons, Ch. Wattawoodcut and Ch. Dilhorne Norseman of Melvaig.

One tends to associate most of the CHE lines with the Exfords and therefore with tricolours and blue merles. This has not always been the case as there were many sables bred at Exford including Ch. Exford

Piskiegye Taw and the C.C. winner Hornet of Exford whose male tail Line today is predominantly tricolour with Ch. Drumcauchlie Bumble Boy's son, Ch. Salroyds Buzzer becoming a Key sire on that Line, Ch. Westaglow Nijinsky, also by Hornet of Exford does not have a direct male tail Line to the charts but features through a Monkswood family of bitches.

Ch. Salroyds Buzzer

In relation to present day pedigrees, via Ch. Wattawoodcut's line, which is predominantly sable, the Line is continued through Ch. Greenscrees Swordsman and his son Ch. Greenscrees Nobleman.

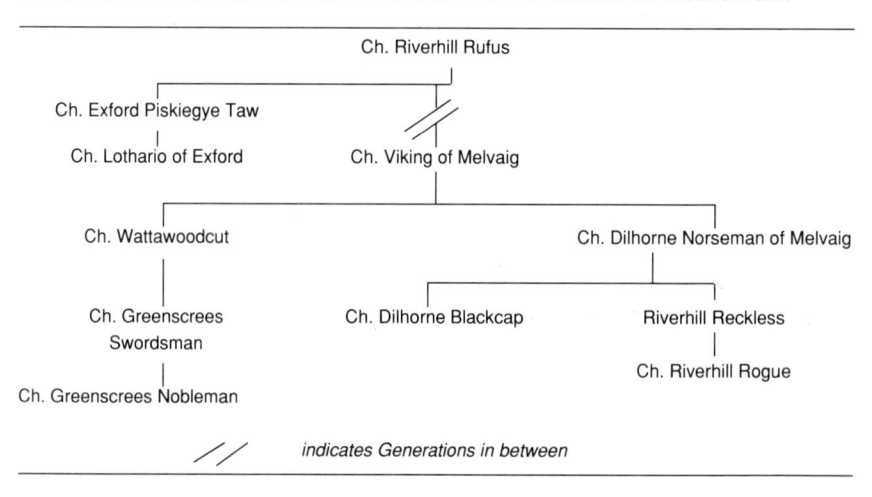

```
                              Ch. Riverhill Rufus
                         ┌──────────────┴──────────┐
   Ch. Exford Piskiegye Taw                       //
            │                                      │
   Ch. Lothario of Exford              Ch. Viking of Melvaig
                         ┌──────────────┴──────────────────────┐
       Ch. Wattawoodcut                         Ch. Dilhorne Norseman of Melvaig
            │                         ┌──────────────┴──────────┐
       Ch. Greenscrees           Ch. Dilhorne Blackcap      Riverhill Reckless
         Swordsman                                               │
            │                                            Ch. Riverhill Rogue
   Ch. Greenscrees Nobleman
```

// indicates Generations in between

Ch. Dilhorne Blackcap (born: 1955)

Blackcap produced the majority of his winners after he was six years old. He produced seven Champions, all blue merles or tricolours. When mated to Ch. Francehill Glamorous he produced Ch. Francehill Silversmith and Felthorn Francehill Pretty Polly who although not a C.C. winner features in the Charts Family, 9 (Part 1), being the granddam of Ch. Felthorn Beachcomber and therefore behind contemporary Felthorns. When Blackcap was mated to Ch. Francehill Glamour Girl, a daughter of Ch. Francehill Glamorous by Marble of Exford, he produced Ch. Francehill Painted Lady, thereby completing three generations of Champion bitches.

Ch. Dilhorne Blackcap

Blackcap is another example of a sire who features very significantly in the middle of pedigrees, being the sire of dams. The dam of Ch Hildlane Winters Night, Hildlane Misty Dawn, a C.C. winner herself, was by Blackcap. Winters Night has bred on through Shelridge Gatecrasher, himself a sire of dams who has bred on and influenced the present day successful Rockaround blue merle kennel.

Mrs Cynthia Charlesworth, Blackcap's owner and breeder, only bred one Champion sired by him, the bitch Ch. Dilhorne Bluecap, although he was the sire of the dam of others. Bluecap's daughter, Ch. Dilhorne Bluemirth won an unheard of record seven C.C.s. I considered her one of the nicest bitches I had seen at the time. Dilhorne Blue Dame, by Blackcap, was the dam of Ch. Dilhorne Blue Midnight and his full brother Ch. Dilhorne Bluenobleman.

Another Blackcap daughter, Ch. Bramble of Wytchfields, a tricolour, was regarded by some as being the most ideal Sheltie. She was the dam of Stargazer of Wytchfields who sired Ch. Exford Pipestyle Mystic Star, or E.P.M.S. as she was known.

Blackcap's influence has been felt not only in the aforementioned Rockaround kennel but also in the Felthorn, Scylla and Shelridge kennels.

Ch. Riverhill Rogue (born: 1957)

Rogue was another key blue merle within the present day merle pedigrees. Neither he nor Blackcap feature in the Charts as direct male tail Line but their influence is still very strong in the middle of the pedigrees. His most significant son was:

Ch. Riverhill Rogue

Ch. Kinreen Blue Kestrel

Ch. Kinreen Blue Kestrel (born: 1960)

Ch. Kinreen Blue Kestrel was significant in founding the successful blue merle Shelert line as well as being the grandsire on the dam's side of Ch. Sharval The Delinquent. One of Mrs Marion Marriage's foundation bitches, Scylla Swan Princess of Callart was a daughter of Ch. Riverhill Rogue.

So, it can be seen that even though Ch. Riverhill Rogue and Ch. Dilhorne Blackcap do not appear in the present day Charts their influence still has a very great bearing on present day pedigrees.

Ch. Greenscrees Nobleman (born: 1966)

This red gold dog is another that no longer features in the direct male tail Line but is very much an influence on many pedigrees. The Forestlands owe much to Nobleman, he sired Ch. Forestland Briar and Forestland Thor. Ron and Jean Fitzsimons' first Champion, Ch. Snabswood Slainthe was by Nobleman. Slainthe has since bred on to add such a dominantly golden sable line at WillowTarn as well as the Snabswoods.

Ch. Greenscrees Nobleman

The other branch of the CHE Line that comes down from Ch. Uam Var of Houghton Hill is through the sable C.C. winner Hornet of Exford to Ch. Drumcauchlie Bumble Boy (born 1975), a tricolour, and on another branch to Ch. Westaglow Nijinsky, a sable. Both who are prominent in todays pedigrees but with definite colour bias. The Nijinsky line being predominantly sable and the Bumble Boy line is tricolour. The Bumble Boy line is becoming more active through his son:

Ch. Salroyds Buzzer (born: 1977) who was owned and campaigned by Mrs Cynthia Charlesworth of the Dilhornes. Buzzers son, Ch. Paramali Rustler has bred on through Forestland Poacher to Ch. Rockaround Night Hawk, another stud dog who is genetically clear of C.E.A. as well as producing quality stock. The blue merle bitches, Ch. Rockaround Sky Lark and Rockaround Sky Light and the tricolour Ramtin Heidi Hi are all by Night Hawk.

Another son of Ch. Salroyds Buzzer was Ch. Longdells Petrocelli who

Ch. Paramali Rustler

died at the early age of seven but left sons Ch. Longdells Petoski and Ch. Mountmoor Blue Boy, both still consistent winners at the present time.

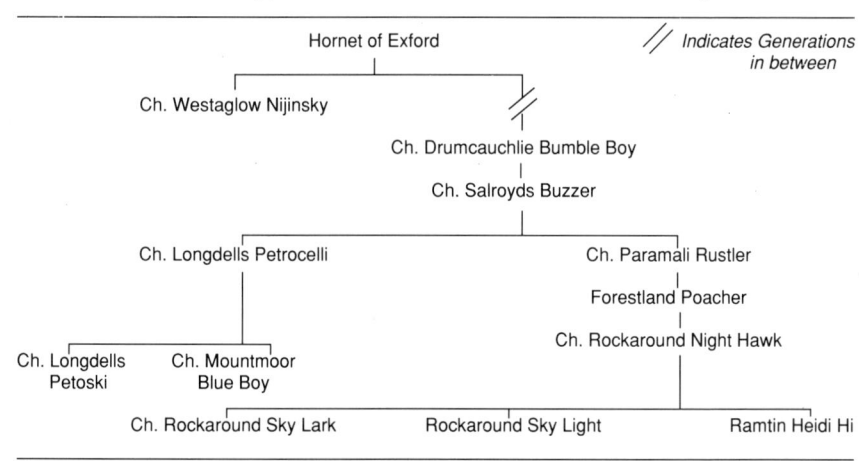

```
                        Hornet of Exford                    // Indicates Generations
                              |                                    in between
              Ch. Westaglow Nijinsky
                                     //
                              Ch. Drumcauchlie Bumble Boy
                                     |
                              Ch. Salroyds Buzzer
                                     |
          Ch. Longdells Petrocelli              Ch. Paramali Rustler
                    |                                    |
                    |                           Forestland Poacher
                    |                                    |
                    |                           Ch. Rockaround Night Hawk
  Ch. Longdells    Ch. Mountmoor                         |
    Petoski         Blue Boy
          Ch. Rockaround Sky Lark    Rockaround Sky Light        Ramtin Heidi Hi
```

Studying the Charts from previous Handbooks it is interesting to see how some lines will disappear and then after a space of some years they will come alive again. But all the time the stronger, more dominant lines are increasing.

Ch. Dilhorne Norseman of Melvaig. Born 1953

Ch. Ebony Pride of Glenhill, winner of 9 C.C.s. Born 1956,
by: Hartfield Herald. ex: Una of Tintobank

Helensdale bitches - 1959

Ch. Janetstown Jacqualine. Born 1961, by: Helensdale Braw Lad.
ex: Janetstown Lousea Seaton. Bred by Miss Jan Godrich,
owned by Mrs. Jenny Durose

Bath 1963.
Miss Joan Herbert and Ch. Sea Urchin of Shelert. Judge: Miss Olwen Gwynne-Jones.
Mrs Marion Marriage and Ch. Black Swan of Scylla

Miss Joan Herbert and Miss Beryl Herbert at home with some of the Shelerts, 1963
All sables - the blue merles and tricolours came later

Ch. Riverhill Rather Dark and Ch. Riverhill Raider aged 5 months. Born 1963, by: Riverhill Ranger. ex: Ch. Riverhill Rather Rich

Four Riverhill Champions: Ch. Riverhill Rather Dark, Ch. Riverhill Raider, Ch. Riverhill Richman, Ch. Riverhill Rather Nice. All ex: Ch. Riverhill Rather Rich, owned and bred by the Misses P. M. and F. M. Rogers

Riverhill Rolling Home. Born 1959, and his son Ch. Antoc Sealodge Spotlight, born 1962. Spotlight won 11 C.C.s.

Ch. Jefsfire Freelancer aged 12 years. Born 1966, by: Glenmist Golden Falcon ex: Ch. Heathlow Luciana, bred and owned by Kath and Alan Jeffries

Ch. Monkswood Moss Trooper. Born 1967, by: Ch. Riverhill Raider ex: Ch. Deloraine Dilys of Monkswood, bred by Mrs Evelyn Knight and Miss Mary Davis, owned by Miss Mary Davis

The Classic Shetland Sheepdog.
Ch. She's My Fancy at Shelert. Born 1971. by: Ch. Such A Spree at Shelert ex: Scarcely Fancy of Shelert, bred and owned by the Misses Beryl and Joan Herbert

Ch. Janetstown Journalist. Winner 6 C.C.s. Born 1969, by: Janetstown Willum ex: Janetstown Jefsfire Sophia, bred and owned by Mrs Jan Moody. Seen here with a Janetstown Pedigree Ryeland

Ch. Drannoc Susiley Spacegirl. Born 1969, by: Ch. Jefsfire Freelancer ex: Chevinsdale Shining Star, bred by Mrs Pugh and owned by Miss Molly Hall

Ch. Ferdinando of Myrehewe. Born 1973, by: Ch. Jefsfire Freelancer ex: Drannoc Flower Girl. Bred by Miss Molly Hall and owned by Miss Irene Beaden

Ch. Midnitesun Justin Time. Winner of 11 C.C.s and sire of 5 Champions. Born 1973, by: Midnitesun Good News ex: Midnitesun Party Piece, Bred and owned by Mrs Rose Wilbraham

The Families

To date there are nine active Families that trace the bottom line of the pedigrees, these are called the female tail Line. Active Families are Family 1 (part I), 3 (parts I & II), 5, 6, 8 (part I & II) and 9 (part I & II), 16 and 24 (part I & II).

A study of the Families reveals that the major influential lines to present day kennels are influenced by certain Key bitches.

Family 9 is the most prolific with three main branches from Ch. Blue Blossom of Houghton Hill (born 1929) who have become Key bitches in their own right. They are Ch. Fascinator of Exford, Riverhill Rhythmic and Riverhill Rouge.

Family 9 (part II) is based on Riverhill Rouge who was the great-granddam of Ch. Riverhill Rare Gold and Riverhill Realgar, both Key bitches in their own right.

The most consistent Families come down from the Helensdale, Exford, Riverhill and Shelert kennels with Beckwith, Felthorn, Forestland, Francehill, Kyleburn, Monkswood, Myriehewe, Snabswood and WillowTarn taking over.

The concentrated breeding of the Helensdales during the 1950s had a great influence to the present day through Ch. Helensdale Gentle Lady and Helensdale Mhairi Dhu.

A group of Helensdale bitches

Ch. Helendale Gentle Lady, Family 13 (part I) was the dam of both Ch. Helensdale Bhan and Ch. Helensdale Ace and therefore features strongly in the middle of pedigrees. At the present time the only active direct line from her is to Mary Gatheral's Herds kennel and Ch. Herriot of Herds and Herds It's Hindsight.

Helensdale Mhairi Dhu, Family 1 (part II,) (1985 Charts) does not feature currently but she was the dam of Ch. Alasdair of Tintobank and Aimili of Tintobank, both by Ch. Helensdale Ace. Aimili was the granddam of Heathlow Hippolyta who, mated to Ch. Francis of Merrion, produced the litter sisters Ch. Heathlow Luciana and Heathlow Lavinia. Luciana became the foundation of the Jefsfire Shelties. She was bought by Kath and Alan Jeffries as a result of an advert in a local paper. Intended as a pet for Kath's mother she so impressed them that her mother had to wait for another puppy. Already in Rough Collies, the Sheltie fitted in well at Jefsfire. Little did they know what a fantastic bitch she was to be. She was successfully campaigned to her title. In her last litter she produced that superb dog Ch. Jefsfire Freelancer. He was the sole survivor of the litter. His offspring are now widespread.

Lavinia was owned by Mrs Mabel Reed of the Lathmere kennel. Both Luciana and Lavinia are linked in the pedigrees of the present day Jesfires via Ch. Jefsfire Rich Reward. Lavinia, bred on to the female tail Line to Ch. Haytimer of Hanburyhill at Hartmere and Ch. Hartmere Harris Tweed.

The Sumburgh kennel of Mrs Rosemary Morewood was the last to be based on pure Helensdale breeding. Helensdale Vanessa was purchased from Jimmy Saunders and was to become the last Helensdale Champion. A very successful kennel was built up at Sumburgh in a very short space of time. Vanessa was born in 1960 and when mated to Helensdale Frolic produced Ch. Sumburgh Sirius. He features greatly in the pedigrees of Ellendale and Forestland. The kennel is now no longer in existence but they made a significant contribution during the sixties and seventies with one particular bitch, Sumburgh Cherry Blossom (Family 9). She was a rich red gold daughter of Ch. Skye of Whytelaw and consistently produced stock who have bred on through the middle of pedigrees.

Probably the most influential Family at the present time comes down from the Riverhills, particularly through Riverhill Rouge and Riverhill Rhythmic. Through Rouge, Ch. Riverhill Rare Gold now appears in the Charts as a separate branch of her own. Family 9 (part II). Rhythmic's branch is most prolific being behind present day Kyleburns and Ch. Kyleburn Golden Eagle, Ch. Midnitesun Justin Time, Ch. Rhinog The Gay Lancer, the Glenmist and Landover kennels and, via Ch. Monkswood Meridian, to Ch. Longdells Petoski.

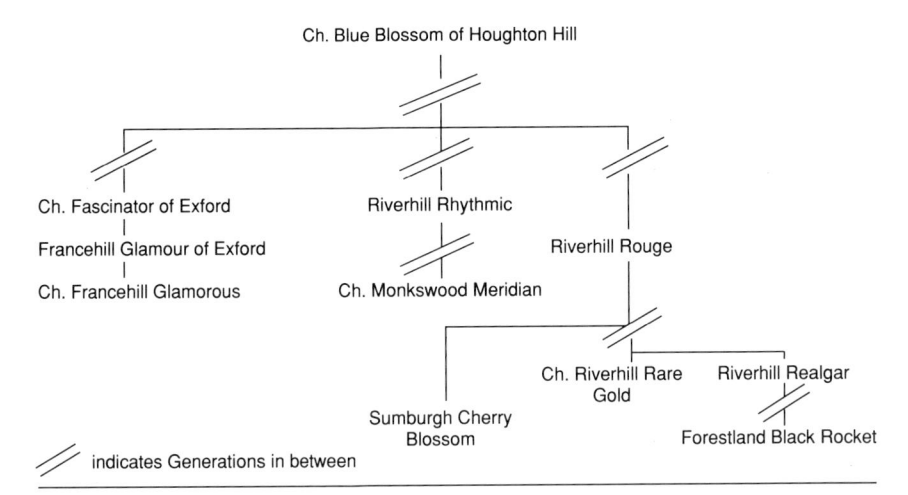

```
                    Ch. Blue Blossom of Houghton Hill
                                │
              ┌─────────────────┼─────────────────┐
              │                 │                 │
Ch. Fascinator of Exford   Riverhill Rhythmic     │
     │                          │           Riverhill Rouge
Francehill Glamour of Exford    │                 │
     │                    Ch. Monkswood Meridian  │
Ch. Francehill Glamorous        │                 │
                    ┌───────────┴─────┬───────────┴──┐
                    │                 │              │
                    │          Ch. Riverhill Rare   Riverhill Realgar
                    │               Gold             │
               Sumburgh Cherry                       │
                  Blossom                   Forestland Black Rocket
   ⁄⁄ indicates Generations in between
```

The most active side of Family 5 today is descended from another Riverhill bitch, Riverhill Reinette. One branch from her produced Ch. Riverhill Royal Flush who went on to the Misses Herbert as a foundation for the Shelert kennel. She became a Key bitch in her own right and is behind nearly all of the Shelerts, if not on a direct female tail line, certainly as the dam of Ch. Midas of Shelert.

Another branch through, Riverhill Rusilla, produced Ch. Riverhill Ratafia. Rusilla was the dam of Riverhill Rohais who when mated to Ch. Jefsfire Freelancer produced Janetstown Jefsfire Sophia, who is behind all the current Janetstowns of today. She was the dam of Ch. Janetstown

Strikin' Midnight of Shelert, Such A Surprise at Shelert, Scarcely Cricket at Shelert (the first blue merle Shelert), and Ch. Samantha of Shelert

Journalist and was great grandmother to Ch. Jasmine of Janetstown through Janetstown Jubilee. Journalist's litter sister, Janetstown Jocelyn's descendents are still breeding on for the Janetstowns and other kennels.

Ch. Janetstown Journalist, Janetstown Jorrocks, Ch. Jasmine of Janetstown

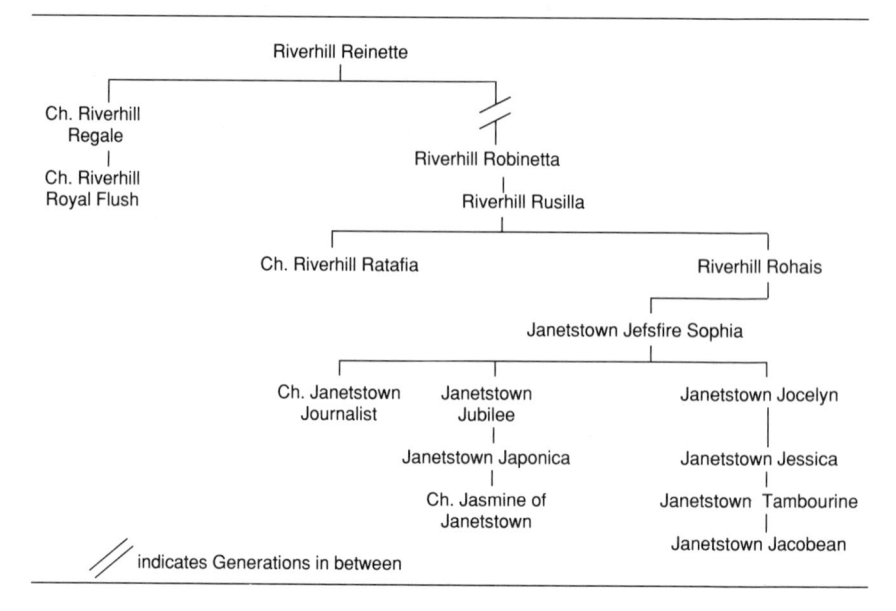

```
                          Riverhill Reinette
                                 |
         ┌───────────────────────┴───────────┐
   Ch. Riverhill                             ╳
      Regale                                 |
         |                          Riverhill Robinetta
   Ch. Riverhill                             |
   Royal Flush                       Riverhill Rusilla
                                            |
                          ┌─────────────────┴─────────────┐
                   Ch. Riverhill Ratafia              Riverhill Rohais
                                                          |
                                              ┌───────────┴───────────┐
                                         Janetstown Jefsfire Sophia
                                                          |
              ┌───────────────┬──────────────────┬────────┴────────┐
         Ch. Janetstown   Janetstown                    Janetstown Jocelyn
            Journalist     Jubilee                              |
                              |                        Janetstown Jessica
                       Janetstown Japonica                      |
                              |                        Janetstown Tambourine
                       Ch. Jasmine of                           |
                         Janetstown                     Janetstown Jacobean
```

╳ indicates Generations in between

40

Ch. Jasmine of Janetstown never produced a daughter so now only features as the dam of a sire in the middle of pedigrees. Her son, Janetstown Jorrocks, has bred on through his son, Ch. Jazzman of Janetstown and his son Colmae Jazz Juke of Janetstown.

Ch. Riverhill Rugosa is a Key bitch being at the head of part II of Family 24. Several branches come down from her to the present day kennels of Franwick, Herds and Sonymer. More significantly Rugosa's daughter, Riverhill Rosalie, also went to the Shelert kennel and produced many branches of Shelert bitches including Ch. Slipper Satin of Shelert.

Family 6 is based on another Riverhill bitch, the tricolour Riverhill Rubicon whose branches extend to the present day kennels of Arcot, Beckwith, Glaysdale, Mohnesee, Ramtin, Shelmyth and via Monkswood to Hartmere and Milesend.

Over a span of forty six years, 1934-1980, the Riverhills produced 29 Champions, 15 of whom were bitches, and 15 other C.C. winners.
Regrettably the Riverhill kennel is no more. Many present day kennels owe so much to the consistent stock produced by the late Misses Patience and Felicity Rogers.
Luckily the breed is left with a legacy of bloodlines that are important to present day dogs and bitches in all parts of their pedigrees.

The Exford kennel of the late Mrs Constance Sangster was a continuation of her mother's Houghton Hill. Current kennels who owe much to the Exfords, particular through Ch. Fascinator of Exford, a branch of Family 9, are the kennels of Drumcauchlie, Francehill, Felthorn, Longdells, Mountmoor, Shelbrook, Shelridge and the Stornaway beauty and obedience kennel.
Francehill Discreet of Exford, one of the branches of Family 8, has seen the continuance of the Francehills as well as being the female tail Line to Kyleburn, Marklin, Penrave, Santrev and Tuffeigha.
Another main branch of Family 8 is from Dilhorne Bluepearl whose descendents include the majority of the Dilhornes and the sable side of Lythwood through Ch. Lythwood Sea Nymph.
Also coming down from the Houghton Hill's and Family 8 are the prolific families of Ruscombe, Snabswood and WillowTarn and through the Westaglows to Marnham.

Family 8 (part III) comes down from the Key bitch, Merry Maid of Whytelaw who is behind the Key sire Ch. Salroyds Buzzer as well as the current kennels of Sonymer and Newsprig and Penrave.

Family 16 features the bitch C.C. record holder, Ch. Shelderon Kiri as the only recent current female line. The most prominent branch comes from the Key bitch, Heatherbell of Callart whose son Ch. Orpheus of Callart is a Key sire in his own right. Ch. Scylla Vaguely Blue, Ch. Scylla Scottish Rifle, Ch. Cowellekot Crown Prince of Stormane, and the bitch Ch. True Delight at Tirrick all come down from Heatherbell.

Ch. Riverhill Rare Gold (centre) with her sons Riverhill Ranger (left) and Riverhill Rolling Home (right)

Ch. Riverhill Rare Gold (born 1954) Family 9 (part II) must be one of the most successful brood bitches ever. So many of the top kennels of today owe their strong bitch Families to her.

She heads several generations of Champion bitches. Her one daughter, Ch. Riverhill Rarity of Glenmist, was the dam of Ch. Gypsy Star of Glenmist who is on the female tail Line to Sonymer, Sanvar and Shelfrect as well as being in the middle of many other pedigrees.

Another branch from Rare Gold is Ch. Riverhill Rash Promise, another who has become a Key bitch. She features in the middle of pedigrees, being the granddam of Ch. Riverhill Ricotta, the sire of Ch. Haytimer of Hanburyhill at Hartmere.

Rash Promise's daughter by Ch. Monkswood Moss Trooper produced the glamorous sable Riverhill Riskall Family 9 (part II). She went to the late Mrs Josie Rae who bred the tricolour Rodhill Elfin Moon. She was sold to Gwen and Irene Beaden as their foundation bitch and has become a Key bitch for the successful Myriehewe kennel. She was the dam of both Ch. Myriehewe Spanish Romance and Ch. Myriehewe Spanish Galleon from Tracelyn. Another son, Myriehewe Magic Moments of Milesend moved with owner Mrs Joyce Miles, to Kent, bringing the Rare Gold Family back home.

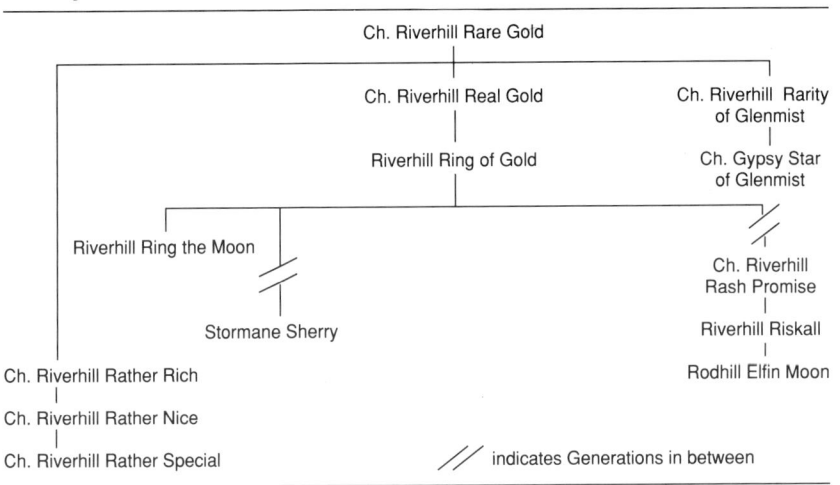

```
                        Ch. Riverhill Rare Gold
         ┌───────────────────────┴───────────────────────┐
                        Ch. Riverhill Real Gold                 Ch. Riverhill Rarity
                                   │                               of Glenmist
                        Riverhill Ring of Gold                  Ch. Gypsy Star
                                   │                               of Glenmist
         ┌─────────────────────────┤                                    //
  Riverhill Ring the Moon          │
                        //                                      Ch. Riverhill
                        /                                       Rash Promise
                 Stormane Sherry                                Riverhill Riskall
  Ch. Riverhill Rather Rich                                     Rodhill Elfin Moon
  Ch. Riverhill Rather Nice
  Ch. Riverhill Rather Special         //  indicates Generations in between
```

Mrs Rosemary Marshall's Forestland foundation bitch was a granddaughter of Ch. Riverhill Rare Gold's sister, Riverhill Realgar. Four generations of Forestland breeding produced the tricolour Forestland Black Rocket. She was a significant Key bitch as she produced

Left to Right: Rockaround Skylight, Ch. Rockaround Skylark, Rockaround Daylight, Rockaround Valentine Sky & Ch. Rockaround Crystal Sky

43

Centre: Forestland Honeysuckle, with her children, left: Ch. Forestland Briar and Forestland Thor and right: Ch. Forestland Target, Forestland Master Buck and Ch. Forestland Tassel. In front Forestland Rowan

Rockaround Stormy Day, the foundation of the present day successful Rockaround kennels of Mrs Jean Angell. Stormy Day was in fact a Forestland but was registered as a Rockaround allowing Mrs Angell to re-establish her kennel. The Rockarounds are now one of the leading kennels specialising in blue merles and tricolours.

Forestland Black Rocket also produced Forestland Saffron who was the dam of the C.C. winning Forestland Honeysuckle. A third branch from Black Rocket was to Forestland Black Lark. Plans were made to breed for a bitch that would be suitable to mate to Ch. Paramali Rustler. By mating the sable Ch. Forestland Briar to the tricolour Forestland Black Lark, Forestland Mink resulted and she was then mated to Rustler and produced Forestland Poacher who has become such a significant stud dog being the sire of Ch. Rockaround Night Hawk.

Honeysuckle was a sixth generation of Mrs Rosemary Marshall's breeding and has been responsible for many branches of significant dogs and bitches of all colours.

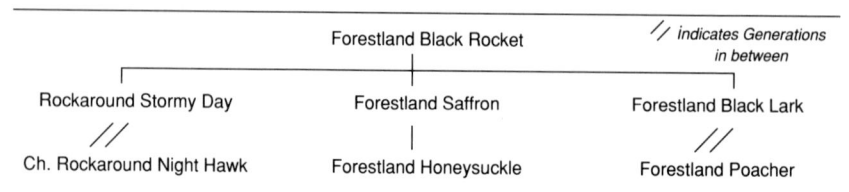

	Forestland Black Rocket		// indicates Generations in between
Rockaround Stormy Day	Forestland Saffron	Forestland Black Lark
//		//
Ch. Rockaround Night Hawk	Forestland Honeysuckle	Forestland Poacher

With Forestland Poacher being the sire of Ch. Rockaround Night Hawk it can be seen how the breeding has been linked back to Forestland Black Rocket.

Stormane Sherry

Stormane Sherry has very far reaching branches to her family having that charming bitch, Ch. Drannoc Susiley Spacegirl descended directly from her. She influenced not only the Stormane kennel but features significantly in the present day kennels of Lythwood, Monkswood and Myriehewe.

Riverhill Ring of Gold, a granddaughter of Rare Gold, is in direct female tail Line, with branches to Blenmerrow, C'urC'in and Edglonian. A third branch was through Riverhill Ring the Moon, that most prolific of bitches, who was Mrs Phyl Pierce's Philhope foundation bitch. She produced eight bitches who feature in the present day Charts. Philhope Moonmaid of Monkswood, by Riverhill Rolling Home, is behind the Glensanda kennel and Philhope Charming Moon, by Ch. Jefsfire Freelancer, went to Mrs Joan Coup's Alwillans kennel as a foundation.

As Ring the Moon was on breeding terms from the Rogers, one bitch by Rolling Home went back to Riverhill to become the last but one

Riverhill Champion, she was Ch. Riverhill Ring the Bell.

Ring the Bell's tricolour son, Riverhill Ringer, is behind many prominent Lines being the sire of Ch. Herriot of Herds and Newsprig Gold Ringster who is behind so many of the successful Hartmere bitches. Her daughter Philhope Moonmaid of Monkswood was mated to Monkswood Marauder (litter brother to Ch. Monkswood Moss Trooper) produced the tricolour Monkswood Moonshiner who is behind the Felthorn bitches and the multiple C.C. winner Ch. Mountmoor Blue Boy.

The most active part of Family 3 (part II) is Felthorn. Through Felthorn Marionette, a very prolific line of bitches is successfully breeding on.

Felthorn bitches. Felthorn Marionette with her daughters. Left to right: Ch. Felthorn Button Moon, Felthorn Moonbeam, Felthorn Marionette and Ch. Felthorn Lady

The Shelert kennel rarely sold bitches and therefore the majority of influence from that kennel was through their stud dogs. Sheila Baker was one of the few people to obtain a bitch who subsequently bred on for the Shemaur kennel, now residing in South Africa. Spending Spree at Shelert bred Ch. Brantcliffe Gem of Love who was steered to her title by owner Mrs Joan Coup. Gem of Love bred on for the mutual benefit of the Alwillans and Mrs Barbara Karp's Skerrywood kennel.

The blue merle, Such Witchery at Shelert was sold to Mrs Ronnie Thompson of the Glencharms on breeding terms. Such Witchery was a product of Ch. Such A Spree at Shelert and Ch. Samantha of Shelert and has become a Key dam in her own right with a direct line to Ch. Shelerts Such A Gambol and via the Glencharms to 'Super Gran', Ch. Glencharm Witch's Brew of Melcette, so-called because she did not win her first C.C. until she was seven years old, winning four C.C.s and a consistent winner in all-breed veteran Stakes classes. She is granddam to the dual C.C. winning blue merle, Witch's Frost of Lyndene at Benravia.

The C.C. winning blue Such A Myth at Shelert lived at the Rhinog kennel of Miss Diana Blount and bred on to many successful Rhinogs. Such A Myth was mated to the tricolour Ch. Rhinog the Black Watch and produced the C.C. winning Rhinog Blue Gossamer and the tricolour Int. Ch. Rhinog The Guardian who was exported to Sweden to Per and Birgitta Svarstad. I judged The Guardian in Stockholm as a twelve year old and I can only say that Sweden's gain was definitely our loss. His influence on Swedish Shelties has been tremendous.

Ch. Slipper Satin of Shelert (born 1959) is descended from Riverhill Rugosa the Key bitch of Family 24 (part II). Her biggest claim to fame is that she was the dam of that great sire Strikin' Midnight at Shelert who influenced so many kennels and features in all parts of pedigrees.

Ch. Shelerts Sands of Delight

Not only has she bred on through her family to Ch. Shelerts Sands of Delight, a great favourite at Shelert, but to Shelert Sands of Time who has produced for Mrs Margaret Norman Ch. Francehill Goodwill and Ch. Francehill Flora Dora, dam of Ch. Francehill Florentine. She also influenced the Herds line, being on the female tail Line to Ch. Herds Hurdler.

Yet another Riverhill bitch is responsible for Family 24 (part II). The merle, Riverhill Rosette had two branches to two sable merles. The one branch through Riverhill Roguish, a blue merle, bred on to the Dilhornes. The other branch through Riverhill Rosamund, whose descendents include the Hildlanes, now no more, but nonetheless significant to present day kennels. The C.C. winning Jack Point of Janetstown is descended from Riverhill Rosamund through one branch from Rosamund via Hildlane Black Sprite. A second branch from Rosamund through Allensway 'Bitta' Sweet at Dippersmoor has bred on to several generations of successful Dippersmoors and Ch. Jazzman of Janetstown.

The Breed Standards 1908 - 1986

DURING the 1920's each of the Shetland Sheepdog clubs had their own breed standard and it was inevitable that these would vary. A number of Collie breeders had taken a fancy to the Shetland Sheepdogs, keeping and breeding them alongside their larger dogs. No doubt the mixing of the two breeds produced an attractive smaller version of the Rough Collie and by close breeding produced a more specific type. With the introduction of the Rough Collie it was not long before the size was raised and the type of head changed, becoming longer and leaner.

Each breed evolves on how breeders and judges interpret the standard. When judges describe a dog in their critique stating that a point is correct, when it is not, the novice owner will presume that the judge is right and thereafter breed for that point. In the past breeders relied on their eye and experience, knowing a good dog when they saw one, and willingly passing on their knowledge to novices. Today it has become more scientific and each person will try and interpret the standard their own way rather than appealing for help from the experienced. People are judging after having been in the breed a very short time. Far sooner than 25 years ago.

Dogs that win in the show ring will be seen by others as being correct. Therefore it is the judges that are responsible for fluctuations in the type of dog produced. Being forgiving about a fault is seen as acceptable. These judges, perhaps in their ignorance, are responsible for perhaps condoning a point when it is incorrect.

Frequently the novice exhibitor will say that they have read the standard, looked at their own dog and then come to the conclusion that there is nothing wrong with him. This is purely their interpretation and if you think about it you can really make anything fit if you want to see it in a particular way. The really fascinating part of breeding and judging is trying to find that ideal dog that most fits the Standard.

I have included all of the Standards from the first issued in 1908 by The Shetland Sheepdog Club up to the present day. It can be seen how some aspects have remained and others, such as the height, have altered over the years.

Earlier Standards

THE SHETLAND SHEEPDOG CLUB, 1908

The type and points of the Shetland Sheepdog shall be similar to those of the **Rough Collie** in miniature. The height shall not exceed 15 inches. A Register shall be kept of members' dogs from 12 to 15 inches.

THE SCOTTISH SHETLAND SHEEPDOG CLUB, 1909

The general appearance of the Shetland Sheepdog is that of an **ordinary Collie** in miniature. In height **about 12 inches** and weight from 10 to 14 pounds. There are two varieties - the rough coated and the smooth coated. The smooth coated dog only differs from the rough in its coat which should be short, dense and quite smooth.

THE ENGLISH SHETLAND SHEEPDOG CLUB, 1914

The general appearance of the Shetland Sheepdog is **approximately that of a show Collie** in miniature. Ideal height 12 inches.

Standard and Points

OF THE

SHETLAND SHEEPDOG.

(from the 'Shetland Sheepdog' by Beryl Thynne, 1916)

The following are the points and description as adopted by the English Shetland Sheep-dog Club and the Scottish Shetland Sheep-dog Club: -

1. - The skull should be as near as posible flat, moderately wide between the ears, and gradually tapering towards the eyes. There should only be a slight depression at stop. The Cheeks should not be full or prominent.

2. - The Muzzle should be of fair length, tapering to the nose, and should not show weakness or be snipy or lippy. The nose must be black, whatever the colour of the dog may be.

3. - The Teeth should be sound, and near as possible level. Very slight uneveness is permissible.

4. - The Jaws clean cut and powerful.

5. - The Eyes should be of medium size, set somewhat obliquely, and close together, of almond shape, and of brown colour - full of intelligence and expression.

6. - The Ears should be small, and moderately wide at the base, and placed fairly close together on top of the skull. When in repose they should be carried thrown back, but when on the alert brought forward and carried semi-erect, with the tips drooping forward.

7. - The Neck should be of fair length, muscular, and somewhat arched.

8. - The Body should be moderately long and level, with well sprung ribs and strong loins; chest deep.

9. - The Forelegs should be straight and muscular, with a fair amount of bone.

10. - The Hindlegs should be muscular at the thighs, with well-bent hocks.

11. - The Feet should be oval in shape, soles well padded, and the toes arched and close together.

12. - The Tail should be moderately long with abundant hair, carried low when the dog is quiet, with a slight upward swirl at the end, but gaily carried when the dog is excited, but not over the back.

13. - The Coat must be double - the outer coat consists of hard hair; the under coat, which resembles fur, is short, soft and close. The mane and frill should be very abundant, the mask or face smooth, as also the tips of the ears. The forelegs well feathered, the hindlegs above hocks profusely covered with hair, but below the hocks fairly smooth. What is commonly known as smooth-coated specimens are barred.

14. - Any Colour except brindle is permissible.

15. - The General Appearance of the Shetland Sheep-Dog is that of the modern show collie *in miniature* (collie character and type must be adhered to). Ideal height, 12 inches at maturity, which is fixed at 10 months old.

FAULTS.

Domed skull: large drooping ears; weak jaws; snipy muzzle; full or light eyes; crooked forlegs; cow hocks; tail carried over the back; under or over-shot mouth.

SCALE OF POINTS.

Head and Expression	15
Ears	15
Neck and Shoulders	5
Legs and Feet	10
Hind Quarters	10
Back and Loins	5
Tail	10
Coat and Frill	15
Size	15
	100

1923
Type confirmed but height expressed as "from 12 to 15 inches, the ideal height being 13½ inches".

1930
General appearance altered to "Should resemble a Collie (Rough) in miniature".

The Shetland Sheepdog.

STANDARD OF POINTS

(from the English Shetland Sheepdog Handbook, 1935)

Revised 1920 and (height) 1923

The Shetland Sheepdog should resemble a Collie (Rough) in miniature, from 12 to 15 inches, the ideal height being 13½ inches.

Skull flat, tapering towards the eyes.

Muzzle long, tapering towards the nose, stop slight, cheeks flat.

Teeth level, jaws clean cut and powerful.

Eyes brown, of almond shape, set obliquely and close together.

Expression alert, keen, intelligent.

Ears small, placed high, carried semi-erect with tips forward.

Neck long, muscular and arched.

Body compact, back level with well-sprung ribs and strong loins; chest deep, shoulders flat, straight front.

Forelegs straight with good bone, pasterns flexible without weakness.

Hindlegs muscular at thighs with well-bent stifles, giving a racy appearance.

Feet oval, toes arched and close together, soles well-padded.

Action lithe and graceful, speed and jumping power great for size of dog.

Coat double, the outer coat of long hair, the under coat short, soft and close. Mane and frill abundant, forelegs well feathered, hindlegs above the hocks profusely covered but smooth below, face smooth.

Tail long with good brush of hair; carried down with upward swirl at tip.

Usual Colours:-
Tricolour, *i.e.,* Black with Tan and White markings.
Black & Tan, *i.e.,* Black with Tan markings.
Black & White, *i.e.,* Black with White markintgs.
Sable.
Sable & White, *i.e.,* Sable with White markings.
Blue Merle.
(White markings may be shown in the blaze, collar, frill, legs, feet and brush tip; all or some.
Tan markings may be shown on eyebrows, cheeks, legs, stifles and under tail; all or some).
The nose black whatever the colour of the dog.

NUMERICAL STANDARD OF POINTS
Head and Expression 15
Ears 15
Neck and Shoulders 5
Legs and Feet 10
Hindquarters 10
Back and Loins 5
Tail 10
Coat and Frill 15
Size 15

100

In 1965 the English Shetland Sheepdog Club, the Scottish Shetland Sheepdog Club and the Northern Counties Shetland Sheepdog Club joined forces to draw up an official standard for the breed. Prior to that time The Kennel Club had recognised the standard that the E.S.S.C had drawn up from the time that the breed was recognised. Over the years there were some adjustments made but it was not until 1950 that The Kennel Club drew up an official book of standards. The Shetland Sheepdog standard in that book acknowledges the E.S.S.C. Before then there was no official K.C. standard.

The 1965 Standard was very much more comprehensive even if one or two points were not quite correct. It has been included as a further guideline to breeders and judges.

1965 Breed Standard

Characteristics

To enable the Shetland Sheepdog to fulfil its natural bent for sheepdog work, its physical structure should be on the lines of strength and activity, free from cloddiness and without any trace of coarseness. Although the desired type is similar to that of the Rough Collie, there are marked differences that must be noted. The expression, being one of the most marked characteristics of the breed, is obtained by the perfect balance and combination of skull and foreface, size, shape, colour and placement of eyes, correct position and carriage of ears, all harmoniously blended to produce that almost indefinable look of sweet, alert, gentle intelligence. The Shetland Sheepdog should show affection and response to his owner; he may show reserve to strangers but not to the point of nervousness.

General Appearance
The Shetland Sheepdog should instantly appeal as a dog of great beauty, intelligence and alertness. Action lithe and graceful with speed and jumping power great for its size. The outline should be symmetrical so that no part appears out of proportion to the whole. An abundance of coat, mane and frill, with shapeliness of head and sweetness of expression all combine to present the ideal Shetland Sheepdog that will inspire and secure admiration.

Head and Skull
The skull should be refined and its shape when viewed from the top or side is a long, blunt wedge, tapering from ear to nose. The width of the skull necessarily depends upon the combined length of skull and muzzle, and the whole must be considered in connection with the size of the dog. The skull should be flat, moderately wide between the ears, showing no prominence of occipital bone. Cheeks should be flat and merge smoothly into a well rounded muzzle. Skull and muzzle to be of equal length; central point to be the inner corner of the eye. In profile the topline of the skull should be parallel to the topline of the muzzle, but on a higher plane due to a slight but definite stop. Lips should be tight. Teeth should be sound and level, with an evently spaced scissor bite.

Eyes
A very important feature giving the expression to the dog. They should be of medium size, obliquely set and of almond shape. Colour dark brown, except in the case of merles, when blue is permissable.

Ears
Should be small and moderately wide at the base, placed fairly close together on the top of the skull. When in repose they should be thrown back, but when on the alert brought forward and carried semi-erect with the tips dropping forward.

Neck
The neck should be muscular, well arched and of sufficient length to carry the head proudly.

Body and Quarters
From the withers the shoulder blade should slope at a 45-degree angle, forward and downward to the shoulder joint. At the withers they

are separated only by the vertebrae but they must slope outwards to accommodate the desired spring of ribs. The upper arm should join the shoulder blade at as nearly a right-angle as possible. The elbow joint to be equidistant from the ground and the withers. The forelegs should be straight when viewed from the front, muscular and clean with strong bone. Pasterns strong and flexible. The body is slightly longer from the withers to the root of the tail than the height at the withers, but most of the length is due to the proper angulation of shoulders and hindquarters. The chest should be deep, reaching to the point of the elbow. The ribs well sprung but tapering to their lower half to allow free play of the forelegs and shoulders. The back should be level, with a graceful sweep over the loins and the croup should slope gradually to the rear. The thigh should be broad and muscular, the thigh bones to be set into the pelvis at right angles, corresponding to the angle of the shoulder blade. The stifle joint, where the femur bone joins the tibia bone, must have a distinct angle. Hock joint to be clean cut, angular and well let down with strong bone. The hock must be straight when viewed from behind.

Tail
Set on low, tapering bone, must reach at least to the hock joint, with abundant hair and slight upward sweep; raised when the dog is moving, but never over the level of the back.

Feet
Oval in shape, soles well padded, toes arched and close together.

Gait
The action of the Shetland Sheepdog should denote speed and smoothness. There should be no pacing, plaiting, rolling or stiff, stilted up and down movement.

Coat
Must be double, the outer coat of long hair of harsh texture and straight, the under coat soft (resembling fur) short and close. The mane and frill should be very abundant and forelegs well feathered. Hind legs above the hocks profusely covered with hair but below the hocks fairly smooth. The mask or face smooth. What are commonly known as smooth coated specimens are barred.

Colour
Tricolours should be an intense black on the body with no signs of ticking: rich tan markings on a tricolour to be preferred. *Sables* may be clear or shaded, any colour from gold to deep mahogany, but in its shade the colour should be rich in tones. Wolf sable and grey colours are undesirable. *Blue merles:* clear, silvery blue is desired, splashed and marbled with black. Rich tan markings to be preferred, but their absence not to be counted as a fault. Heavy black markings, slate coloured or rusty tinge in either top or undercoat is highly undesirable. General effect should be blue. White markings may be shown in the blaze, collar, chest frill, legs, stifle and tip of tail. All or some tan markings may be shown on

eyebrows, cheeks, legs, stifles and under tail. All or some of the white markings are to be preferred whatever the colour of the dog, but the absence of these markings shall not be considered a fault. *Black and white* and *Black and tan* are also recognised colours. Over markings of patches of white on the body are highly undesirable. The nose black whatever the colour of the dog.

Size

Ideal height measured at the withers 14 inches for bitches, 14½ inches for dogs. Anything more than one inch above these heights to be considered a serious fault.

Faults

Domed or receding skull; lack of stop; large drooping or pricked ears; over-developed cheeks; weak jaw; snipy muzzle; not full complement of teeth; crooked forelegs; cow hocks; tail kinked, short or carried over back; white or white predominating; pink or flesh coloured nose; blue eyes in any other colour than merles; nervousness; full or light eye; under-or overshot mouth.

Ch. She's My Fancy at Shelert - An ideal Sheltie - well balanced and typical head.

The current Breed Standard, 1986

The Official Standard reproduced by kind permission of The Kennel Club.

The Kennel Club decided to rationalise all the breed standards in 1984. A new standard was drawn up with the co-operation of all the breed clubs and the latest version was published in 1986, not without a great deal of discussion as the breed clubs were very anxious for it to be right. One or two points have been changed. Other relevant details were deleted.

The most important changes were the reference to the length of the back and further detail to the description of blue merle's eye.

The reference to the Rough Collie was taken out which is unfortunate as it does give a visual idea of type. There has always been some sort of reference to the Collie throughout the breed's history. Originally there was reference to the Show Collie until that was changed in 1930 to read 'should resemble a Collie (Rough) in miniature.'

Also removed from the 1965 Standard was the list of faults which included reference to the amount of white allowed. It stated that 'white should not predominate'. There is no reference made about how much white, in relation to solid colour, is allowed in the current Standard.

I hope that the following analysis and explanation of the Standard will assist those who are breeding and judging. However long you have been in the breed you should repeatedly read the Standard.

Remember that no dog is perfect, in spite of those people who tend to see their dogs through rose coloured spectacles. Seeing the dog as a whole rather than fixing on a particular point has to be the first consideration. Breed type will be seen instantly by the experienced eye. The balanced dog with the correct expression will automatically take the eye of the judge.

The first paragraph of the standard refers to 'General Appearance' which is where the reference to the Rough Collie has been deleted.

GENERAL APPEARANCE
Small, long haired working dog of great beauty, free from cloddiness and coarseness. Outline symmetrical so that no part appears out of proportion to the whole. Abundant coat, mane and frill, shapeliness of head and sweetness of expression combine to present the ideal.

A 'long-haired working dog' could conjure up visions of a shaggy creature with hair everywhere. One of the particularly appealing aspects of the breed is the fact that they have that neat double coat but have a clean smooth-haired face, legs and feet.

The outline is the shape of the dog when viewed in profile, or side, and should be graceful without being either cloddy or heavy. The expression is a very important feature giving the breed its unique appeal.

CHARACTERISTICS:
Alert, gentle, intelligent, strong and active.

TEMPERAMENT:
Affectionate and responsive to his owner, reserved towards strangers, never nervous.

These two headings could really be combined as one of the main characteristics of a Sheltie is his temperament. To say that they are 'active' is an understatement and 'alert' can sometimes be interpreted as being sharp.

Breeders of Rough Collies who have Shelties say that compared with the Collies the Shelties are noisy and busy. On the other hand when a Sheltie person has a Collie they tend to regard them as quieter and slow.

Shelties are really very gentle creatures, extremely intelligent and willing to please. A gentleness, devotion and reponse to his owner is in contrast to that sometimes underlying reserve towards strangers. The often extrovert character can still display this reserve when faced with an unknown situation. In the past this has been interpreted as nervousness but there is a dividing line between reserve and nervousness. Temperament has improved enormously over the last thirty years.

As a breed Shelties are excellent at obedience, agility and trial work because of that intelligence and willingness to please.

HEAD AND SKULL:
Head refined; when viewed from top or side a long blunt wedge, tapering from ear to nose. Width of skull in proportion to length of skull and muzzle. Whole to be considered in connection with the size of dog. Skull flat, moderately wide between the ears, with no pronouncement of occiputal bone. Cheeks flat, merging smoothly into well rounded muzzle. Skull and muzzle of equal length, dividing point inner corner of eye. Top-line of skull parallel to top-line of muzzle, with slight but definite stop. Nose, lips and eyerims black. The characteristic expression is obtained by the perfect balance and combination of skull and foreface, shape, colour and placement of eyes, correct position and carriage of ears.

The head is such an important feature of the Shetland Sheepdog and much emphasis is made of it in the standard. There is more written into the Sheltie standard about the head than many other breeds and the correct expression plays a major part in creating the true Sheltie type. It is that often elusive combination of balance of the head, the shape, colour and placement of the eyes and the way that the ears are placed and carried which gives that soft gentle melting expression. Getting the head right can be very difficult; having, for instance, a round, badly placed eye or prick ears can ruin the whole effect.

The size of the head should be in proportion to the rest of the dog. From a judging point of view the tremendous variation of type, particularly in the head can vary in different areas of the country due to the influence of particular stud dogs.

How much 'refinement' is required in the skull? A narrow skull is less likely to be flat and is more likely to have too little stop. The width of the head and skull very often follows right through the whole of the dog, therefore; 'narrow skull, narrow body'. 'Broad skull, wide body'.

The stop which 'breaks' too far down the muzzle can rise between the eyes and can appear to be more 'straight through' rather than being on two separate planes. The eyebrows can sometimes hide this fault.

A soft, gentle, melting expression

The narrow overlong head with a small eye can look out of proportion and give the wrong expression as much as a square broad skull with too much stop and bold eyes. The flat skull is quite rare and does not tend to have the prominent occipital bone, which is the protruding bone at the back of the skull.

To have flat cheeks can seem almost impossible but can be found when there is enough fill of foreface and a well-placed, correctly shaped eye. If the dog carries too much weight it can show in bulging cheeks.

The rounded muzzle should be as it says and not be boney or have veins that stand out. There should be no snipeyness i.e. the foreface should not be narrow with the nostrils protruding too far over the underjaw.

There should be sufficient depth and width of underjaw to accommodate the teeth.

When the Standard says that the skull and muzzle should be of equal length, this should be self explanatory as should the fact that the width of the skull between the ears should be equal to the length of the skull

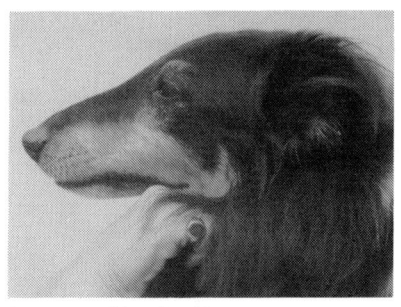

Incorrect Head - Drop nose, stop starts along muzzle and rises between the eyes. Receeding skull, and too deep through skull."

measured from the inner corner of the eye to the occiput.

The Standard calls for a blunt, wedged shaped head, being neither triangular nor oblong.

One has to view the head from the side to be able to see the parallel lines of the skull and muzzle. When doing this one can calculate the amount of stop. A receding or domed skull can be seen easily, as can the 'dished face' which is when the end of the nose turns upwards. Equally incorrect is the 'drop' nose when the very end of the nose drops away. A very ugly fault is the Roman nose when the whole of the head is convex, rising between the eyes and dropping away at the tip of nose.

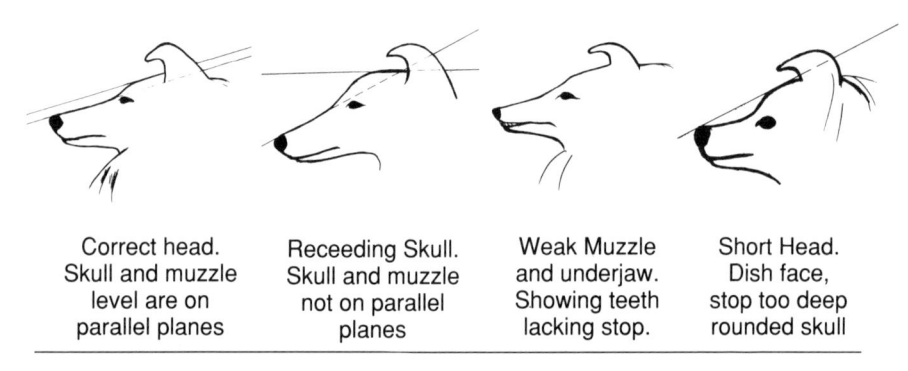

| Correct head. Skull and muzzle level are on parallel planes | Receeding Skull. Skull and muzzle not on parallel planes | Weak Muzzle and underjaw. Showing teeth lacking stop. | Short Head. Dish face, stop too deep rounded skull |

MOUTH:
Jaws level, clean, strong with a well developed underjaw. Lips tight. Teeth - sound with a perfect, regular and complete scissor bite i.e. upper teeth closely overlapping the lower teeth and set square to the jaws. A full complement of 42 properly placed teeth highly desired.

A scissor bite is described very well. There should not be a gap at all between the top teeth and the bottom teeth when the mouth is closed. It should not be undershot, overshot or even level which would cause the teeth to become worn down. A lack of underjaw is all too frequently seen, which can give an overshot mouth. A lack of depth of underjaw emphasises the rather ugly fault of showing the teeth. The lips should be tight but covering the teeth, equally, they should not sag at the corners.

It seems to be more common to see the narrow jaw which results in squashed-up incisors and even missing incisors. When the incisors become very confined there can be a tendency to get a 'wry' or 'undershot' mouth, giving a bad bite.

A 'wry' mouth is when some of the bottom teeth protrude in front of the top teeth. The underjaw being too narrow to accommodate all of the teeth.

Undershot is a reverse scissor bite i.e. when all of the bottom teeth protrude beyond the top teeth.

A full complement of 42 teeth is not always seen, missing premolars are becoming more prevalent and can be put into the same category as any other structural fault. Although one can forgive the odd missing tooth when judging it is rather alarming to see large gaps at the sides and it is not uncommon for the majority of premolars to be missing.

The crooked canine, or fang, is seen all too frequently and should be heavily penalised. This can be due to failure of milk teeth to shed at the right time.

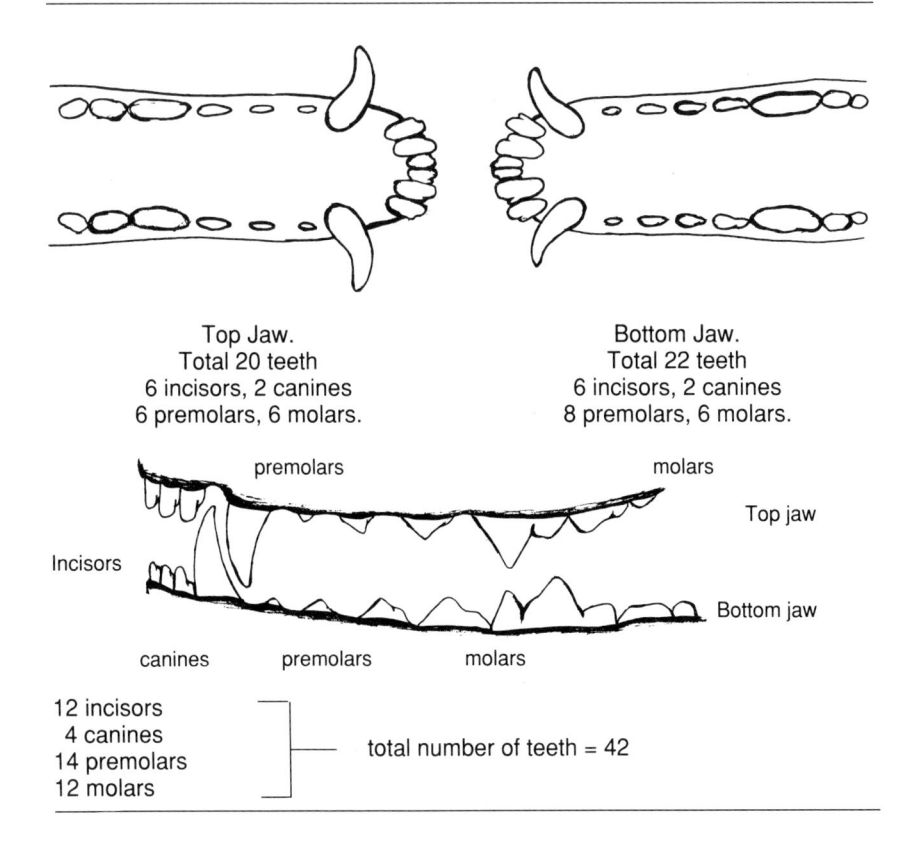

Top Jaw.
Total 20 teeth
6 incisors, 2 canines
6 premolars, 6 molars.

Bottom Jaw.
Total 22 teeth
6 incisors, 2 canines
8 premolars, 6 molars.

12 incisors
4 canines
14 premolars
12 molars

total number of teeth = 42

EYES:
Medium size, obliquely set, almond shape. Dark brown except in the case of merles, where one or both may be blue or blue flecked.

The size, colour and shape of the eye is instrumental in giving the true expression. The large, round eye can give a very startled, hard look and the over small, or button eye can give a mean and sometimes empty look. The light or amber eye is not attractive and very wrong, giving an untypical expression. Some dogs have darker wider rims which can give the impression of a larger eye when they have not. If this accompanies a bold eye the effect is accentuated making it appear bolder still.

When there is a total lack of pigment, more often than not seen in the golden sables, the eye can look piggy. This is seen during the winter months or when the dog is lacking condition.

The golden sable with gold eyelashes and correct dark brown eye will be able to hide an otherwise bold eye.

A tricolour will need always to have a well shaped, dark eye due to the surrounding black. A light eye on a tri is very obvious.

The china blue eye in the blue merle can be very attractive providing the shape and placement is correct. Odd coloured eyes, one blue and one brown or dark brown with blue flecks are quite permissible, as well as the usual dark brown eye.

A blue or blue fleck in a sable's eye is a major fault and more than likely means that some blue/sable crossing has occurred somewhere way back in the pedigree.

The placement of the eye is usually governed by the width of the skull and the amount of foreface. The broader skull can give more of a flat-on set, or forward facing eye usually accompanied by a round more protruding eye. This is often accentuated when there is a lack of fill of foreface.

The lean narrow skull can give a small sunken eye and a mean look.

EARS:
Small, moderately wide at the base, placed fairly close together on top of the skull. In repose, thrown back: when alert brought forward and carried semi-erect with tips falling forward.

When alert the ideal amount of ear tip is approximately one third of the ear. The tips of the ears should always be pointing forward. They should not be folded down on the cheeks like a Spaniel or lifted too high to expose the inside of the ear. The tips should not point sideways. They should not be low set on the side of the head or have a fold in the back which can cause them to twist outwards from the base of the ear.

They should never be pricked which can so easily happen with the ear that is too small or thin leathered.

Pricked ears are a very bad fault and totally ruin the expression. It is a waste of time trying to show the dog that has ears that are permanently up. Ears have improved enormously in the breed over the last 25 years but can still be a problem.

The standard does actually say that they should be *'fairly* close together on the top of the head'. Not 'tight' or 'bang on top' or 'nearly touching' as so many people misguidedly think. The very tight ears can give a rather sharp look. One can refer to ears as 'needing to be tighter' which is probably a kind way of saying that they are down the side of the head.

Left: Pricked ears spoil the expression.

Right: Correct ears giving desired expression.

NECK:
Muscular, well arched, of sufficient length to carry the head proudly.

The correct length of neck will give the Sheltie a good head carriage that somehow gives the sort of presence, air of authority, that 'look at me' look that can make all the difference to the shape and outline of the dog.

A long neck on an up-to-size dog can make it look even bigger, even though he may be the correct height at the shoulder. A short neck gives a square stuffy appearance. The good neck usually accompanies a well angulated forehand and shoulder. Equally the short neck can go with a lack of angulation and short upper arm.

The amount of coat can also alter the apparent amount of neck. The heavy coated dog can appear to be lacking in neck and the heavy coated short-necked one will lose it completely.

FOREQUARTERS:
Shoulders very well laid back. At the withers only separated by vertebrae, but blades sloping outwards to accommodate desired spring of ribs. Shoulder joint well angled. Upper arm and shoulder blade approximately equal in length. Elbow equi-distant from ground and withers. Forelegs straight when viewed from front, muscular and clean with strong bone. Pasterns strong and flexible.

There can be as much emphasis made of the shoulders as being the only cause of poor forehand conformation when it is the combination of the whole of the front. When one describes the 'front' in a critique it tends to mean the straightness of the front legs, when viewed from the front, as opposed to the whole of the 'forequarters'. The forelegs should not be over on the knee when viewed from the side.

The forequarter is the combination of the shoulder, upper arm, width and depth of chest and the front legs including the pasterns.

One needs to handle both good and bad to appreciate or even understand. As the good ones are few and far between it is small wonder that the indifferent ones are accepted as correct.

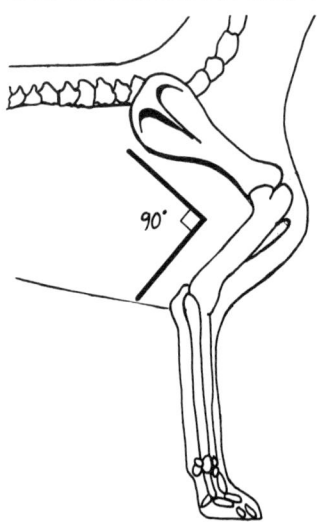

The shoulder blade and the upper arm should be of equal length. This fact is often overlooked or perhaps it is due to the lack of understanding. If the upper arm is short then there will not be sufficient reach when moving. There will be a short, stilted up and down, hackney-type action.

There should be an angle of 90 degrees at the *point* of the shoulder, taking the measurement from the withers to the point of the shoulder, then from the point of shoulder to the elbow. The elbow would then be well under the dog.

When the angle at the point of the shoulder is more than 90 degrees it will mean that the shoulder is more upright. This combined with a short upper arm gives the dog a squarer look when viewed from the side, throwing the forelegs forward with the dog unable to stand with his forelegs underneath himself giving the appearance of the forelegs being in a direct line from the ears rather than the withers.

Correct angulation of shoulder

The distance between the withers and the elbow and the elbow to the floor should be the same. The shoulder blades should meet clearly at the withers.

Correct Front    Narrow body fine bone    Crooked front    Wide in front out at elbows

So often the shoulder blade along with the upper arm, is condemned as being the overall fault when there can be other contributory factors such as the width and depth of the ribcage.

Whereas one does not wish to see a square dog when viewed from the front, neither do we wish to see the very narrow dog that looks as though both front legs are coming out of one hole.

The front legs when viewed from the front should be straight with sufficient bone without being overdone. There should not be a foot turning out or in. The dog with loose elbows and pin-toeing in movement is very wrong as well as being very uneconomic and ugly.

Pasterns

The pasterns should be of sufficient length to allow flexibility and smoothness when moving. They also act as a shock absorber. The short pastern will often accompany the upright shoulder and hound foot. The long thin pastern will often accompany poor bone, lack of muscle and the hare foot.

> **BODY:**
> **Slightly longer from point of shoulder to bottom of croup than height at withers. Chest deep, reaching to point of elbow. Ribs well sprung, tapering at lower half to elbow to allow free play of forelegs and shoulders. Back level, with graceful sweep over the loins; croup slopes gradually to the rear.**

The reference to the length of the back has been a bone of contention for several years as it was wrongly described in the 1965 standard. It is one of the most important changes made to the new Standard. The old standard wrongly stated that 'The body is slightly longer from the *withers* to the root of the tail than the height at the withers'. This has been changed to 'Slightly longer from point of shoulder to bottom of croup than height at withers.'

So often it has been interpreted as needing to be *long* whereas it should be *moderately* long. It was described as moderately long in the pre- 1965 standard. The description in the current standard is now correct, being more specific and can easily be measured. The result of that mistake in the 1965 standard seemed to bring about a number of rather long, low slung dogs with short legs as many people had interpreted the standard literally.

The chest should be deep but there are many dogs that are very lacking in this department. 'Shelly' is an expression not often used in the breed today, 'shelly' means that the body is weakly formed, narrow with no depth and lacking in substance.

The body and rib cage should not be rounded or *tube* like nor *slab* sided and narrow. There should be sufficient width between the shoulders to allow for heart and lungs. The rib cage should then taper gradually to the sternum which should reach down to the level of the elbow. Again, those who have never actually handled a dog with a good depth of chest do not understand what they should be looking for.

That the back should be level is self explanatory but it is essential to have that graceful sweep over the croup to give the correct outline. The Rough Collie standard calls for a slight rise over the loin which gives a different outline. Excess hair over the loin and croup can sometimes give a bad topline and squared off look to the rear end and needs to be checked when judging.

The loin is the coupling, being the area between the last rib and the pelvis.

HINDQUARTERS:
Thigh broad and muscular, thigh bones set into pelvis at right angles. Stifle joint has distinct angle, hock joint clean cut, angular, well let down with strong bone. Hock straight when viewed from behind.

The well constructed, fit dog will have plenty of muscle to drive if he has sufficient width in his pelvis with well set on thigh bones. It is to my mind that the hindquarters in many of the dogs today are becoming too light and narrow. This, combined with a femur that is set into an incorrectly angled pelvis gives a very ugly rear end, with the resulting cow-hocks and straight stifles which will then give the outline a more squared off appearance.

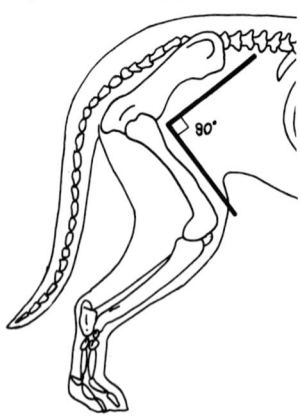

Correct angulation of hindquarters

The stifle should have a distinct angle being neither too exaggerated nor too straight. The over-angled stifle can give cow-hocks due to the feet being too far from the body, the weight being wrongly distributed. The feet will turn out and the hocks turn in.

It does state, categorically, that the hock joint should be clean cut, in other words it should be well defined but there does seem to be a tendency for this to be less than distinct. When it says that the hock should be well let down it means that the distance between the hock joint and the foot should not be too great. The hock to the foot should be perpendicular to the ground. If the hock is too high then it will give the dog the appearance of being 'up' on the leg and often goes with straight stifles.

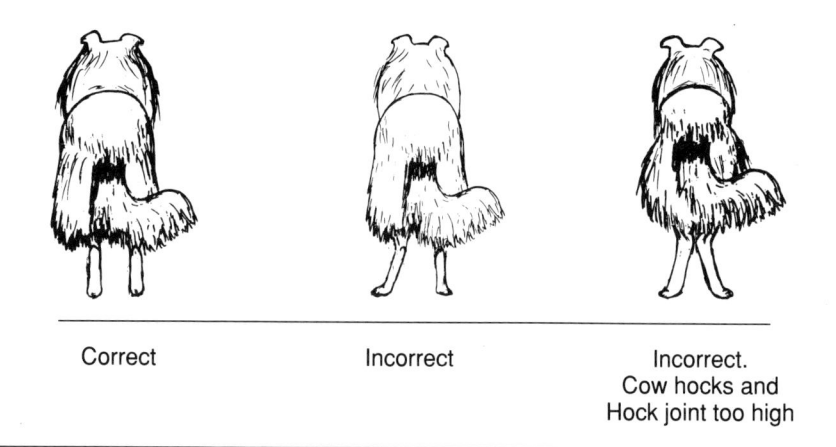

Correct   Incorrect   Incorrect.
                                  Cow hocks and
                                  Hock joint too high

TAIL:
Set low; tapering bone reaches to at least hocks, with abundant hair and slight upward sweep. May be slightly raised when moving but never over the level of the back. Never kinked.

The tail is a continuation of the spine and in the Sheltie it should reach the hock joint. It is the bone that should reach the hock not just the feathering. It is rare to find the correct length of tail which is important to give the final finish to the graceful outline.

The short stubby tail gives a squared-off appearance to the outline, is unattractive and incorrect.

The carriage is dependent on the set of the tail, the high set tail will usually accompany poorly angulated hindquarters and straight stifles. The majority of Shelties raise their tails when on the move but it should never come over the level of the back like a Spitz.

The correct upward sweep can only be achieved if the tail is of sufficient length. It should never be twisted in a rigid hook as opposed to the attitude of carrying the sweep slightly to the side. A kink is when the vertebrae are misplaced and is a serious fault, therefore the whole length of the tail should be checked at birth and when judging.

FEET:
Oval, soles well padded, toes arched and close together.

The elegant oval, well padded foot should merge smoothly with pastern and legs. The rounded foot on a short pastern will give a hound foot. The 'hare' foot is a flat foot on weak pasterns and is extremely ugly. Hare feet will splay as the dog ages. The nails are always long and do not wear down on a hare foot.

I often think I can guess how a dog moves by the shape of his feet and the way his nails grow. I once had a dog in to groom whose nails were shorter on the left side of both his front feet. I was to discover that when this dog was taken for a walk, apart from pulling on the lead all the time, he always went the same route round the roads, turning left at each junction. He pulled on the lead so much that all his weight was over on his left with the result that the nails were worn down on one side!

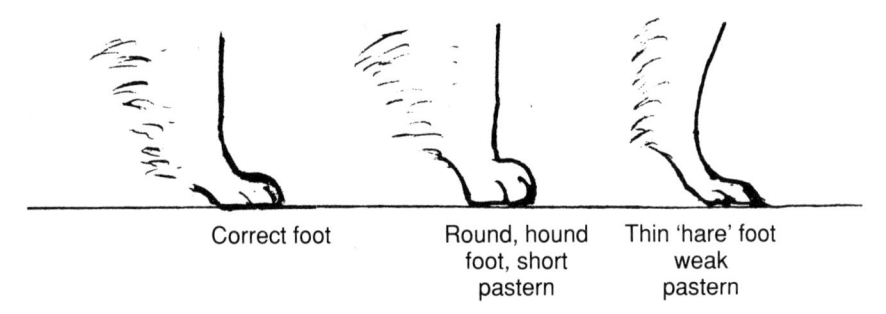

| Correct foot | Round, hound foot, short pastern | Thin 'hare' foot weak pastern |

As most of the drive comes from behind the nails on the hind feet will tend to be worn down more than the nails on the front.

GAIT AND MOVEMENT:
Lithe, smooth and graceful with drive from hindquarters, covering the maximum amount of ground with the minimum effort. Pacing, plaiting, rolling or stiff up and down movement highly undesirable.

To see the well made dog move is a delight. The legs should not be lifted any higher than necessary therefore being economical of effort. When a well constructed dog, who has the neccessary shoulder placement and length of upper arm, is doing an extended trot there will be the maximum amount of reach. Fewer steps are taken over a given distance without any bouncing up and down but giving the impression of floating across the ground in a 'Daisy-cutting' action.

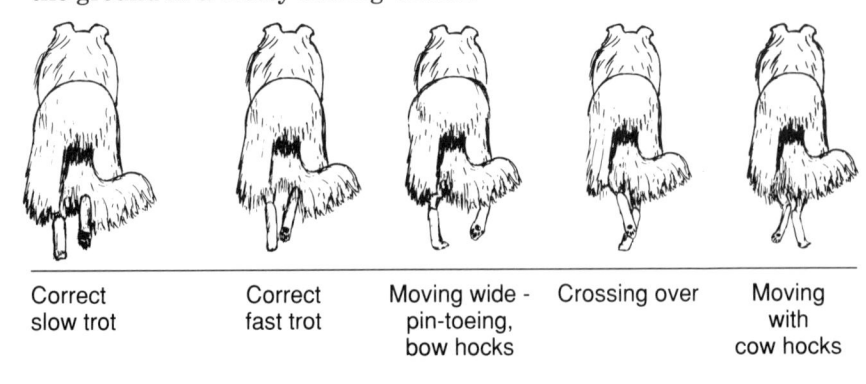

| Correct slow trot | Correct fast trot | Moving wide - pin-toeing, bow hocks | Crossing over | Moving with cow hocks |

When going away the feet should not cross or splay outwards. 'Pin-toeing' is pigeon toed and is wrong, as are cow or bow hocks or wide behind.

When moving towards the judge the front legs should be straight, there should be no swinging or throwing of a foot to the side and the legs should never cross over. At a brisk trot the feet will merge so that the inner part of the foot touches an imaginary central line. In other words single tracking. Unfortunately many see crossing over in front as single tracking, which is wrong.

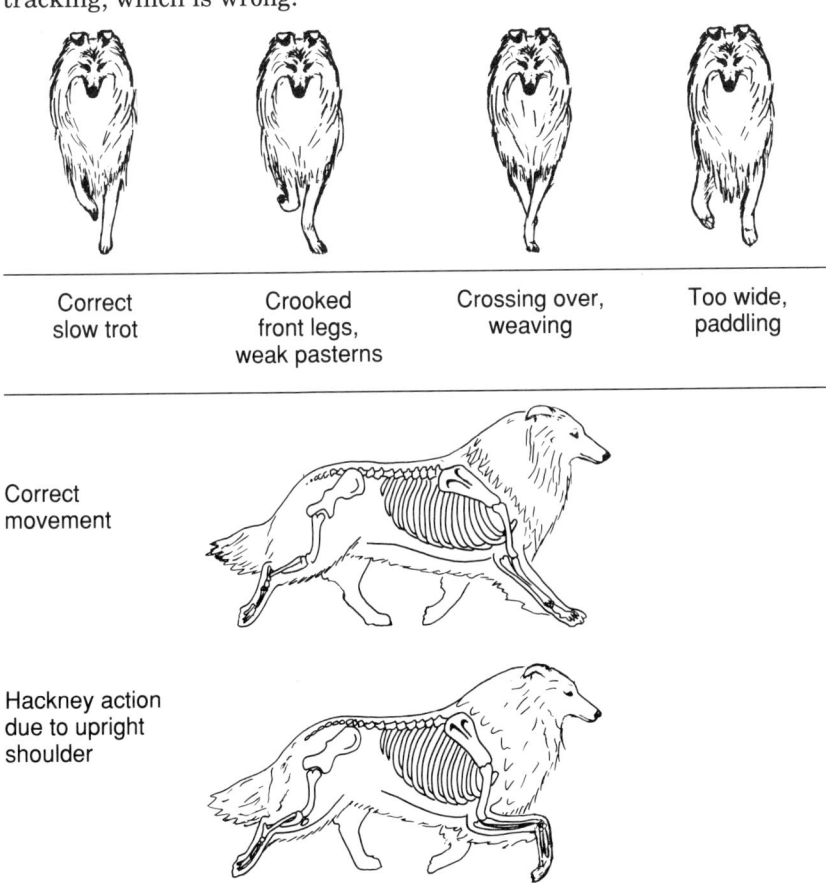

| Correct slow trot | Crooked front legs, weak pasterns | Crossing over, weaving | Too wide, paddling |

Correct movement

Hackney action due to upright shoulder

Pacing

Pacing is when both legs on the same side move forward together. In other words the legs are moving laterally, not diagonally. When a dog does this the body tends to roll as the weight is thrown from one side to the other.

Why do they do it? With our breed it can be that it is a habit which is usually formed when there are several dogs out on leads together.

Because the dogs are all moving at the same pace this pace may not suit each individual. The walk then becomes an amble or pacing. If the dogs are exercised individually and at the correct speed then diagonal movement is maintained.

Pacing - both legs on the same side move forward together

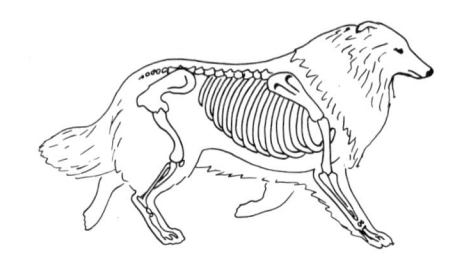

Crabbing

Crabbing is when the dog is over-reaching behind and has to swing the whole body sideways so that the hind feet do not hit the front feet. This can happen when a handler tries to move the dog too quickly, misguidedly thinking that if they go quickly the dog is moving well and covering the ground. Each dog will have his own comfortable pace to move his best.

In the show ring a dog can crab due to anticipation of moving round in a circle or turning left when doing a 'triangle'. The dog that has been constantly to ringcraft classes and been shown a great deal can easily drop into the habit of leaning inwards when moving.

COAT:
Double; outer coat of long hair, harsh textured and straight. Undercoat soft, short and close. Mane and frill very abundant, forelegs well-feathered. Hindlegs above hocks profusely covered with hair, below hocks fairly smooth. Face smooth. Smooth coated specimens highly undesirable.

A correct double coat is the Sheltie's crowning glory. Generally it will keep tidy and be able to withstand all weathers. The coarser top coat acts as an outer jacket and the soft, dense undercoat is the thermal underwear. The undercoat will lift the top coat giving more of a stand-off effect at the same time as providing insulation.

It is often misguidedly thought that the Sheltie should have as big a coat as possible. There should not be so much coat as to hide the true shape of the dog. It should be a well fitting coat to enhance the shape and general appearance.

The present day Shelties have much bigger coats than their

predecessors, often being totally impractical for general maintenance, but looks good in the show ring. There are varying opinions as to how much coat is acceptable and different lines produce different types of coat both in quality and quantity.

Whereas there should be sufficient coat there should not be so much as to hide the true shape of the dog, nor too little, lacking undercoat.

The Standard calls for an abundance of coat in General Appearance but it is the mane and frill that is mentioned as being 'very abundant' in this section specifically on coat.

The top coat should always be straight and harsh. It should not be soft or wavy. The two often go together and can be seen more in bitches when growing a totally new coat after a litter. As the coat lengthens it can become straighter. However, if the coat is soft then it is likely to remain wavy which is a fault.

If the top coat is too soft it will give little protection from the elements and absorb any wet. The overlong, drapey top coat gives a very grand effect in the showring but is not correct and is totally impractical. It can allow the dog to become entangled in undergrowth and is not so easy to keep groomed and tidy.

The coat that is loose and open, not dense, will not give the right amount of protection and insulation. Equally the soft silky top coat will not repel any moisture.

The reference to the hair below the hocks says that the hair should be 'fairly smooth'. Each individual dog can grow a different amount of hair here, some barely growing any and others growing so much that the scissors are out nearly every week.

The pet Sheltie with plenty of untrimmed hair below the hock can look quite old and down at heel. Trimming will rejuvenate the appearance of an old dog.

A long well feathered tail gives the finishing touch to a graceful outline. The hair on the tail tends to be much longer in bitches as are the more 'profuse' petticoats. The dogs will tend to have a more 'abundant' mane and frill making him look dominant and majestic.

COLOUR:

SABLES: Clear or shaded, any colour from pale gold to deep mahogany, in its shade, rich in tone. Wolf sable and grey undesirable.

TRICOLOURS: Intense black on body, rich tan markings preferred.

BLUE MERLES: Clear silvery blue, splashed and marbled with black. Rich tan markings preferred but absence not penalised. Heavy black markings, slate or rusty tinge in either top or undercoat highly undesirable; general effect must be blue.

BLACK & WHITE and BLACK & TAN: are also recognised colours. White markings may appear (except on black and tan) in blaze, collar and chest, frill, legs and tip of tail. All or some markings are preferred (except on black and tan) but absence of these markings not to be penalised. Patches of white on body highly undersirable. All colours are enhanced by being rich in tone.

Sable and White

Sables can be such a variety of lovely colours, they can also be quite uninteresting. The clear golden sable with a full white collar is the ultimate in many people's eyes. Equally the richly shaded or deep mahogany can be very striking, particularly if accompanied by a full white collar to set it off. Practically any shade of sable is acceptable, from the very pale honey or wheaten colour through the many shades of goldens and browns to dark shaded.

Wheatens usually have excellent pigmentation around the eyes and lips. The wolf sable is incorrect. This is when the colour appears to be grey. Defining which is wolf and which is wheaten can cause some debate because when a wheaten is out of coat it can take on a grey hue.

At all times they are classed and registered as SABLES.

Sable and White (Golden)
'Jack Point of Janetstown'

Tricolour

Tricolours are generally not so popular with the general public as they tend to regard the breed as being sable. Like all of the colours there are some most attractive ones as well as being some very dreary ones.

The overall effect can be dependent on the markings. In tricolours the tan should be rich in tone, having the whites really white can enhance the overall effect.

The tan points can appear on the eye brows, the cheeks, legs, stifles and under the tail. These tan points are preferable but not necessary. Some tricolours with only a few tan hairs can appear to be black and

Sable and white (Shaded)
'Ch. Jazzman of Janetstown'

white. Excess tan around the muzzle can give an optical illusion making the dog appear to be lacking in foreface. A total lack of tan around the head is quite legitimate but can sometimes detract from the expression if the eye colour is too light.

It is important that the black should be very black with no hint of 'rusting' or 'ticking' with grey hairs. The depth of black can vary. Some are never a good black, others always regain the jet black with a new coat. The general condition of a tricolour can be immediately obvious. The clean healthy coat will shine, the coat 'on the blow' will be dull and lifeless.

Tricolour
'Ch. Reubicia Orion'

Blue Merle

The colouring of a blue merle is all important and the blue must be a good, clear, crisp silvery blue not solid slate grey or muddy grey with brown tips to the coat. The whole essence of the merle, apart from the blue, is the splashes of black, or 'marbling' which should be well broken up. There should not be a predominance of black or large black patches over the blue. The amount and position of black markings on the head can sometimes detract from the expression. The tan points need not neccessarily accompany the merle but do help to enrich the overall effect.

Blue Merle
'Ch. Rockaround Crystal Charm'

Black and White, Black and Tan

Black and Tan is very rare these days. The black and white has become more evident in recent years. As with the tricolour the black should be a really dense black with no sign of rusty tinge.

White Markings

It is everyone's ultimate aim to have the full white collar which is so much a part of the Collie markings. To have the full Collie markings can be a great asset in the show ring as well as being aesthetically desirable.

The amount and position of the markings is all important. To have a white blaze on the face is not a fault. Over the years there have been fluctuations in the fashion, or preference to a white face. Those not used to living with white on the faces of their dogs say they find it difficult to assess the expression when judging. This is noticable when a Collie person judges our breed as it is very rare to see a Rough Collie with a blaze in the ring.

The offset blaze can sometimes detract from the expression particularly if the eye is not quite right. The famous Ch. Helensdale Ace had the most uneven blaze but had a sweet expression. Ch. Myriehewe Spanish Galleon at Tracelyn had a very broad but even blaze which did not detract from his lovely eye and expression. He became a Champion winning many C.C.s including one at Crufts. He continued winning and collecting C.C.s as a veteran. Any grey hairs that would otherwise be evident around the muzzle are not seen due to the white.

The 1965 Standard stated that 'all or some' of the full Collie markings are to be preferred. That includes not only the white blaze but the white up the stifle. The white on the stifle is a point that is still controversial yet quite legitimate.

The amount of white carried is critical as there should not be more than 50% of white. In the old Standard it stated in the list of faults that 'white should not predominate'. Any reference to the amount of white was omitted in the latest Standard.

White over-markings or patches of white on the solid colour of the body are called mismarks. This is a very serious fault.

Mismark - Over patches of white, white predominates, attractive, but wrong!

The smutty muzzle on a sable is quite legitimate providing it does not detract from the expression.

Ticking or freckles on the white, particularly the legs, on all colours, are entirely acceptable.

SIZE:
Ideal height at withers: Dogs 37 cms (fourteen and a half inches); bitches 35.5 cms (fourteen inches). More than 2.5 cms (one inch) above or below these heights highly undesirable.

Although there is a one inch leeway either side of the ideal the Standard is quite specific about an 'ideal height'. The relationship of the build and balance of the dog to the height is not often taken into consideration. The thirteen inch bitch, at the shoulder, can look too small if the head is small and there is insufficient bone. The thirteen inch bitch that has a bigger head on a long body with a big coat is incorrect because the balance will be wrong. Equally the fifteen and a half inch dog will look too big if he has a large head and long body. Both are correct in their height but fail in other respects. The smaller headed, finer boned male may get away with being half an inch over size.

FAULTS:
Any departure from the foregoing points should be considered a fault and the seriousness with which the fault should be regarded should be in exact proportion to its degree.

The previous standard listed specific faults which are now in the category of 'undesirable' but they are still faults. Whilst not wanting to encourage 'fault' judging it is helpful to be aware of the faults in the breed whether or not one is judging or breeding.

The faults listed in the old standard are: domed or receding skull; lack of stop; large drooping or prick ears; over-developed cheeks; weak jaw; snipey muzzle; not full complement of teeth; crooked forelegs; cow hocks; kinked tail, short or carried over the back; white or white colour predominating; pink or flesh coloured nose; blue eyes in any other colour than merles; nervousness; full or light eye; under- or overshot mouth.

NOTE:
Male animals should have two apparently normal testicles descended into the scrotum.

As entirety was not mentioned in the previous standard it needs to be pointed out that it is a fault and should be treated as such. When one or both testicles are not descended, it may be forgiven by the occasional judge when the dog is a puppy but is unacceptable in an adult. It can be one of the most heartbreaking sides of keeping a dog for show when it fails to become entire.

76

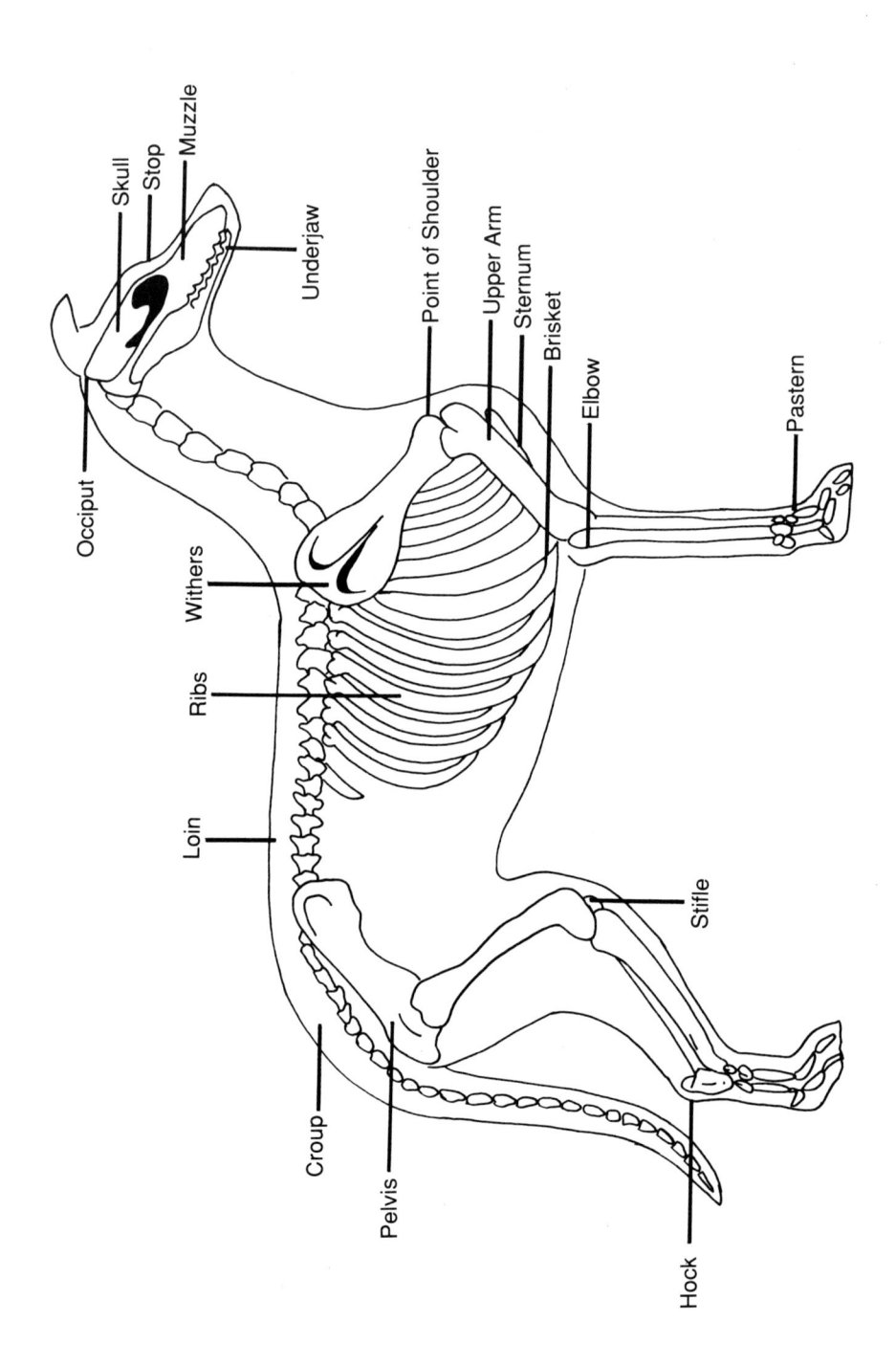

Buying the Sheltie Puppy

ANYONE thinking of buying a Sheltie should have a securely fenced garden and not be out at work from 9 am to 5 pm.
Always buy from a reputable breeder. The Shetland Sheepdog Clubs or The Kennel Club will supply a list of breeders.
Never go to a kennels where puppies of all breeds are bought in for resale. You may have to travel a distance or wait until there is a puppy available. If you are going to have the dog for the next fifteen years waiting for a few days or even weeks is a small price to pay to get the right puppy.
Do your homework,. You need to be sure that the breeder is reputable, that the puppies are well bred, with a decent pedigree and have been well reared. If necessary go and see several kennels to find out about type and temperament. It can vary.

Dog or Bitch

You will then need to decide whether you want a dog or a bitch. The majority of people will have a personal preference purely because they like what they know, but I have known them to change when there is no choice and they have been equally satisfied.
We, as a family, prefer the dogs and it was only by chance that I first kept one, having always had bitches in the family for as far back as I can remember. I was in the situation that if I did not keep the only surviving dog of a litter then I would lose my original breeding line, He proved an enormous success and attached himself to my husband, who had never had anything to do with dogs before we met. Very diplomatic!
The males are probably more of a family dog and will divide their attentions equally. Somehow one's attentions are always drawn to the dog puppies in the litter and many other breeders will say the same.
If you are gardeners and are contemplating a dog you will have to accept that his leg lifting may destroy your conifers, but equally a bitch can leave brown patches on the lawn from her urine. With the anti-dog lobby of today you must train your dog to relieve itself in the confines of your own garden, not in public places.
The Sheltie bitch will probably attach herself more to one particular member of the family. Dogs are probably more outgoing and perhaps more suitable to a predominately male household.
It is often said, to my mind misguidedly, that a bitch will not wander. They will tend to stay pretty close to you at all times. Anyone who

knowingly allows their dog to wander whether it be male or female is irresponsible and should not have a dog at all, so the argument should not arise. If, however, a bitch in season should get out she can be equally intent upon seeking out a mate as a male dog.

If you are thinking about mixing a dog and bitch and have no intention of breeding then one or other can be neutered. It must be thought out in advance how to deal with the problem.

If by any chance you wish to show or perhaps have a litter from your bitch, then be guided by the breeder. The breeder who has the breed at heart will be conscious of any inherent problems and will be aiming to improve their existing stock. If you have decided on a bitch and the breeder wishes to 'keep tabs' on her then a sensible gentleman's agreement over breeding can work very well. The majority of dedicated breeders will be aiming to breed something that will be good enough to be shown if not to be a Champion. Their aim is to improve the breed, not to produce puppies purely for the pet market.

I say majority because there can be an element of commercialism in the show world and people have been caught in the past by paying very large sums of money for bitch puppies that are tied up with a very complicated breeding term arrangement. Not all breeding term arrangements are bad - but beware.

Whoever the breeder may be, there are certain things to be aware of when you visit. There are some horrendous places where people keep too many dogs in the most appalling conditions. Too many people accept it as the norm but I am sure that anyone with any feeling for animals cannot fail to have heard about puppy farmers who from time to time are exposed by the media. Avoid them. If you find yourself at one of these places you do not have to make any excuse, just get out quickly before your heart rules your head. I have known people buy something because they have felt sorry for it, only to regret it.

Choosing the Puppy

Colour

The most popular Sheltie colour is sable and white. Tricolours, predominantly black with tan points and white markings are not so common and blue merle, a silvery blue with black overpatches, tan points and white markings are more rare.

If you are trying to replace a very much loved Sheltie that was a particular colour keep an open mind about the colour of the next one. All too often too much effort is made to find a carbon copy of the previous dog. This will be an impossibility as they are all so very different, if not in colour then certainly in personality. Every dog is different and what counts most is the temperament.

If your previous Sheltie was a sable do not be put off if a breeder offers you a tri or merle puppy. You are not compelled to buy the first puppy you see so go and see them. The personality and temperament of the puppy is all important. You may be very taken by it or you may not and will have definitely decided to pursue the hunt for a sable.

Sheltie puppies are most appealing

Size

Sheltie puppies are most appealing and the majority of people will buy the first puppy that they see. To predict the adult size of Sheltie puppies is extremely difficult, therefore those that see an appealing eight week old puppy may not neccessarily give too much thought as to its eventual size. It is not unreasonable to ask the breeder whether they think a puppy is going to end up big or small. Some people would only want a correct sized or smaller adult whereas others prefer a larger dog. The honest and experienced breeder should be able to give some sort of indication. If you are in doubt then go and see other puppies.

Health

When viewing your prospective puppy do see that the puppy is happy and clean, well covered with the coat healthy and sweet smelling.

Being able to see the mother and or the father can give you some idea about colour, type and temperament.

Handle the puppy and feel whether or not it is nicely rounded, I prefer to see a fat puppy at eight weeks. The puppy who is skinny, has a pot belly, running eyes and a staring coat has not been reared well with regard to feeding and worming.

If the puppy smells and the coat is stuck up with excrement that is purely bad management, for which there is no excuse.

Shelties have an inherited eye problem, about which the majority of responsible breeders are most concerned. Puppies can be screened for CEA, Collie Eye Anomaly, from the age of six weeks and it is not unreasonable to ask the breeder for details of such an examination and the results of the parents' examination. If neccessary ask to see the certificate from the eye specialist. If a puppy is mildly affected the condition will *not* progress as the puppy gets older and will *not* affect him as a pet and valued member of the family, (See page 205 CEA).

The majority of puppies sold at eight weeks old have not been vaccinated. If the puppy has been vaccinated then it is reasonable for the cost of the vaccination to be added to the purchase price, unless otherwise stated.

Before actually purchasing your puppy:

* Do your homework
* Go and see several breeders, even if they do not have a puppy to sell
* Decide whether you want a dog or a bitch
* Decide on the colour
* Decide the size, if neccessary
* See the parents or relations
* See that the puppy is clean and healthy
* Check that he has been wormed
* Ask whether the pups eyes have been tested
** Do not be afraid to say if you are not sure and would like to have time to consider. The majority of caring breeders would rather you were completely satisfied before taking away one of their puppies

Bringing up the Sheltie Puppy

The New Puppy

At the time of purchase the breeder should have supplied you with:
* A receipt
* A pedigree
* A diet sheet
* Registration certificate

The only person who can register a puppy with the Kennel Club is the breeder. If the registration documents have not come back from the Kennel Club it is usual for them to be forwarded at a later date. As a number of successful breeders are not always up to date with their paperwork it is not unreasonable for you to remind them if it has not been received within a couple of months.

Settling the puppy in

Preparations should have been made for the arrival of the new baby puppy, beforehand. The correct food to be fed should have been ascertained from the breeder before collection and purchased so that there is continuity of the diet. Nothing will upset him more quickly than a dramatic change in feeding. Keep to the diet recommended. If in doubt pick up the phone and ask the breeder's advice.

* A bowl of water should always be available and changed daily
* Place the bed in a quiet position
* Vaccinate as soon as possible
* Do not allow him to run up and down stairs

Allow him to have plenty of sleep and rest, both day-time and night-time.

Feeding the New Puppy

It is essential that a diet sheet should accompany the puppy when going to his new home. Apart from the trauma of leaving the rest of the litter and finding he is on his own, a dramatic change of diet can have some devastating results.

Before you collect the puppy check with the breeder exactly how the puppy has been fed so that the correct food can be bought. Alternatively the breeder may give you a supply of food if it is not readily available.

There should be a bowl of clean, fresh drinking water available at all times.

Do not give him great bowlfuls of milk. His digestion can very easily be upset by too much milk, they do not need it.

Do not give large meals, this will guarantee an upset tummy. Small meals, little and often, are the best. Four meals per day for the eight week old is usually recommended,(see page 144).

For the first few weeks keep to the basic diet recommended by the breeder, then when the puppy is well and truly settled you can decide what form of feeding will suit both the dog and you.

These days there are a myriad of prepared foods that are ready to feed. The tinned Chum Puppy Food and mixer has excellent results particularly if fed from the outset of weaning and can then be fed until at least eight months prior to giving an adult diet.

The complete foods such as Go-Dog or Pedigree Chum Formula are excellent products which assure firm stools and give a consistent, balanced diet.

The Puppy Pen

It is essential for puppies to have their regular rest during the time of rapid growth, a separate pen is required so that they can be allowed to sleep and rest without any distractions. It cannot be emphasised enough how important this is. The exhausted puppy will curl up and sleep anywhere.

The exhausted puppy will curl up and sleep anywhere

The purchase of some wire puppy playpen panels provide an excellent portable pen, or an individual panel can make a gate across doorways. They have several uses even when puppy has grown up. They will fold flat for easy storage and can be used indoors or outdoors.

I find them useful even for the adults because if the puppy learns at an early age about his pen he will accept being in it as part of his routine. It can be a place of safety.

Maybe he will need rescuing from overactive children or be prevented from becoming mixed up with the new paint!

Puppy's Bed

It is not really a very good idea to purchase an expensive bed for the

Puppies in their playpen

eight week old puppy as it will be demolished within a very short space of time, apart from which a bed that is suitable for the baby puppy will not be big enough when he is an adult. A cardboard grocery box, with the side cut out, is the ideal bed as this can be changed when chewed or soiled and the size can be increased as he grows.

The baby puppy who has suddenly found himself alone without the comfort and warmth of his litter mates will appreciate a small box that is made snug with some old jumpers laid inside. A covered hot water bottle in the bottom of his bed for the first few nights can help him to settle.

As the puppy grows up a sensible bed is the moulded plastic type that will withstand a certain amount of chewing without being a hazard.

An excellent type of bedding, albeit quite expensive, is made of nylon fur and is greenbacked. Vetbed is marketed as dog veterinary bedding and used by dog and cat breeders everywhere.

It is reasonably indestructable, does not hold any moisture, washes well and dries quickly. If you do purchase this type then do buy the more expensive sort as you will get what you pay for. The cheaper varieties will matt up easily and the pile is not so dense. When washing in the washing machine do not put through the hot wash. Wash on a low temperature programme and brush through the pile before drying.

Bean bags are not a good idea for the young teething puppy as they are easily chewed and it is not easy trying to clear up millions of polystyrene beans! However, they do enjoy them when they are older.

House Training

The most impressionable age for a puppy is between six and eight weeks. How the breeder manages the litter during those two weeks can be critical to the length of time it takes to house train a puppy.

Constant vigilance and anticipation on the part of the owner is essential.

Vigilance - in watching the puppy's every move and when he starts to wander around with his nose down then put him outside either by calling him out or picking him up and placing him onto the grass.

Anticipate and be aware of his natural need to relieve himself. It is an automatic reaction for a young puppy to spend a penny as soon as he wakes up, just as he will want to defecate soon after a meal. The length of time between the meal and defecation will lengthen, as the number of meals are reduced. There is more bowel control as the puppy grows older.

When the puppy has gone to his new home the idea of using a sheet of newspaper placed strategically by the door can be an excellent one. Put down when you are not in the same room as the puppy so that if he is caught short he can use it. When you are in the same room then you should take the paper up. Watch him carefully and when he starts to move towards the door, and the paper, you can open the door and let him out. At the same time give the command 'out'. If you give a command each time then the puppy will know what you mean. Always give the same command.

The trick is to not allow the puppy to even get that far, but anticipate him and take him out at the time he should be due to relieve himself.

I will always try and accompany the puppy onto the grass. Not only to show him where to go but so that I can tell him what a 'good boy' he is every time.

Being creatures of habit a routine can soon become established.

Some puppies will learn quite quickly whereas others simply do not seem to get the message. I do find that the winter puppy is somehow easier to house train than the summer puppy. The longer nights mean that the puppy will rest more due to the dark. The summer puppies wake with the light and will be charging around well before you are ready yourself, with the resulting mess.

When a puppy has gone to his new home any difficulty in house training should be noted and advice from the breeder sought. Every puppy can be different. A urinary problem is not uncommon in the form of cystitis and veterinary advice should be sought if there is no response to the alternatives, (see page 215).

Ch. Shelto Sheraleigh. Born 1975, by: Moonraker from Mistmere ex: Exbury Larkspur. Winner of 7 C.C.s. Bred and owned by Mrs Diane Moore

Ch. Shetlo the Gay Piper. Born 1979, by: Ch. Rhinog The Gay Lancer ex: Ch. Shetlo Sheraleigh. Bred and owned by Mrs Diane Moore

Ch. Jasmine of Janetstown, aged 8½ years. Winner of 10 C.C.s including the C.C. at the English Shetland Sheepdog Club Championship Shows in 1979 and 1984 (also Best in Show). The breed bitch Record holder 1984-1988.
Born 1975, by: Lysebourne Quick March, ex: Janetstown Japonica.
Bred by Mrs Lo Frosch and owned by Mrs Jan Moody

Ch. Sharval The Deliquent aged 11 years. Born 1968, by: Carousel of Melvaig ex: Sharval Cilla Black. The breed C.C. record holder 1971-1985 with 16 C.C.s. Bred and owned by Mr Albert Wight

Ch. Rhinog The Gay Lancer. Born 1972, by: Ch. Sharval The Delinquent ex: Ch. Rhinog Waltzing Matilda. Bred and owned by Miss Diana Blount. Sire of 4 Champions and behind many other winners in both UK and Sweden

Ch. Scylla Scottish Rifle. Born 1978, by: Ch. Rhinog The Gay Lancer ex: Scylla Starry Halo. Bred and owned by Mrs Marion Marriage. Winner of the C.C. at the English Shetland Sheepdog Club Championship Show in 1981 (also Best in Show) and 1984.

Janetstown Jorrocks (left), bred and owned by Mrs Jan Moody. Born 1980, by: Ch. Scylla Scottish Rifle ex: Ch. Jasmine of Janetstown (centre). Janetstown Apple Juice (right) a granddaughter of Jorrocks, by: Ch. Marksman of Ellendale.

Ch. Jazzman of Janetstown.
Born 1985, by: Janetstown Jorrocks
ex: Dippersmoor Dreamtime.
Bred by Mr R. G. Bradley and owned
by Mrs Jan Moody.

Colmae Jazz Juke of Janetstown. Born 1987, by: Ch. Jazzman of Janetstown ex: Golden Sun of Colmae. Bred and owned by Mrs Margaret Collett.

Ch. Sandpiper of Sharval. Born 1976, by: Ch. Sharval The Delinquent ex: Chamwood Gay Girl. Bred by Mr and Mrs W. Young and owned by Mr Albert Wight. Winner of 14 C.C.s and 3 Working Groups. The only Sheltie to win more than one Group and Best in Show at an all-breeds Championship Show, Belfast 1978.

Ch. Lythwood Sky Master. Born 1981, by: Ch. Sandpiper of Sharval ex: Lythwood Snaffey. Bred and owned by Mr Derek Rigby.

Ch. Lythwood Sea Nymph. Born 1977, by: Heathlow Harvest Time at Lythwood ex: Lythwood Tar Baby. Bred and owned by Mr Derek Rigby.

Ch. Lythwood Scrabble. Born 1984, by: Ch. Lythwood Spruce ex: Ch. Lythwood Sea Nymph. Bred and owned by Mr Derek Rigby.
Best in Show, Shetland Sheepdog Club of Northern Ireland 1986.

A very distinctive Sheltie characteristic - the smile!

Snabswoods out exercising with Mrs Jean Fitzsimons, 1979.
Ch Snabswood Slainthe is on the right.

Diarrhoea in the recently rehomed puppy frequently happens. Do not change the diet from the one recommended by the breeder until the puppy is settled. If looseness is not due to the diet and persists it will want sorting out quickly. Whilst the puppy is in that sort of state any hope of house training him will be impossible. Again seek the advice of the breeder and/or your veterinary surgeon. I have dealt with the subject of diarrhoea elsewhere, (see page 200).

Some puppies are quicker than others and the older puppy that is still dirty at night can be moved to a different room to sleep. This can very often have the desired effect. If I have a puppy that is being run on and is in the house during the day but still persists in messing his kennel at night, bringing him into the kitchen to sleep can do the trick. Use a puppy pen, not too big, and put his bed in there and pop him in very last thing at night. One is then in a very good position to creep downstairs in the morning, so as not to wake him up, and put him out as quickly as possible.

I must say that I do find dogs easier to house train than bitches. A bitch can sometimes not be too clean until they have a season.

A change of home for the adult kennelled bitch who is persistently dirty can be quite miraculous. One particular bitch that I thought would never learn was sleeping on her new owner's bed within twenty four hours and never disgraced herself.

Points to remember:
* Anticipate and take outside regularly
* Accompany the puppy to the place you wish him to go
* Always give the same command
* Always give praise
* Do not change the diet too quickly

Lead Training

Lead training can start at twelve weeks. A fine rounded leather collar should be put on and worn for long periods. If the puppy sleeps on his own then leaving the collar on all the time will not hurt. It is easier to get the puppy to move when on the lead for the first time if he is used to having a collar round his neck. If you put a collar and lead on the first time you want to go out then he will spend most of the time sitting down scratching his neck and collar.

A very fine lead with a small light-weight clip is preferable to a cumbersome heavy lead that will weigh too heavy round the puppy's neck.

It is more difficult to lead train in your own garden as he will not understand why he is being restrained when at other times you allow him his freedom. Going outside his own territory is easier as he will have more incentive to stay close to his owner. Find a quiet road and take him a few hundred yards to start with, then carry him then put him down again. Having another dog or member of the family walking ahead will encourage the young puppy to move forward. As he follows do not let the lead go tight, follow the puppy sensibly. As he becomes more confident then a little pressure on the lead may be used for guidance. Talk to him all the time, using an encouraging tone of voice. The whole exercise should be fun and made into a bit of a game. When the brakes are on give a pull and then relax the lead. Repeat several times until he moves forward with you.

The puppy that lies on his back with his legs in the air can pose a problem. Bribery with a tit-bit can be most effective provided he is really hungry.

The young puppy should only have a minimum amount of formal exercise so it should be a case of little and often.

Car Training

In the main Shelties are good travellers, preferring to accompany their owners and sit in the car for hours on end rather than be left at home. Unfortunately there are the exceptions, this tendency seems to run in certain lines.

Early training can set a pattern for life but can so often be neglected, possibly due to the fact that one does not consider taking a very young puppy out. Hence, the first three times that he goes in the car are when he goes to the vet for his injections. How can one blame a puppy for associating going in the car with a nasty man who sticks needles in him.

Tension and nerves contribute towards travel sickness therefore to have the dog relaxed in anticipation of enjoying himself is half the battle. The baby puppy should go for car rides as often as possible, even if it is only half a mile at a time. If someone can nurse him then that will give him the security that he needs. If a few undramatic journeys can be accomplished then there is every prospect that he will become a good traveller.

The young puppy should be:
* Taken out on regular journeys
* Nursed by a passenger
* or, given his own box on the floor

Avoid
* Only taking him out when going to the vet or to kennels
* Feeding prior to a journey
* Travelling the very young puppy in the back part of an estate car
* Driving quickly on a twisty road

The dog who continues being sick or dribbles into adulthood can be a major problem. However, giving travel sickness tablets can be effective provided the right one for the dog can be found. The products that are most widely used within the Sheltie fraternity are:

'Sealegs'. These are effective without making the dog drowsy. This is better for show dogs who need to be on their toes at the show. Dosage is one tablet for adult dogs, given the night before then again an hour before the journey if necessary. Puppies need half the dose.

'Shaws' Travel Sickness tablets are also effective and will help the dog to sleep, but only for an hour or so. This may be sufficient to relax him. Do give at least an hour and a half before setting out.

The dog that resists going near the car can be put into the vehicle for short but increasing periods whilst it is stationary in the drive. Try giving him his meal in the car rather than the normal place.

Daily walks can start with a short journey in the car rather than walking straight off the premises. The association with the car and a walk can often overcome any travel sickness problem.

When all else fails and desperation point has been reached and an essential long journey must be undertaken then a visit to the vet may be needed. Any medication given for the show dog should be tried out before the day of the show in case it has a bad effect.

As soon as possible give him his own bed or blanket positioned in the car where you will always want him to travel. Some Shelties dislike things whizzing past the car and can appear quite demented; if this is the case then the floor is a very suitable place. Be firm about making him stay in his place from the outset. The dog that leaps around the car all of the time is dangerous and is no pleasure to have around.

A portable travelling cage is a safe way of transporting a Sheltie in the rear of an estate car or hatchback. It allows him his own bed and prevents him being thrown around.

Kitchen roll and towels are essential and should be taken on every journey.

REMEMBER - never leave a dog in a car when the sun in blazing. Even if the outside temperature is quite cool, the inside of a car can heat up very quickly to horrendous temperatures in a relatively short space of time. During hot spells in the summer give very careful consideration as to whether the dog needs to accompany you. He may well be better off at home.

If the journey is really necessary always carry a cool box with ice and water in case of lengthy jams on motorways.

Buying an Adult Sheltie

There can often be a very valid argument for having an older dog. Notwithstanding the possibility of having one that is already housetrained, there is the advantage of not having to give so many meals, as would be the case with a young puppy.

The older dog may take a little time to settle. Usually a month is needed to become familiar with his surroundings.

Older Shelties settle very well in new homes, particularly if they have come from a kennel with a large number of dogs. I think that they are better off as they will get all the attention when rehomed, rather than having to take their place amongst a crowd.

The adult dog or bitch may be available for a number of reasons. Not having made the grade for the showring is the most usual reason. It is not until the puppy is over six months that the breeder can make his decision.

Alternatively, there is the brood bitch who is ready to be retired from breeding. Many sensible breeders will be aware that their faithful broods will be far better off sharing someone else's lap than spending the rest of her days in a kennel. The only thing to beware of is that the wholly kennelled dog may not settle easily if it has never been off the premises or been in a house. The new owner who takes on a dog in these circumstances and perseveres will be greatly rewarded. I am glad to say that the age of the large kennel is more a thing of the past and most Shelties are used to being indoors at some time or another. Most breeders have their Shelties living as part of the family.

The majority of Sheltie owners usually end up with more than one dog. Two is a convenient number, three can be a crowd. Shelties can become very noisy if there are too many around. If you have difficult neighbours nothing will aggravate relations more quickly than noisy dogs. Many people have moved house to get away from complaining neighbours.

Introducing a dog puppy into a household with one dog is alright but introducing an adult male to another adult male could create problems. A similar thing can happen with bitches, but it is less likely.

Responsible Dog Ownership

* Control your dog at all times
* Do not allow your dog to be a nuisance to others
* Do not allow him to bark unnecessarily
* Keep on a lead when on the road
* A collar and identity tag should be worn when outside the home
* Clean up after your dog
* Vaccinate annually
* Worm regularly
* Feed sensibly
* Exercise regularly
* Groom regularly
* Never leave a dog in a parked car during hot weather
* At any sign of illness consult your vet
* When booking your holiday do organise the dog at the same time and book him into a good licenced kennel where they understand our breed

Any person who is thinking of buying a dog for the first time should be aware of their responsibilities to those who do not have and do not like dogs. The 1980's saw an upsurge in the anti-dog lobby so any way that the dog owning public can be protected, in the same way that the anti-dog are protected, should be pursued. There is more emphasis on educating the public to responsible dog ownership than ever before.

As in most things it is *not* the responsible people who are to blame.

The Neighbours

To say that any Sheltie should not bark is asking the impossible. When there is more than one dog in the home the likelihood of more noise is increased. It is therefore unwise to allow any excess barking that will aggravate the neighbours.

Never allow your dog to run up and down the garden fence for hours on end. Leaving him with the run of the garden whilst you go out is a recipe for trouble. Even when he is left in the house it is wise to confine the dog to one room. When you are out you will not be aware of any noise he may be making but persistent barking can be classed as a nuisance.

Dogs and Collars

Your dog should always wear a collar with an identity disc or tag when outside your home. This should be common sense as there can be so many instances whereby a dog can be lost.

Dogs on Leads

Local authorities each have different bye-laws with respect to where dogs must be kept on a lead. This could be just on roads or could include parks and open spaces. To my mind no dog should be off the lead on any public highway. A loose dog, however normally reliable, can so easily be distracted. I have heard too many tales of woe about the one time the dog went on to the road. He only needs to do it once.

It is an offence to allow a dog to chase farm animals. When in the country dogs should always be on a lead where there are livestock. Farmers and landowners have a right to protect their animals and the law gives them the right to shoot any dog they think is harrassing their stock or even if in the same field off the lead.

Clean up after your Dog

All dogs should be trained to relieve themselves on their own ground. In the past it has been the accepted thing to take the dog out for a walk last thing at night to relieve himself. Nowadays the dog should relieve himself in his own garden prior to going for a walk.

Local authority bye-laws are becoming increasingly strict about dogs fouling in public places. Any accidental excrement deposited in a public place should be removed by the person in charge of that dog.

There are a myriad of Pooper Scoopers on the market but I find that it is easier and cheaper to carry a supply of polythene bags and sheets of kitchen roll. The sheet of kitchen roll can be placed over the excrement then put your hand into the polythene bag, grasp the paper and contents and then pull the bag inside out. A tie will seal the bag and it can then be carried to a litter bin or taken home for disposal. Your hands will still be clean.

At home all excrement should be picked up daily from the garden and disposed of.

Do not allow males to urinate in public places. It is a natural tendency for males to mark an area but they should be discouraged. Open gardens in suburbia are targets for the unleashed dog who will always make for the garden, particularly with conifers, owned by an anti-dog person.

Dogs in Cars

Never leave a dog in a parked car during warm sunny weather. Even with a window open the inside of the car can reach an exceedingly high temperature within a very short space of time. Always carry water and ice packs on long journeys during the summer in case of lengthy hold-ups on motorways.

Kennelling

Do not leave your Sheltie with a friend or neighbour when going on holiday unless they are familiar with the dog and their premises are secure. A licenced boarding kennel that is sympathetic to our breed is the safest place. The worried Sheltie can be the most expert escapoligist and can then be a hazard to the motorist. Apart from which your dog's life could be at jeopardy if on the loose.

Insurance

Breeders and owners should always take advice on insurance.

For a small amount per annum third party cover can be obtained. For an additional cost vet's fees can also be covered.

Feeding

SHELTIES are notorious as a breed for getting an upset tummy. This is made more evident because of their long tail and petticoats which can become easily soiled and rather smelly! Being sensible about your dog's diet should ensure that he always has firm stools. Most dogs will cope with the same food day in day out. There is no real necessity to keep changing the diet. It is purely the whim of the owner who feels that they themselves would prefer a change.

The fussy eater will usual live as an individual in a rather doting home where his owners think that if he does not eat he will starve. They then keep trying something a little more tasty until the bowl is cleared. Most of the time these little rascals will lead their owners on to such an extent that they get precisely what they want! Conventional dog food, when given, is rejected. What the owner does not realise is that the dog will not starve. The majority of the time these owners will also try to feed the dog too much when he does not need it and is not really hungry.

When a so-called 'fussy eater' comes into the kennels they are often accompanied by a variety of goodies. The dog will probably not eat for the first day anyway. Being fat enough means that a day's starvation does them no harm at all. In fact many canine dieticians recommend one day a week without food as a general regime.

I will then feed small but tasty meals and by the end of their stay they will eat normally. Back home with their owners they will quickly revert to their old habits.

A well balanced, high quality diet is required throughout a dog's life. How he is reared as a puppy and the care taken in feeding the dam even before the puppies are born can, I am sure, have an influence on his future life.

All my adult Shelties get two meals per day. The main meal in the morning (because it suits me) and a smaller 'token' meal in the late afternoon or early evening. The second meal is because when there are puppies or youngsters about who require a meal at that time the adults also require recognition. I am convinced that Shelties 'do' better on the two meals and the second meal can be used for regulating weight. The 'teenager', who can drop weight very quickly, can be fed more at his second meal.

The single pet Sheltie will have more of a tendency to obesity than two or three dogs living and playing together.

Today there are many excellent products on the market from canned meat to dry complete foods.

Meat should always be accompanied by a mixer biscuit or equivalent carbohydrate, baked brown bread can be a useful standby. It is well known that Shelties cannot tolerate the amount of meat to biscuit ratio recommended by many of the tinned food manufacturers. A general guideline for Shelties is 1/3 meat to 2/3 biscuit.

Knacker's meat should always be well cooked to ensure that there is no chance of transferring any infection from the beast to the dogs.

There are many excellent dry complete foods on the market. These are completely balanced with the correct amount of protein and carbohydrate, with vitamins and minerals incorporated. Different products have varying percentages of protein content with puppy and breeding diets having a higher protein content than a general maintenance diet.

18%-20% protein content is recommended for general maintenance with 24% for more active dogs and 29%-30% for growing puppies.

There are fewer digestion problems when a complete diet is consistently fed. The loose flake type is popular, but tends to be excreted in similar form. It also allows small particles to accumulate around the teeth and gums causing periodontal problems.

The expanded variety I find excellent. It can be soaked or, if given dry, gives them something to chew, keeps teeth and gums clean and appears to be more digestible with fewer stools.

If a complete food is given there is no necessity to add anything else. Any addition, such as meat, will unbalance the diet.

Feeding the Veteran

As dogs get older their dietary requirements change. Shelties can be prone to early kidney problems so feeding the veteran a lower protein content diet is advisable.

Where there is a kidney or arthritic problem fish or white meat should be fed if meat and biscuit is normally given. There should also be a higher ratio of biscuit to meat.

The complete food manufacturers now seem to be more aware of the dietary requirements of the veteran and have accordingly brought out appropriate products.

Where there is an obesity problem bran or boiled brown rice can replace the biscuit.

Remember that the elderly dog may not be taking as much exercise as in earlier years so the amount of food should be regulated to prevent obesity.

Supplements

Most dog food manufacturers state that all the essential vitamins and minerals are incorporated but many people cannot resist adding the many calcium and vitamin supplements available. I use one product for the growing puppy and for the in-whelp bitch. A good diet should be sufficient for the average adult dog. During winter months when there seems to be a total lack of sunshine I buy a large tin of Vetzyme yeast tablets and give a course at the recommended dosage to the entire kennel. When the tin is finished they will not have any further supplementation unless the dogs are being frequently used at stud or the show dogs are out of coat. One hears of people feeding all and everything hoping it will bring the coat back quicker and better. It is like trying to watch the kettle come to the boil, it will appear to take an interminable time but in the end it will come. The dogs that are not being shown will always have the most marvellous coat when you have not been trying!

Table 1 Dietary supplements

	Nutrient	Dosage	Dangers
Proprietary supplements	Minerals and/or vitamins	As directed	Toxic in excess
Yeast tablets	B group vitamins	As directed for man but scale to dog size by weight	None
Cod liver oil	Vitamins A,D,E	Less than one 5 ml teaspoon per week for largest dogs	Toxic in excess
Vegetable oils	Essential fatty acids	One per cent of dry matter of diet (e.g. five per cent of meat diet)	Become rancid with time
Bone meal	Calcium, phosphorus	¼oz per lb meat	May cause malformed bones in excess
Seaweed tablets	Iodine	As directed	Little
Garlic tablets	?	?	?
Raspberry tablets	?	?	?

Table 2 Vitamins

Vitamin	Dietatry source	Main functions	Results of deficiency	Results of excess
Fat Soluble Vitamin A	Fish oils, liver, vegetables	Vision in poor light, maintenance of skin	Night blindness, skin lesions	Anorexia, pain in bones (malformation)
Vitamin D	Cod-liver oil, eggs, animal products	Calcium balance, bone growth	Rickets, osteomalacia	Anorexia, calcification of soft tissues
Vitamin E	Green vegetables, vegetable oils, dairy products	Reproduction	Infertility, anaemia, muscle weakness	n/k
Vitamin K	Spinach, green vegetables, liver, in vivo synthesis	Blood clotting	Haemorrhage	n/k
Water Soluble (B group) Thiamin (B_1)	Dairy products, cereals, organ meat	Release of energy from carbohydrate	Anorexia, vomiting, paralysis	n/k
Riboflavin (B_6)	Milk, animal tissues	Utilization of energy	Weight loss, weakness, collapse, coma	n/k
Niacin	Cereals, liver, meat, legumes	Utilization of energy	Anorexia, ulceration of mouth (black tongue)	n/k
Pyridoxine (B_6)	Meat, fish, eggs, cereals	Metabolism of amino acids	Anorexia, anaemia, weight loss, convulsions	n/k
Vitamin (B_{12})	Liver, meat, dairy products	Division of cells in bone marrow	Anaemia	n/k
Folic acid	Offals, leafy vegetables	As B_{12}	Anaemia, poor growth,	n/k
Pantothenic acid	Animal products, cereals, legumes	Release of energy from fat/carbohydrate	Slow growth, hair loss, convulsions, coma	n/k
Biotin	Offal, egg yolk, legumes	Metabolism of fat and amino acids	Loss of coat condition (scaly skin, scurf)	n/k
Choline	Plant and animal materials	Nerve function	Fatty infiltration of liver, poor blood clotting	n/k

n/k = not known in dogs

Table 3 Minerals

Mineral	Dietary sources	Main functions	Results of deficiency	Results of excess
Calcium	Bones, milk, cheese	Bone formation, nerve and muscle formation	Poor growth, rickets, convulsions	Very high levels - bone deformities
Phosphorus	Bones, milk	Bone formation, energy utilization	Rickets (rare)	Symptoms of calcium deficiency
Potassium	Meat, milk	Water balance, nerve function	Poor growth, paralysis, kidney and heart lesions	Muscular weakness?
Sodium/chlorine	Salts, cereals	Water balance, muscle and nerve activity	Poor growth, exhaustion	Thirst, high blood pressure (if intake maintained)
Magnesium	Cereals, bones, green vegetables	Bone formation, protein synthesis	Anorexia, vomiting, muscular weakness	Diarrhoea
Iron	Eggs, meat (liver), green vegetables	Part of haemoglobin (oxygen transport)	Anaemia, low resistance to hookworm infestation	Weight loss, anorexia
Copper	Meat, bones	Part of haemoglobin	Anaemia	Anaemia in other mammals, hepatitis in Bedlington Terriers
Zinc	Meat, cereals	in digestion, tissue maintenance	Hair loss, skin thickening, poor growth	Diarrhoea
Manganese	Tea, nuts, cereals	Fat metabolism, many enzyme functions	Reproductive failure, poor growth	Poor fertility in other mammals, albinism, anaemia
Iodine	Fish, dairy produce	Part of thyroid hormone	Hair loss, apathy, drowsiness	In other animals, symptoms similar to deficiency
Selenium	Cereals, fish meals	Associated with vitamin E function	Muscle damage	Toxic

Dogs may also require molybdenum, fluorine, tin, silicon, cobalt, nickel vanadium and chromium in very small amounts.

Grooming

Routine Grooming

The coat of the Shetland Sheepdog is his crowning glory enhancing his appeal and creating attention and interest wherever he goes. Keeping the coat clean and well groomed ensures that he will look his best and be pleasing to the eye at all times.

Regular grooming is essential for keeping any dog clean whether it has a long coat like a Sheltie or a smooth coat like a Dalmatian. The effect of brushing removes dirt and stimulates the hair folicules which will supply the natural oils for the coat. An accumulation of dirt and natural oils over a period of time will create a 'doggy' smell if not removed. Shelties benefit from weekly attention, and will appreciate more if given and needed.

The smoother coated breeds never seem to be groomed regularly as they will look tidy most of the time which is why they will tend to have more of a 'doggy' odour than a Sheltie. With the Sheltie it is very apparent from his appearance when grooming is neccessary.

Frequent grooming can be very therapeutic for both dog and owner. It allows the owner to maintain a rapport with the dog at the same time as discovering any problem not normally visible beneath the coat. Any growth or skin complaint such as eczema or the occasional tick or infestation of fleas can be found at grooming time. A brush that is run through a coat where there are fleas present will disturb them making them obvious.

My own dogs are brushed weekly or whenever needed. When moulting they need more regular brushing and combing to help get rid of the old coat and help in the new coat. Swirls of Sheltie hair around are evidence of a moult. Regular bathing at that time helps to loosen and remove the old coat and at the same time stimulates the new coat. When all the old coat has gone, and the new coat seems to be taking an age to get to any length, a bath will revitalise it and make all the difference.

Grooming Equipment

* Brush - Mason Pearson Universal
* Slikker brush
* Combs
* Coat Dressing
* Talcum powder or chalk
* Scissors
* Thinning Scissors
* Stripping knife
* Nail clippers
* Grooming mat
* Towels

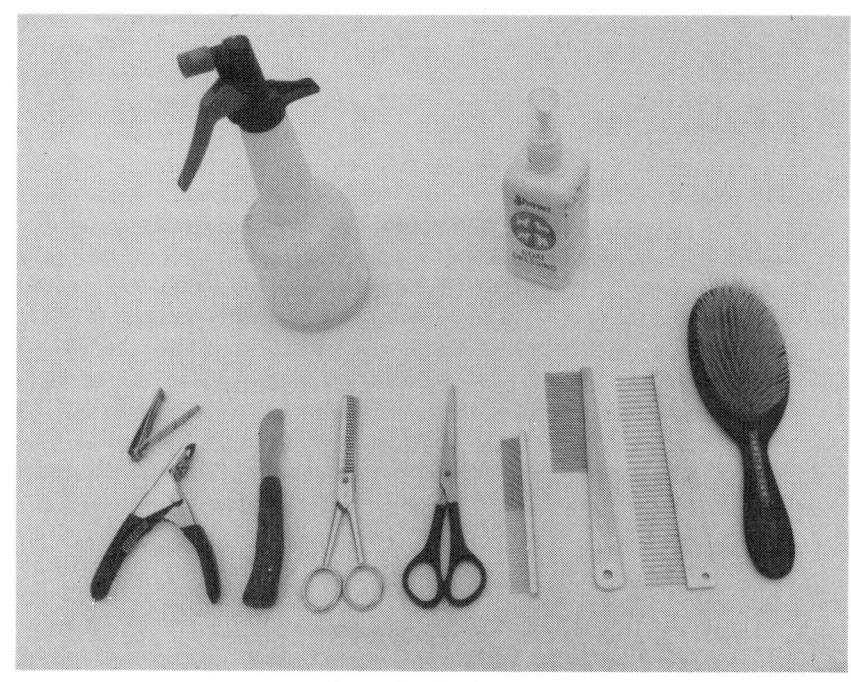

Grooming Equipment

The Brush

The most vital part of the grooming kit. A nylon or nylon and bristle brush on a rubber cushion is most suitable for the double coat on the Sheltie. The very best type is a Mason Pearson Universal, which is all nylon and marketed for humans. They are obtainable through any pharmacist or at the shows but may have to be ordered. I personally have been using these brushes since I first started in the breed. They will last for years therefore justifying their initial expense. The action of the Mason Pearson works in a way that gets right down to the undercoat at the same time as the top coat and giving the coat a lift. They are used world wide by Sheltie and Collie folk as well as for other breeds. The Mason Pearson brush comes with a separate cleaning brush which is useful when washing the brush. It is advisable to wash any brush regularly if a coat dressing has been used as it will prevent the rubber cushion rotting.

The Slikker brush

A fine wire brush resembling a carding comb. Effective for loosening matted undercoat in the neglected dog. Not recommended for the regular grooming of the show dog as it will break the coat.

Combs

I use three types of comb. These can be bought individually or in combinations.

a) A wide toothed comb is useful to gently go over the top coat as a final touch. Also to use when removing dead coat during a moult.
b) A medium toothed comb for combing the frills at the back of the front legs and behind the ears.
c) A very fine comb that is sold as a cat comb. This small comb can come as a dual width and is excellent for combing through the short hair that is on the head, legs and the ears. It can also be used behind the ears when there is an excess of fine hair.

Coat Dressing

Over the years I have tried many of the products on the market but always come back to the original Shaws Coat Dressing as it suits the Sheltie coat particularly well. It can be obtained with a pump spray or in bulk and then decanted into a spray bottle.

An oil based dressing is totally unsuitable and will make the coat greasy and lank. Tricolours can react to certain coat dressings causing the coat to become dull.

The use of a coat dressing will make grooming easier, separating the coat as it deodorises, leaving a pleasant smell.

Rain water has a most beneficial effect on the Sheltie coat which is evident after they have been out in the rain. Any rain water that has been gathered should be filtered (a coffee filter paper works well) before it is put into a spray bottle.

It must be emphasised that Kennel Club regulations state that no substance should be left in the coat, when the dog is being shown, that will alter the texture of the coat. Whereas a grooming spray may be used at home it is advisable to only use rain water at a show. No one is quite sure what is acceptable. Random tests can be made at shows. If the results are proved positive the penalty is disqualification.

Talcum Powder and Chalk

A very useful aid in the general care of the coat but only at home. Kennel Club regulations prohibit the use of chalk or powder when a dog is being shown. The ban is unfortunate as the Sheltie that has had his whites touched up with a chalk block prior to entering the ring can be so greatly enhanced.

At home, talcum powder is useful to use as a cleaner, i.e. the undercarriage of a dog where urine has accumulated and gives off an odour. Sprinkle on the talcum then brush off immediately. It can be used to help remove a pungent smell which persists even after washing. This could be if pants have been dirtied, which can happen rather frequently with Shelties, or when they have done the unmentionable act of rolling in something foul!

A liberal dusting of chalk or talcum powder is beneficial on the very soft hair behind the ears. This fine hair can often become greasy, therefore the powder or chalk will absorb any grease. It will also allow a better grip to be made when using finger and thumb to pluck away any excess hair.

Chalk or talcum powder can be useful as a cleanser where bathing is undesirable. A thorough damping with water or coat dressing and then a liberal coating of powder can be rubbed well in and thoroughly brushed out. The powder will have absorbed the damp and dirt leaving the coat clean and sweet smelling.

Talcum powder is excellent when cleaning up puppies, but beware of any powder getting in their eyes.

Scissors

A good pair of small hairdressing scissors are a must to keep feet and heels tidy. Keep these scissors only for cutting hair. Nothing will ruin a good pair of scissors quicker than being used for other household jobs such as cutting paper and string.

Always keep the blades clean of mud or grease by wiping them after every use. If they rust they will lose their efficiency. A drop of oil on the blades will keep them clean and prevent any rust.

Practice makes perfect where trimming is concerned. When using scissors only take a little off at a time. Any hair removed can take a long time to grow and it will always take much longer when you want it to grow!

Thinning Scissors

These have a serrated blade and will not cut away so much hair in one go. They can be used instead of scissors below the hock and for thinning excess hair behind the ears. They can be easier to use for those unfamiliar with wielding a pair of scissors. Although I dislike them and seldom use them I can see why they are used. It is purely a preference.

Stripping Knife
The one piece knife that has a serrated blade I find quite efficient but they can be very sharp and I would not recommend them to the totally inexperienced groomer. I could never get on with the type that had a razor blade between two combs.

Nail Clippers
The guillotine type of clipper is most suitable as it is easier to see the exact place that one is cutting. Their action does not allow the nail to split in the same way as the scissor type.

Pincer clippers, sold as a pocket clipper for humans, are useful only for baby puppy claws that are like very fine hooks. As with the scissors, keep them clean and rust free by wiping the blades after every use and keeping oiled.

A Mat for grooming
A piece of carpet or a car mat kept specifically for dog grooming should be included in the kit. This is so that the dog does not slip when standing on the table.

Towels
Common sense hygiene means that your Sheltie should always have his own towels which are separate from those used by the family.

Grooming the Puppy
It is a very important that the Sheltie puppy is groomed from the time he is eight weeks old or even before. Grooming should start as soon as the puppy arrives in his new home and should be a regular occurance. Although there may not appear to be a need the procedure is all part of his training.

As often as possible (or at least twice per week) put a mat onto a table. Stand the puppy on the mat, always keep a hand on him to prevent him jumping off. Do not let him lean on you, make him stand on all four feet. This might sound ridiculous but puppies can lean with a foot off the mat not allowing you to handle him properly. If he stands on three legs pick up the opposite foot so that he has to put the other foot down. When he is settled gently run a hand from his head down his back and over his tail.

For the potential show puppy this can be a double lesson. Learning to stand on the table in the correct position for a judge to examine him as well as for grooming. They soon become very used to the exercise and it is a good discipline. Do not forget to make it fun, giving lots of praise, and do not overdo it so that they become bored.

After just standing on the table you can start to gently use a brush.

After a week or so gently start to comb behind the ears. Always make a general fuss of him before putting him on the floor so that he associates grooming with attention.

As your puppy grows up and becomes used to being on the table you can then progress by changing the way that he faces. This is helpful when more thorough grooming is needed. Always have the same routine and try to position him on the mat in the same way each time i.e. first facing to the left to do the left side then face to the right to do the right side. Then the rear end should be available to brush the tail and petticoats. Lastly the dog should face the front to do the bib. He is then in a position to be able to accept praise and fuss. Tell him what a good boy he is. Praise and even more praise. By having a routine such as this the dog will generally stand still. The mould will be set for the rest of his life.

When using a coat dressing on a very young puppy do not use the actual spray, as this will frighten him. Put the dressing onto the brush before brushing. Talcum powder is very useful when grooming a young puppy.

The fluff on a puppy will start to look less as the puppy grows up. If the fluff is turned back at about twelve weeks the new coat can be seen starting to come through by the skin. An idea of the colour of his adult coat may be apparent. Some puppies will remain very fluffy with the adult coat growing through, gradually overtaking until there is a very respectable coat by the age of six or seven months. Others will lose their puppy coat and appear smooth at around the four to five month stage giving a very leggy appearance. The eventual mature adult coat cannot be gauged by the amount of puppy coat. One of the fluffiest puppies I ever bred had been named Fluffy only to never carry a coat!

When a puppy has lost his baby fluff and starts to grow a new coat that coat will keep well for at least six months before he has his first really good moult around a year old.

The Adult Newly Grown Coat

The newly grown coat will be fresh, be a good colour and will shine. A cursory brush and spray will keep it fresh. In very hot weather that continues for long periods there may be a necessity to spray and brush regularly to prevent the coat drying out too much and to remove the dust. The whites become very difficult to keep clean in prolonged dry periods.

Grooming at Moulting Time

When a Sheltie starts to moult, the undercoat will have lifted from the skin, and if not removed it will look dead, pick up the dirt and the undercoat will mat into lumps.

The first evidence of a coat starting to 'blow' on the regularly groomed dog will be hair in the brush. As there is a tendency to not groom a dog that is in good healthy coat the first signs will be a dulling of the general coat condition. The hair on the tips of the ears will become a different colour as the hair is dead, forming into little tufts as it tries to come away. Also, tufts of undercoat appear on the thighs. Then as the moult progresses the dog will scratch to remove the dead hair. The loose hair will accumulate in their claws before being deposited on the carpet!

It is at this stage that more vigorous grooming is required. Not only with the brush but with a wide toothed comb.

In the case of a badly matted coat or knots behind the ears, the 'slikker' brush that resembles a carding comb, can be used to loosen and help remove the lumps. Combing through will then be easier.

After stripping all the coat out your dog will look and feel so much better.

This type of brush is not recommended for use on the show dog as the wire bristles will break the coat if used over a long period of time.

Brushing

A dog coming into good coat will benefit from regular brushing which stimulates the growth and keeps the coat clean. Good deep brushing with a Mason Pearson Universal brush ensures that the undercoat as well as the top coat, is kept separated, not in 'rats tails' and lumpy. When the coat parts in lines and looks dead, there has not been sufficient deep grooming or the coat is in need of a bath.

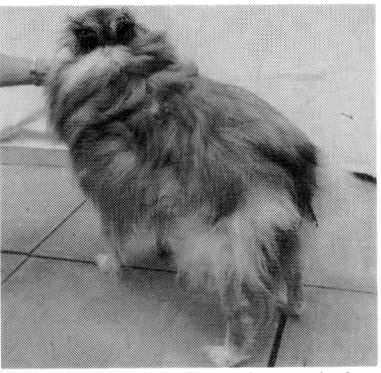

A badly matted coat in need of grooming

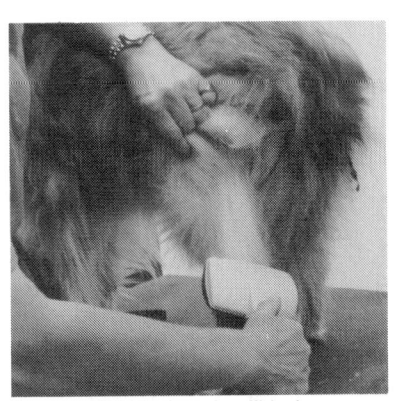

The Slikker brush will help to loosen and remove lumps of matted coat

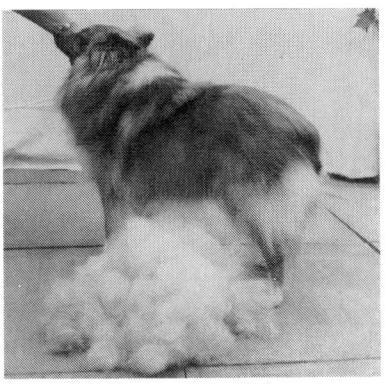

All dead and matted coat removed from the dog

'Deep brushing' means brushing right through both the topcoat and the undercoat.

Deep brushing will 'lengthen' the coat by the action of untangling the undercoat and topcoat. A great deal of dirt can be removed purely by brushing.

If you start brushing over the top then the brush will skim over the topcoat and not get down to the undercoat. Superficially this may look alright but after a while the coat will separate and lie in lumps with the topcoat draped over the top.

Never try to comb without brushing vigorously first as great distress will be caused to the dog.

The most efficient way to deep groom is to first brush all the hair against the lie of the coat from the root of the tail up towards the ears. Give a liberal spray with a coat dressing or rain water and rub well in with the hands or continue brushing in the same direction. Damping the coat will prevent any static from brushing and sweeten the coat at the same time.

Begin brushing with the natural lie of the coat starting just above the hock. Section the hair and hold the brushed-up coat back with one hand and brush downwards *with* the natural lie of the coat. By using a twisting action of the wrist all the bristles of the brush will go through that one section of hair taking in both the undercoat and the top coat. The hair will be 'stretched out' as it is brushed through and the coat will look longer.

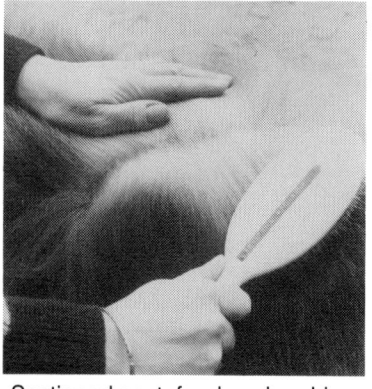

Sectioned coat for deep brushing

Go through that same section two or three times before taking in more coat from a layer immediately above. By doing this the section already brushed will be separated and each layer will merge with the coat already brushed. Keep taking in more and more, layer by layer, until the ears are reached. Repeat on the other side, then do the tail.

Many Shelties dislike having their backends groomed, due to previous rough handling or the dog having expressed a dislike, to the extent that the owner gives in. Do not lift the tail too high or take in too much of the hair of the tail at one time as any pulling will cause discomfort, and make him even more reluctant to be groomed around his rear end. If there is difficulty seek the aid of another person to hold the dog up.

Go through the petticoats again and take in the coat at the top of the tail just above the petticoats so that there is not a lumpy ridge between the sections.

With the dog facing you brush all the mane upwards hold up the hair and starting from almost between the legs brush the coat downwards taking in more, layer by layer, up to the chin. Repeat the procedure up both shoulders, incorporating the soft hair behind the ears. The hair each side of the neck can be very thick and difficult to get at. Turning the dogs head away from you will allow deeper brushing.

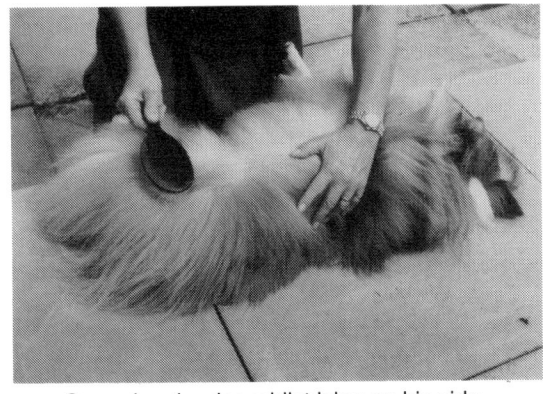

Grooming the dog whilst lying on his side

Brush the frills on the front legs before using a comb.

Some people find it easier to have the dog lying on his side to be brushed, this can be very relaxing for the dog, when he is used to it.

Keep the brush clear of hair by frequently running the wide toothed comb through the bristles. By keeping the brush free of hair the whole length of the bristles will be used to maximum efficiency. If the brush is full of hair then the shortened bristles will skim over the top of the coat. Some people have a theory that to leave the brush full when a coat is moulting will not take too much out. Dead coat hanging off a dog is no good to anyone. It will look a mess and will be deposited all over the place.

The show dog will *not* be enhanced by a dead lumpy coat, it is best being thoroughly brushed and even combed immediately prior to entering the ring. If there is a delay going into the ring keep spraying to keep the coat damp. The damp will hold the coat up for sufficient time for the class to be judged before it flops.

Use the wide toothed comb to give that final touch.

Combing

When I first started in Shelties it was considered a sin to use a comb. The cursory flick over with a brush was all that was required and I was told never to comb my dog as it would remove all the undercoat! Whereas this may have been good advice I do believe there is a definite need for the use of the comb.

It is very important that the coat is well brushed before attempting to use a comb. The brushing will loosen and separate the hair making it easier for the comb to go through.

The *wide toothed comb* should be used for giving a final touch after brushing. It is also a very vital piece of equipment when the coat is moulting, as it will remove vast amounts of undercoat without pulling too hard. If the comb is too fine it will pull the dog too much causing discomfort to the dog.

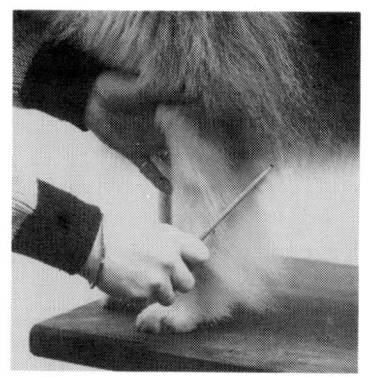

The *medium toothed comb* is the one that will be used most frequently, as it can be used for the frills at the back of the front legs and behind the ears. Remember to brush first. It can also be used to remove the final bits of dead coat when there is no thickness to have to drag through.

The *very fine toothed comb* is a must and should be used to groom those forgotten parts, the short hair on the head, the legs and the ears. It can also be used for the very fine hair behind the ears, but only after thorough brushing then combing with the medium comb.

The amount of dead hair that can be removed from these short coated parts indicates that there is a need for the attention. Dogs' ears are not helped when there are tufts of dead hair on the tips. To avoid this occurring use the very fine toothed comb on the ears every time you groom thus avoiding a dramatic change in the weight on the ears, causing them to fly.

Medium comb to comb frills downards

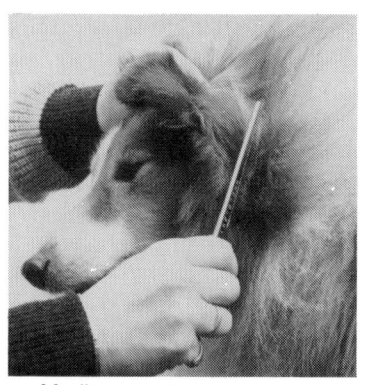

Medium comb used for soft hair behind the ears

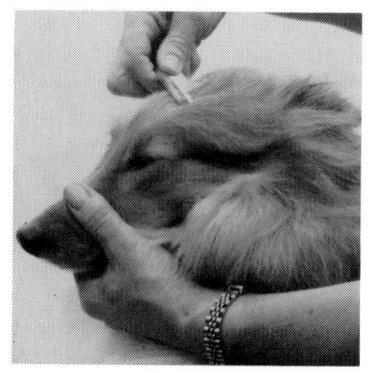

Comb through the short hair on the head with the fine toothed comb

Tufts of dead hair on the ear

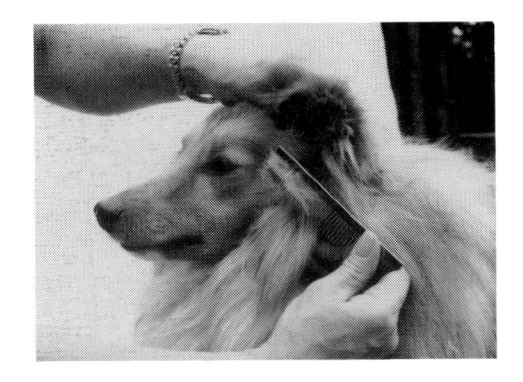

Dead coat combed out of ear

Trimming

The essence of clever trimming is for the dog to look as though he has *not* been trimmed. Some Shelties require more drastic trimming around the feet than others. I certainly like to keep all my dogs' feet regularly trimmed. It should be part of the routine when grooming. Untrimmed feet on any Sheltie can make him look old and down at heel. However, if overdone they can look fine and spindly in bone, or, make an otherwise good shaped foot look round.

For general upkeep the only parts that need to be trimmed are the feet and below the hocks. It has been known for the over enthusiastic, scissor happy, novice to cut the frills off the back of the front legs and the petticoats. Do *not* touch these. It will be a good six months before the dog is restored to his former glory with a new coat.

To obtain perfection in preparation for the show ring a good deal of practice is needed. The last thing one wants is your young hopeful to look as though he has been trimmed with a knife and fork. The dog should look natural and I do not like to see gross overtrimming on our show Shelties. Luckily this does not happen too much in the UK.

The pet Sheltie can be trimmed by his owner, albeit sparingly, and if there is any difficulty then a breeder should be contacted for assistance. The exhibitor needs to be proficient so as not to ruin the chances of the dog. Too much hair removed from one area can upset the whole balance of the dog. If you are going to a show with the new young hopeful it is wise to practice on the other dogs that are not being shown.

Ideally the show dog should be trimmed over a space of time. Taking only a very little off each time and then you have the opportunity to observe the outcome, allowing time to decide whether too much or too little has been removed. If too much has been removed then there can be sufficient time for the mistake to grow out. It is easier to take off a little at a time than try to put some back!

To trim underneath the feet hold the scissors flat against the pads and

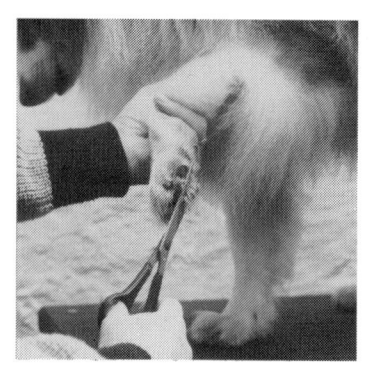

Hold the scissors flat against the pads

Any tufts between the toes can be removed with the points of the scissors

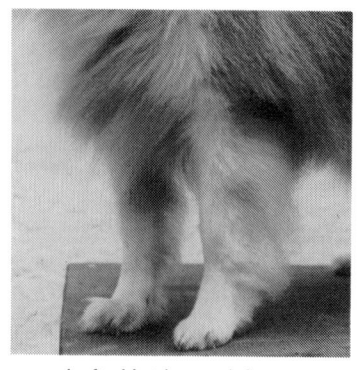

Left: Untrimmed foot,
Right: Trimmed foot

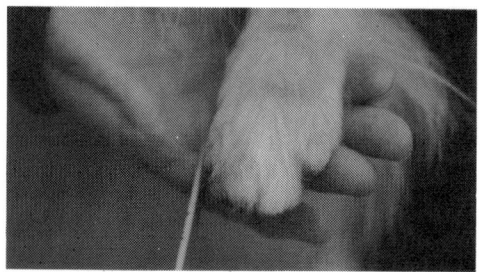

Trim the side of the pad and foot

cut any excess hair level with the pad. Do not cut between the pads. With the top of the foot facing you trim any hair that sticks out beyond each side of the foot by using the scissors in an upward direction, so giving the foot a neat oval shape.

Any tufts that stand up between the toes, above the line of the foot, can be removed by inserting the points of the scissors between the toes and gently snipping away the soft hair. The hair on the top of the foot should *not* be cut as it will lie down when the soft bits between the toes have been removed. Beware not to nick the skin between the toes. If in doubt then this soft hair can be plucked out with finger and thumb.

Do not trim around the nails or trim off the hair that covers the middle two toe nails. To expose the nails will appear to shorten the foot, making it look like a cat or hound foot, which is incorrect.

I personally dislike the practice of trimming an inch or more up the back of the front legs, this can give a rather hard appearance and an illusion of lack of bone or accentuate a straight pastern. If there is so much hair that it makes the dog look down at heel then there is justification in removing a little to give a clean line between the leg and foot. Trim only a quarter to half an inch in a gradual line upwards from the back pad to gently merge with the frill.

To trim below the hocks, brush the hair before combing, this will loosen any matted coat and avoid having to pull too hard with the comb. Comb the hair away from the leg and with the dog standing, trim with the scissors pointing downwards. Do not cut too close to the bone.

In the show ring today there is a tendency, to my mind, for too much hair to be left below the hocks. This can give the effect of too heavy bone or it may be done to diguise light bone. It does not allow the hock joint to be defined and at worst it can give the appearance of being sickle hocked, down at heel and a flat foot.

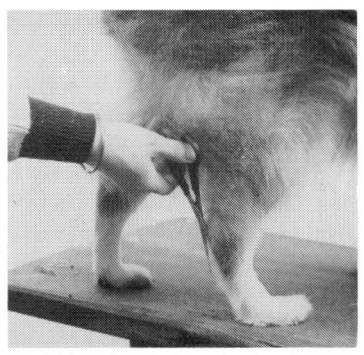

Trimming below the hocks

Untrimmed around the ears

Trimmed and tidy around the ears

Trimming the ears

Any untidy whisps of hair around the ears can easily be removed by holding the hair against the ear and plucking the fronds out with finger and thumb. As the hair is soft, it will break away easily. I find this the best method as very little hair is removed without signs of overtrimming. The use of Thinning Scissors behind the ears should be done carefully and progressively.

Removing matted hair from behind the ears

The only other time that scissors should be used is for removing any hair that has matted into lumps that cannot be brushed or combed out behind the ears. Never try and cut the knot away in one piece. There is a tendency to pull the lump away from the skin but in doing this the skin will not be flat and it is very easy to nick the dog. Therefore it is better to use the point of one of the blades to penetrate the hair between the skin and the matt, then cut through the matt from the skin outwards. The scissor blade will act like a knife cutting the lump of matted hair into several sections. The use of the slikker brush will loosen the matt altogether. Comb with the wide toothed comb, then the very fine comb ensuring that all the dead and matted hair has been removed. Any loose or dead hair that is allowed to remain will matt again very quickly. Any loose tufts or overlong hair can be plucked away with finger and thumb.

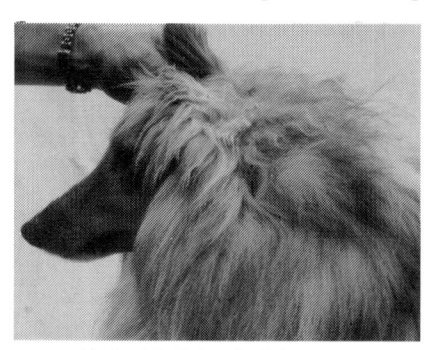

Matted hair behind the ear

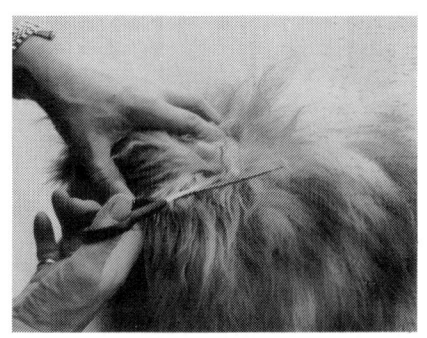

Cut through the matt from the skin outwards

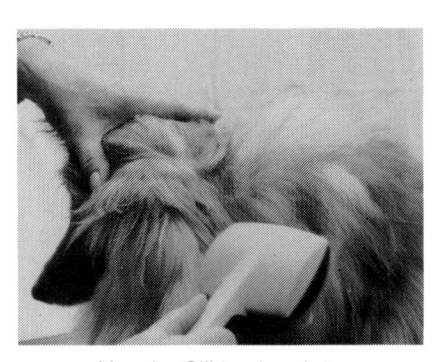

Use the Slikker brush to loosen the matt

Any loose tufts of overlong hair can be plucked away by finger and thumb

The Stripping Knife

The stripping knife can be used to trim around the ears rather than using finger and thumb. The hair to be removed should be held between the thumb and the blade then pulled sharply so that the hair is cut. Alternatively it can be used like a comb, but be careful not to catch the skin or take off too much.

The top of the skull can have a little of the hair removed if the dog appears to have a domed rather than a flat skull due to an excess of hair. Great care must be taken, too much hair removed will alter the colour on the head.

Shelties can very often carry too much coat over the croup, ruining the topline and overall outline. The stripping knife can be used like a comb to remove some undercoat so that the coat will lie down.

Nail trimming

The nails on the front feet will be longer than on the back feet due to more propulsion, when moving, from the hindquarters.

The guillotine type of nail clipper should always be used to prevent the nail splitting. The moving blade should face away from the dog as it is easier for the operator to see where the blade is cutting. It is also possible to hold the nail with the clipper prior to actual cutting, allowing you to check the amount to be cut.

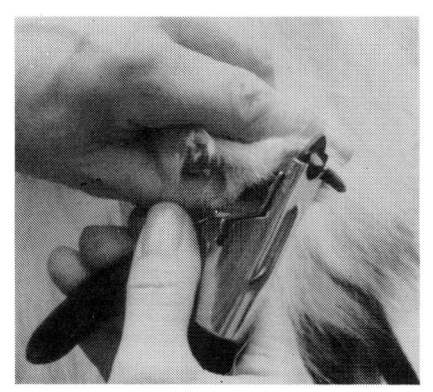

Unpigmented nails are much easier to trim as the 'quick', or vein, is visible. It will be seen to taper towards the point of the nail. When trimming leave a gap between the end of the quick and the blade of the clippers.

Black nails are more difficult to gauge and great care should be taken. If too much nail is removed and catches the quick, profuse and alarming bleeding will occur.

It is best to remove a little from the very tips once a week. As the nail becomes shorter the quick will recede.

Guillotine nail clippers with moving blade in view

When the nail becomes long, thin and hooked with a groove underneath, more can be removed.

Remember to keep dew claws trimmed as they can occasionally grow into the skin if unattended.

If in doubt go to a vet or breeder.

Bathing

There are some people who believe that a Sheltie should never be bathed. The pet Sheltie living as one of the family, apart from regular grooming, will need the occasional bath to keep the coat lively and sweet smelling. When the coat starts to moult it becomes dull and lifeless, sometimes taking weeks for the process to be complete. Dandruff can be seen where the undercoat lifts from the skin and dirt is attracted to dead coat which looks lumpy and feels tacky.

Owners of show dogs are always anxious for the new coat to grow as quickly as possible. Bathing will help to remove loose undercoat, clean up the skin and remove dirt accumulated in old dead coat. It also encourages the new coat to grow. Hot dry spells cause dust to build up in the coat evidenced by the colour of the whites.

As a guide, a twice yearly bath will keep the coat and skin in good condition. The show dog who needs the overall bath should be done at least a week before the show to allow the coat to settle. Too much bathing of the whites will remove the natural oils and cause the coat to flop.

Always groom thoroughly before bathing otherwise the dead coat will matt. Stand the dog in the bath

Stand the dog in the bath

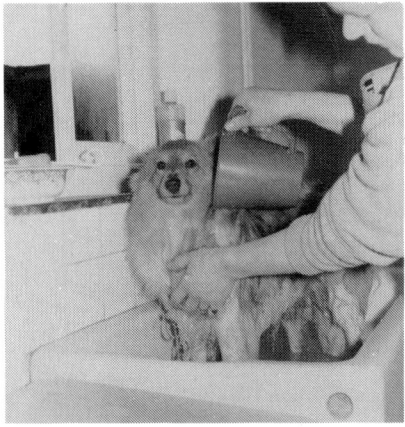

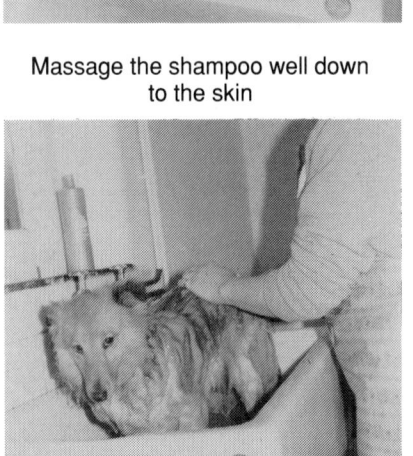

Massage the shampoo well down to the skin

Shaking will remove the excess water

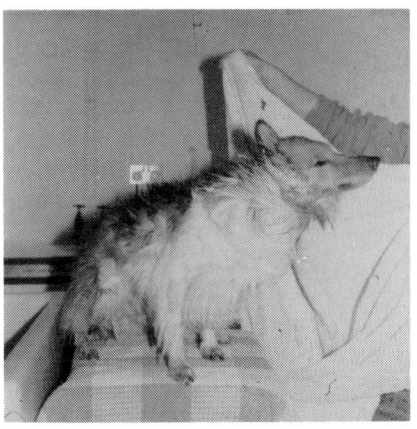

or sink, or on warm days dogs can be bathed outside with several buckets of warm water.

Dilute the shampoo with 2 parts water to 1 part shampoo into a washing up liquid bottle. This helps it to be distributed more economically. The second application of shampoo will penetrate more easily, massage well down to the skin. Rinse thoroughly, squeeze out the legs and allow the dog to shake to remove excess water. Rub well with a towel before drying thoroughly with a hair dryer or fan heater. During warm weather the coat will dry naturally. Brushing and combing will hasten the drying process and remove loose hair. The next day, brush and comb through again.

Remember to wash all the bedding after bathing the dog. A clean bed helps to keep the dog clean.

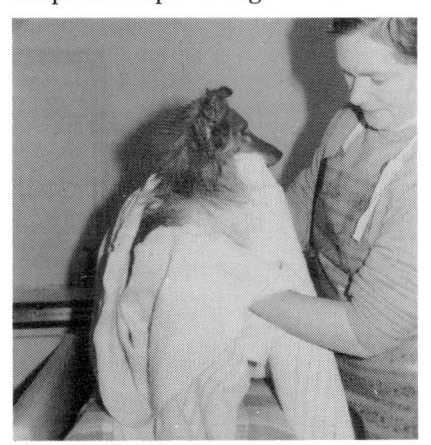

Towel thoroughly

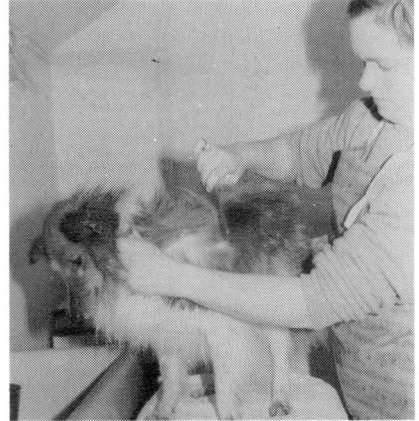

Combing will remove loose hair

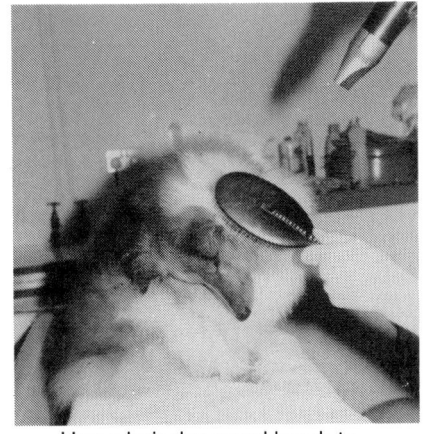

Use a hair dryer and brush to blow dry the coat

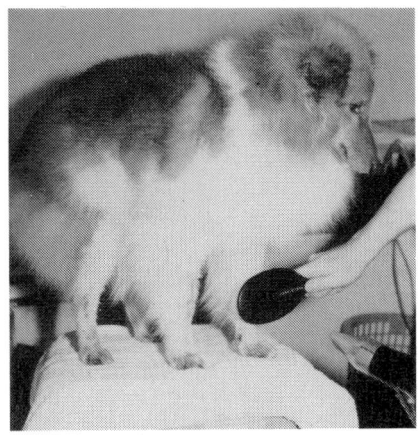

Do not forget the short hair on the legs, the final touch

Keeping Teeth Clean

In recent years teeth appear not to be strong and tend to be prone to problems, mainly due to feeding methods.

Most dogs these days are fed prepared foods where there is no need to tear or chew.

Some dogs will never chew bones or 'hoof' chews to help keep the teeth clean and gums healthy. The result is that teeth become caked with calculus which if allowed to accumulate can cause periodontal problems where the breath is offensive, gums become infected, decay takes place and the teeth can be lost.

Before too much calculus has built up, toothpaste and toothbrush can be used, but where there is discolouration, toothpaste on a piece of damp towelling can be rubbed around the teeth without causing discomfort to the dog. Done regularly the dog will accept the procedure. The toothpaste can be a mild type for humans or one of the proprietary brands marketed for dogs.

Rub around the teeth with toothpaste on towelling

When a build up of calculus is seen it can be removed by using a dental scaler, or the end of a metal nail file which is less sharp if the dog happens to move suddenly. If the gum is caught the dog will be reluctant to allow you to continue.

The scaler should be placed between the gum and the calculus, firmly flick the calculus away, once loosened the rest will chip away quite easily. Use toothpaste on the towelling to polish away any discolouration.

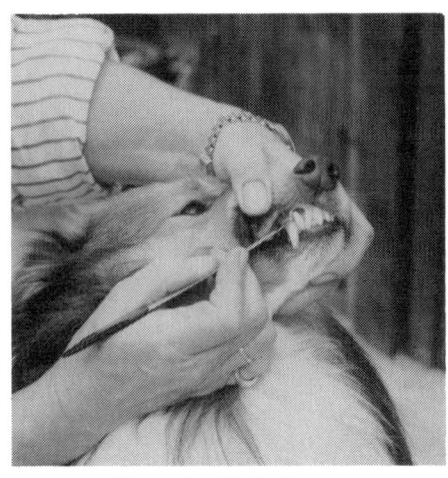

Removing Calculus

Breeding

Breeding from the pet Sheltie

THERE are reasons for and against breeding from the pet Sheltie. The average pet male dog is best never used at stud, it is a case of what he has never had he will never miss. There is certainly a very great likelihood that once he has mated a bitch he will become a nuisance and will quite naturally be more aware of bitches and maybe wander after the scent of an in-season bitch. So it is hardly fair to deliberately use him once.

Those who have thought that they would like to use their pet dog on a friend's maiden bitch usually come unstuck. Stud work is not always as easy as it seems and not a case of simply letting the dog and bitch out into the garden for half an hour. The stud dog needs to be trained from an early age.

If you decide that you would like to have a litter from your bitch do not take her to the most convenient stud dog who happens to live down the road. There are many things to be taken into consideration. Seek the advice from a reputable breeder who will have the knowledge about pedigrees and any hereditary problems to be aware of.

Making a start

To start a kennel of Shelties for breeding and showing, a well bred bitch will be needed as a foundation. Time taken over selection can save generations and years of work. Go to the shows to see all the dogs, talk to as many breeders as possible, visit their kennels to see their other dogs and study the pedigrees.

The foundation bitch should have a good pedigree with several generations of identifiable affixes which will mean that her breeding has been well thought out rather than 'happened' through chance matings of pet bitches. A muddled ancestry means several generations would need to be bred before any progress can be made and consistent quality achieved.

The bitch should be clear of C.E.A. (see page 205). Starting with clear stock gives a basis on which to work.

An eight-week-old puppy cannot be guaranteed as a show specimen although it could be a 'promising' puppy, therefore it should be bought on the basis of its pedigree as well as its promising looks. If it is successful in the ring then that will be a bonus.

If an older bitch of good breeding is available, but has not quite made the grade for showing, she could well prove to be a good brood bitch and foundation for your kennel.

The majority of breeders will only be breeding for themselves so they will naturally keep the best.

Therefore the only way to have a choice is to breed your own.

Planning a Litter

When breeding, careful consideration should be given to the quality as well as the pedigree of the bitch and the stud dog. The breeder should always be aiming to breed the puppy that is an improvement on anything else previously bred.

Relatively few of what one breeds will make the show ring, most of them will become pets. There is therefore a requirement that all puppies bred are sound and healthy with good temperament.

To have a choice in a litter is satisfying but quality not quantity should be aimed for.

Remember that 50% of genes will come from the sire and 50% from the dam. Unfortunately, they do not always blend the way we imagine.

One of the biggest problems when breeding Shelties is the unpredicatable variation in size. From one litter there can be one that resembles a Collie and one very tiny, weedy 'Pommy' type as well as others in between. Unfortunately using a small dog on a large bitch does not result in the puppies being the perfect size. Sensible line breeding and using the correct size breeding stock over several generations can establish more consistent size.

Colour

The colour of the dog and what colour he produces can vary. If, for example, you have a shaded sable bitch and only want a sable litter then using a tricolour or shaded sable dog is very likely to produce tricolours. The dominant sable stud dog will only produce sables even when mated to a tricolour. Equally the clear golden sable bitch could well be dominant sable herself, in which case using a tricolour dog would produce only sables.

The blue merle mating is a very complex subject and needs careful consideration. A basic rule should be that a blue merle should only be mated to a tricolour.

Blue merle to blue merle can produce blue merle or tricolour but there could be predominently white puppies with the possibility of blindness and deafness.

The blue merle to sable can produce tricolour, blue merle, sable or sable merle. The sable merle is not a recognised colour but when mated to either tricolour or blue merle can produce excellent coloured blues. Any sable produced from a merle should be excluded from any future breeding programme because of the possibility of producing blue-eyed sables.

Tricolour mated to tricolour will produce only tricolour. A tricolour can be mated to either sables or blue merles. The merle bred tricolour will not pass on the blue gene if mated to a sable. The sable bred tricolour will not pass on the blue gene if mated to a sable. Similarly, the sable bred tricolour will not produce sable when mated to a blue merle.

Before the word 'genetics' became fashionable most animal breeding was done by 'eye'. The good stockman would know his pedigrees by what he saw in front of him. He would know whether the grandsire had a particular good or bad point and would choose a mate accordingly. He would not accentuate the bad points by doubling up on them, but try to accentuate the good points that he KNEW were behind; this could be done by close breeding or making an outcross.

There are many misguided breeders who think that because a pedigree looks right on paper that it should work.

In-breeding

In-breeding is always the excuse given when an hereditary problem arises. This may be true but good points can also be bred for in the same way. It is more likely to be ignorant breeding which can produce all sorts of defects.

In-breeding is brother to sister, parent to child or grandparent to grandchild as this does not bring in any new blood. In a lesser sense half brother to half sister, can bring in some new blood.

In-breeding can be misinterpreted by the novice as being a good thing. They have probably seen pedigrees where in-breeding and line breeding has been successful and presume that they can do the same.

Just because the same name appears over and over again in a pedigree does not mean it is necessarily a good thing.

A little knowledge can be a dangerous thing and the novice should take advice from the long established breeder before diving in. Those who can remember all of the dogs in a pedigree, going back over several generations, have the advantage over the novice. Knowing what the dogs were like and what they produced allows calculated selection. Leave any in-breeding to the experts - it is not for novices.

Basically, in-breeding is doubling up on a pool of genes. These genes may be good or they may be bad. What one needs to remember is that any point that is doubled-up on will be imprinted. If it is a good point then that is excellent as it will hopefully remain. On the other hand if there is a major fault then it could be generations before that fault is eradicated. Total mediocrity can linger for generations. In-breeding can be highly successful or a total disaster.

The dog who is in-bred to has to be of such outstanding quality for there to be any benefit.

The advantages are that type can be fixed and size brought down. If the result is good then it is an excellent basis on which to build. A super in-bred bitch will have the advantage of maintaining much of her type if mated to a dog on similar lines i.e. coming down from the same Line or Family. Or she can be useful if mated to an outcross dog and then bred back into her line at a later generation.

Line-breeding

Line-breeding is when a particular dog or bitch appears in a pedigree several times but not as a close relative. The chosen dog to whom it is intended to line-breed could be several generations back. When a stud dog is selected the dog that is being line bred to will appear somewhere if not several times in the pedigree of both the stud dog and the brood bitch.

The English Shetland Sheepdog Club Charts are invaluable to anyone breeding Shelties as it can be seen how all Champions and C.C. winners have descended and how certain dogs have maintained a strong line of descendants.

Out-crossing

When a particular point is needed, making an outcross can be beneficial and should be regarded as part of a long term breeding programme. It may take another generation, going back into the original line, before the results can be seen. Even then bad points can be brought in as well as the good points

The Bitch

The Season or Heat (Oestrus)

THE age that a bitch can come into season for the first time can vary. This could be anytime between seven months to two years but more usually it is around nine to twelve months. It is not unusual for a Sheltie to be well over a year old before she has her first season. Thereafter she will come in approximately every six months. Some bitches will come into season every six months, others will have a perfectly normal regular ten to twelve month cycle.

Prior to coming into season she will make her mark by frequently urinating, particularly away from home. This is her way of announcing to every male in the area that she will soon be interesting.

At around the same time her vulva may start to swell slightly before showing any colour, or she may have a slight brown mucous discharge.

The season starts when the colour is a definite blood red discharge 'Colour' is the vaginal bleeding associated with the 'season' or 'heat'. Licking of the vulva is an indication that the bitch is coming into season and she should be inspected regularly to ascertain her first day. With a young bitch at her first season the first indications may be blood on her petticoats. At the onset of bleeding the young bitch can often look quite bewildered and it is not unusual for her not to want to keep herself clean. Normally she will keep herself clean by incessant licking, the older bitch keeping herself cleaner than the maiden.

The season lasts approximately three weeks. During the first week the bleeding will be the most pronounced but she may not be so attractive to a dog at this stage although certain bitches can be very interesting from the first day.

She should be confined to home at once and not taken out for her regular walks, particularly around her own home.

From around eleven days the bitch will come into 'oestrus' this is the time when the bitch will be releasing eggs from her ovaries. She gives off a strong scent and becomes most attractive to the dog. It is advisable to confine the bitch for several days after she has stopped bleeding as it is during this time that she can be mated. It is not unknown for a bitch to be still mateable on her seventeeth or eighteenth day and still conceive. Do not trust the bitch until she is quite clear of her season. One cannot always blame the male for any misallience as bitches can be equally as sexy in their behaviour and will seek out a dog in the same way that a dog will seek out a bitch. It has been known for a bitch to be mated whilst out on a lead!

A change of environment, such as a spell in boarding kennels, can sometimes hasten a bitch coming into season. It is her way of becoming acceptable to a new pack.

The Bitch's Cycle (Oestrus cycle)

Pro-oestrus - The first stage of the season when she is not receptive to the dog. The vulva will become swollen and hard and there will be a profuse blood stained discharge. This lasts about nine days.

Oestrus - This stage is when the bright red discharge starts to fade slightly and the swelling begins to go down. Between the eleventh and fourteenth day ovulation occurs and the bitch is receptive to the dog. In Shelties the optimum time for mating tends to be later than other breeds.

Met-oestrus - For twelve weeks after an unmated bitch has had her season she will undergo hormonal changes and have a false pregnancy. All bitches go through this false pregnancy. The majority will never display any symptoms whereas others will show all the signs of being pregnant. At the end of the twelve weeks of Met-oestrus Anoestrus will start.

Anoestrus - The period where there is no sexual activity. The length of Anoestrus determines the frequency of the seasons. At the onset of Anoestrus it is noticeable that the coat starts to come out and the moult begins.

Silent heat

A careful watch should be made of the bitch who has a 'silent' season and any change in behaviour should be observed. The vulva may become enlarged but there will be an absence of bleeding making it difficult to define the correct time for mating except if the bitch is living with a dog.

As the bitch gets older her seasons may become barely noticeable but she can still be attractive to a dog as though she were in season. It is not uncommon for the elderly bitch to get herself mated.

False or Phantom Pregnancy

This occurs with a particularly maternal bitch around the time that she would be due to have puppies had she been mated. She will behave as though she has puppies even to the extent of producing milk. She may try to dig and make a bed in the same way that she would if she had started in labour, or she may just confine herself to her bed and try to 'mother' a toy, guarding it as if it were a whelp. During this time she should be kept occupied to divert her attention. Long walks and a reduced diet will help to minimise the milk which should dry up of its own accord. The milk should not be removed. bathing with warm water three times a day will reduce it.

Homoeopathic Urtica Urens can be given twice daily for three days to reduce any milk.

The other form of false pregnancy is when a bitch shows all the signs of being in whelp whether she has been mated or not. This is more noticeable to the owner of the bitch that has been mated because they will be convinced that she is in whelp, the abdomen becomes enlarged and the bitch appears to be in whelp only to go down at around six or seven weeks from mating. This is not the same as resorption when the bitch is definitely in whelp and the puppies will be absorbed due to some trauma.

The apparently in-whelp bitch who does not shed the hair from around her nipples during the eighth week after mating will not have puppies.

Spaying of the Bitch

The neutering of a bitch can be done for several reasons:
* Metritis or Pyometra - an urgent operation
* Prolonged seasons
* Continued false pregnancies
* Permanently attractive to males
* Irregular or frequent seasons
* When a bitch is living in the same house as a male
* A bitch that is not required for breeding purposes

Many older Shelties can have Metritis which can develop into Pyometra without displaying any of the usual symptoms. Many Shelties have been lost because this is difficult to diagnose. Spaying or 'neutering' of the bitch is the only treatment but needs to be done quickly.

It is the policy of many kennels to have the older bitches spayed when they are past their breeding age, and are still fit, but before they are too old, removing the risk of an emergency operation due to Pyometra. This makes sense when there are dogs running with bitches in the house. For the pensioner bitch to suddenly have to be outside in a kennel for three weeks, particularly in the winter, is hardly fair.

Where a young bitch is concerned the owner should think carefully before having her spayed. I have heard many a person say how they had regretted the decision as they would have liked to have had a puppy from her at a later date.

There can be a tendency to obesity where a spayed bitch is not particularly active and living on her own without the stimulation of other dogs. Overfeeding is very much a contributory factor to obesity.

Spaying will alter the texture and amount of coat, usually becoming softer and more profuse.

The spayed bitch can be vaguely attractive to males in the same way that a castrated male will be interesting to other males.

Breeding a Litter

Having made a decision to have a litter from your bitch, there are certain things to be ascertained prior to her coming into season.

There should be someone at home for the duration of whelping and rearing of the puppies.

Do not plan a holiday before the whelping. Any change of routine may cause a bitch to resorb her puppies. Before mating the bitch look at the calender and count the nine weeks to when she will be due and for eight weeks after the puppies are born.

Having decided on the stud dog you wish to use it is worth establishing whether your bitch is acceptable to the owner of the stud dog. A discussion about pedigrees should be anticipated so have the bitch's pedigree to hand.

When your bitch's season is imminent check her each day so that you are sure which is her first day.

Phone the stud dog owner the first day of her season. If the dog is booked by someone else you will have to start planning again.

The stud fee should be agreed upon in advance and is paid at the time of the service. The fee is for the use of the dog not for the outcome. A proven stud dog cannot necessarily be blamed if there are no puppies as the result can depend very much on the day of the season the bitch is mated. In the event of a bitch not having any puppies, there is no obligation by the stud dog owner to offer a free stud at the bitch's next season, it is purely a matter of courtesy.

When to Mate

It is the responsibility of the owner of the bitch to be sure that the bitch is ready. A bitch is ready for mating when *she* is ready not when it is convenient for the owner. If she needs to be mated mid-week or on Christmas Day then that is the time she should be mated. More bitches miss due to mating on the incorrect day than any other reason. It is more inconvenient and expensive to have to take her again in six months time.

Count the day that she first shows colour as day one of her season.

Some bitches will swell a great deal and display a very enlarged vulva. The swelling will increase during the first seven days and she will bleed profusely. The vulva will look very inflamed and be very hard to the touch.

For the next few days this will remain the same.

As bitches vary in the amount of discharge and swelling displayed it can sometimes be difficult for the novice breeder to define the right day to take her to the dog. The position of the vulva can be a very good guide.

At around the eleventh to twelfth day the colour will tend to become less bright and appear more watery. The swollen vulva will start to go down. It is unlikely that she is ready for the dog at this stage. Not only does the swelling need to have decreased but the vulva should be soft.

At around the fourteenth or fifteenth day the vulva will have gone down. When the bitch is standing on the floor and her tail is lifted the vulva will appear to be raised up towards the tail. This is so that the vulva is presented for the dog and will be easier for him to enter.

The novice or pet owner will very often have a numerically good litter. This is because

a) the owner has probably missed the first day of the bitch's season and takes her to the stud dog later rather than earlier, or

b) because the owner follows exactly the instructions given by the stud dog owner. The over anxious breeder will often take the bitch to the dog far too early.

There are always bitches that do not 'go by the book' and can confuse the owner particularly if there is not a male in the kennel to act as a tease. If there is more than one bitch in the home very often the bitch, when approaching her optimum time, will ride others around and try and encourage them to mount her. She will do this 'courting' dance several days before she is actually ready. It is always good for a maiden bitch to be able to play these games because when she is presented to the dog for the first time she will not mind being mounted.

When a bitch is standing for another bitch she will be ready for mating about two days later.

When taking the bitch for mating make sure that she is respectably clean and well groomed and has not got dirty pants or fleas.

But, do not wash the bitch's rear end prior to mating as this will destroy any odour that will sexually stimulate the dog.

Before arrival at the stud dog owner's property make sure that she has been allowed to relieve herself. Having an empty bowel will make easier penetration for the dog. Do not exercise her in the stud dog owner's driveway as this will attract unwanted local suitors to the house.

If the bitch is mated early a second mating 48 hours later will help to ensure that she has been covered over her time of ovulation.

The Stud Dog

WHICH stud dog is better than the next? Champions do not necessarily make a Champion. One should be looking into the future when planning a mating.

Pedigree is all important and a careful study of the dog's progeny can give guidelines as to the quality he is passing on. Many people will rush to use the dog of the moment, but the wise discerning breeder will watch his progress for longer and see what he can produce.

The knowledgeable, long established breeder will know at a glance all the dogs in a pedigree. A lifetime in the breed gives them the advantage of knowing exactly what those dogs were like, the sort of progeny they produced and what good and bad points they have perpetuated.

It should be policy to only use or keep a stud dog that has a B.V.A./K.C. certificate pronouncing him clear of Collie Eye Anomaly, (see page 205).

The stud dog who is genetically clear of C.E.A. is very useful but that aspect should be considered with all other points such as temperament, type, size, quality and colour.

Anyone considering keeping a dog for stud should be very selective as it is not good enough to have any old dog at public stud. Unless a dog has been shown, nobody will know he exists. He needs to be a Champion, or have a record of wins, otherwise he will not attract enough stud work to justify his place in the kennel.

It does not make economic sense to keep an inferior dog at stud who will then not be used by other breeders. The space being taken up by the inferior dog could be a place for a better one.

Those who keep a dog mainly for their own use will never progress as there is a limit to how often a dog can be used within a kennel. There comes a time when all the stock will be children or grandchildren of the same dog. There can then be a temptation to do continuous close matings to their own dog because it 'looks good on paper'.

Kennels of bitches can have the choice of the cream of the country's stud dogs whilst the owner does not have the inconvenience of owning a dog.

Age to start Stud Work

The age at which a young dog is ready to mate a bitch can vary. This can be due to lack of maturity and may differ depending on his bloodlines.

Some dogs easily and successfully mate a bitch at ten months old whereas others do not get over excited before they are fifteen months. Unless a dog is interested there is no way that the process can be hurried. The dog living with bitches has the advantage as he will become aroused from the time a bitch starts to show signs of a season.

Stud work is not always as easy as it seems and patience is required to give confidence to the dog. Having an experienced handler to help with the first mating is important, a maiden dog can easily be put off by the nervous owner who is trying to do the right thing. However, it is much easier if, firstly the dog is keen, secondly the bitch is not a maiden, and thirdly she is ready and receptive.

The Mating

The flirtatious bitch will do as much to encourage and stimulate the dog as possible. The flirting and play prior to any mating is all important and will arouse the dog, but do not allow them to flirt for too long before holding the bitch. The young dog should become used to having the bitch handled from the start as not all bitches are receptive and could snap. The successful show dog does not want his face bitten and scarred.

The accomplished stud dog will do sufficient courting to become aroused and will then wait for the bitch to be held before mounting her. With the bitch facing to the handler's left, hold the bitch's tail to the side with the right hand. Place the left hand under the bitch's tummy between her back legs and the first and second fingers either side of the vulva. As the dog mounts and starts to work the bitch can be guided towards the dog. As the dog penetrates he will work closer to the bitch and she may give a sharp cry. At this stage he will become extended and start to swell. Hold both the dog and the bitch firmly together as she may wriggle away before a tie has taken place. The tie can last for several minutes or nearly an hour. Ejaculation is a pumping process which can be felt as a pulse at the root of the dog's tail.

Once the dog has achieved a satisfactory tie he may want to turn himself; or he can be helped by lifting one foreleg across the bitch's back, so that both forelegs are on the same side. The corresponding hindleg can then be gently lifted over the bitch's back so that the two are then standing tail to tail. The bitch should be restrained from wandering around for the duration of the tie by being tethered or held by her owner who can be seated on a chair, it could be a long wait.

The dog who persists in licking the bitch's vulva is trying to stimulate himself from her secretions, this is an indication that she is not ready or has gone over her optimum time.

To assist penetration a smear of vaseline can be placed on the vulva.

When the dog has difficulty in penetrating a maiden bitch there could be an obstruction. Examination could reveal a stricture which may require veterinary attention.

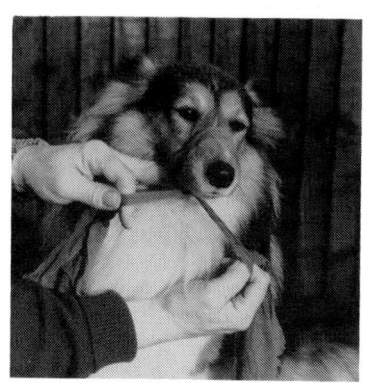

A snappy bitch should be muzzled before anyone is bitten and this can sometimes have a quietening effect upon the bitch. Use a bandage or stocking wrapped twice around her muzzle, crossed under her chin then tied behind her ears.

Muzzle with a stocking

Often there is a difference between the size of the dog and the bitch. If the bitch is smaller than the dog several pieces of carpet can be used to raise her to the level of the dog. If the floor is slippery the carpet can be put under the dog's hindlegs to give him more grip. If the bitch is bigger than the dog and he needs to be raised, several newspapers can be put under the carpet.

The stud dog needs to be trained to stud work and should not be put off by the bitch being handled. At the outset of his stud career he should be encouraged to a routine so that when a difficult bitch is encountered he is not put off. The stud dog who is reluctant may have been told off for unnecessarily mounting another dog and will be cautious about attempting to mount a bitch, however provocative she may be.

Whelping and Rearing

The In-Whelp Bitch

The gestation period is nine weeks.

The first few weeks after a bitch has been mated can be most frustrating. The anticipation of a pending litter becomes more exciting the longer you have been breeding. The long awaited plans have started to be put into action. Is she in whelp or not?

One of the first signs that she has conceived is a continual but very slight light brownish discharge from her vulva, which may remain slightly enlarged.

At around three weeks into the pregnancy she can go off her food as well as becoming a bit more fussy. After another week she will return to her normal eating pattern after which her appetite will be greatly increased.

The in-whelp bitch - increased abdomen and more pronounced nipples

Regular daily exercise should be maintained throughout the pregnancy. This is very important even though towards the end she may be reluctant to want to go. Be very careful about taking her out with a crowd of other boisterous dogs during the last two weeks as any accidental collision could have disastrous results. A gentle but shorter walk on her own will ensure muscle tone.

Do not allow her to jump in and out of the car or on and off chairs when she is obviously heavily in whelp.

By five weeks her nipples will have become more pronounced and slightly pinker and the slight increase in the size of her abdomen can be seen if she is stood up on her back legs and observing whether the normal hollow between her ribs and abdomen has become filled.

When it is evident that the bitch is in whelp be careful how she is picked up. Place one hand under her forechest and the other under her rear. Never lift her under her tummy.

Picking up the pregnant bitch

Clean fresh water should be made available at all times.

After mating, feeding should continue as before and nothing extra need be given. After one month a very gradual increase should be sufficient, gradually increasing to approximately 60% more by the time she is seven weeks.

Whereas it is advised not to get the in-whelp bitch too fat it appears that Shelties need more as they have a tendency to feed themselves rather well before nourishing the puppies, hence the appearance of being somewhat overweight. If there is a good sized litter she will need all the best quality food that she can get.

She will start to show definite evidence of being in whelp from five weeks and be looking more so by six weeks and then gradually increase in size until she whelps.

During the last three weeks she will need a considerably higher protein diet than normal: an increase of meat, or other sources of protein which are easily digested such as fish together with boiled eggs, cheese and, of course, milk. Liver given once per week is a good source of iron, copper and the vitamin B complex as well as protein. Raw grated carrots are excellent.

Because of the increase in the bitch's size, as the pregnancy progresses, the meals should be divided so that she can accommodate the increased amount of food. She should be having at least three meals per day during the last two weeks.

If she vomits her food it could be that she cannot cope with the amount given in one feed, her increased abdomen not giving her enough room for the extra food. It will also be noticed that she will need to urinate more frequently due to pressure on her bladder.

Supplements
It is said that if a proper balanced diet is given then there should be no need to supplement. However, calcium together with phosphorous is important and can be given in the form of 'Stress'. Brewers yeast can be given without any harmful effects and is a great source of the vitamin B complexes. There are a wide selection of combination supplements on the market but *do not overdo them*. The addition of vitamin and mineral supplements should be carefully watched as more harm than good can be done if abused (see page 94).

During her pregnancy the bitch who is well looked after will look in superb condition with her coat shining and be in the best coat that she has ever had. As she looks so well do not forget to groom her. The bitch who is used to regular grooming will enjoy the attention at the same time as allowing you to check her over.

One to two weeks before she is due to whelp it will be noticed that she will shed the hair from her tummy, leaving a clean area for the puppies to be able to find the nipples. She will scratch the hair out in great lumps so it is a good idea to keep this area gently combed through.

Two weeks before the bitch is due to whelp she should be introduced to the whelping box which should be positioned where you intend her to whelp.

A very successful whelping box can be of wooden construction or a very large cardboard box obtained from the supermarket or grocers. This should be big enough for the bitch to be able to lie *fully outstretched*. A suitable hole can be cut out of the side for the bitch to get in and out.

The advantage of a cardboard box is that it is clean at the outset and can easily be replaced when soiled. The use of the temporary puppy panels around the box will allow her privacy.

Useful Homoeopathic Remedies for the In-Whelp Bitch

Homoeopathic remedies can safely be used for the in-whelp bitch (see page 215).

Caulophyllum
A useful homoeopathic remedy which can be given as one dose weekly from mating with an extra dose during the final week. Or one tablet daily from five weeks and then one at the onset of labour. Eases the birth.

Pulsatilla
To prevent uterine inertia give two tablets per week from five weeks.

Arnica
Two doses during the final week of pregnancy and 3 doses per day for two days after whelping. This will help during delivery and assist her recovery.

Sepia
One dose of Sepia will help to quickly restore the uterus to normal.

Diagnosing Pregnancy

For those anxious to confirm a pregnancy there are four methods.

1. Abdominal Palpation
The fertilised eggs become implanted in the uterus 16 days after ovulation. A vet may be able to confirm that she is pregnant at 21 days by abdominal palpation when the foetal units can be felt, as though they are a string of large peas in each horn. This 'pea' stage may not be easy to detect at precisely 21 days from mating as many bitches are often mated well before they have ovulated, and as spermatazoa can remain viable within the bitch for at least seven days or more, one's calculations for estimated time of birth could be a week out. Also, as Shelties tend not to have large litters, being able to feel the odd one is not so easy.

2. Ultra-Sound
Diagnosis by ultra-sound between 24 and 28 days after mating is a safe method. However, the accuracy can be very dependent on the skill of the operator, particularly in estimating the number in the litter.

3. X-Ray
X-rays to confirm pregnancy should be avoided where possible as there can be a radiation risk to the puppies. The skeletons of the puppies will only show up after 45 days. Not to be recommended.

4. Wait and see
Under normal circumstances I will simply wait to see for myself whether a bitch is in whelp or not. Time alone will tell.

Resorption

Where it is obvious, or it has been confirmed, that a bitch is in whelp and then fails to produce, any puppies that died intra-uteri will have been resorbed. This is one of the most frustrating things and happens more often than we imagine. After a bitch has been mated any trauma should be avoided.

* Do not go on holiday and/or put the bitch into kennels
* Do not take her to shows
* Do not take her on excessively long walks
* Do not send her to a stranger for whelping
* Avoid unnecessary medications
* Avoid anything out of the normal routine

Whelping

It is always a good idea to inform your vet that there is a whelping imminent. If it is a weekend then it is useful to find out who will be covering in an emergency as this may not be your regular vet.

Equipment required for Whelping

* Whelping box
* Infra-red heat lamp. Preferably a dull emitter
* Plenty of newspaper
* Vetbed
* Towels
* Scissors - sterilised
* Hot water bottle
* Cardboard box
* Glucose

It is a natural instinct for a bitch to try and find what she thinks is the most suitable place to whelp. This may not be the place that you had in mind. Many bitches will prefer somewhere that is dark such as a cupboard, under some inaccessible piece of furniture or even somewhere in the garden or under the garden shed. Shelties have their own ideas and may prefer the settee or your bed!

You will have to be firm with her and confine her to the whelping box designated to her some weeks beforehand. This should be in a quiet draught proof corner that is not too light.

A corner of the kitchen is ideal with a portable pen surrounding the box to prevent her from wandering around trying to find the place where *she* wants to whelp. If she whelps where you cannot get at her, such as under the shed, there will be difficulties in giving any assistance if it is required. One hears horror stories of each puppy being born in a different room. Be firm with her and make her stay in her pen.

A quantity of paper in the bottom of the whelping box will give her something to dig up when she starts in labour. Other bedding can be removed when furious digging gets underway, leaving only the newspaper.

I never knowingly leave a bitch to whelp on her own so at the first signs I will sleep in the same room, not leaving anything to chance.

Whatever time she starts she does not need an audience. If the confinement is during the day it is best not to appear to be watching her. Find something else to do, such as the ironing or writing letters, whilst keeping a watchful eye on proceedings.

About 24-48 hours, before the start of labour the bitch's temperature will usually drop. Normal temperature being around 38.5°C (101.5°C) it can drop to around 36°C (97°F). She may become restless and uneasy and the vulva becomes more prominent and flacid and a sticky discharge will be seen.

The first indication of partruition is when a bitch refuses her food. This first stage of labour could go on for twenty four hours during which time she may dig up her bed, shred the newspaper and pant. The digging could go on for some time and it is not unusual for you to be waiting and watching, often for most of the night, before she goes into the second stage. At the second stage she will pant more and show signs of definite contractions with her back arched whilst straining to expel the puppy.

As each puppy is born it will be in a sac, a fluid filled membrane, which the bitch should tear open then lick the puppy until it is clean and dry. The time lapse between each puppy can vary and it may not be noticed

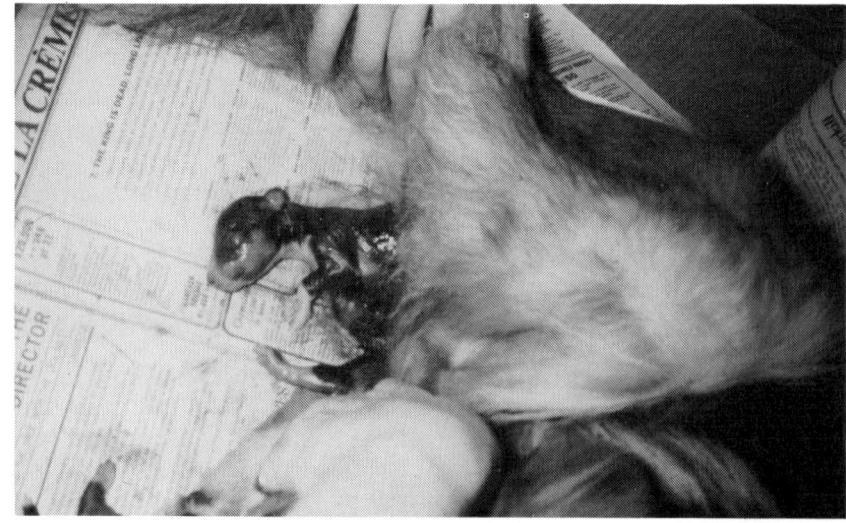

A newly born puppy

Yorkshire Shetland Sheepdog Club Championship Show, Parade of Champions 1982.

From left to right. Mrs Constance Sangster with Ch. Roaming of Exford, Mrs C. Hindley with Ch. Imp of Lynray, Miss Peggy Ure with Ch. Kyleburn Star Sound, Mrs Carole Ferguson with Ch. Mountmoor Jeanie McCall, Mrs Mona McConnell with Ch. Shelverne Spun Gold, Mrs Jean Fitzsimons with Ch. Snabswood Slainthe, Mrs Margaret Searle with Ch. Francehill Andy Pandy, Miss Botterill with Ch. Shezlynn Brown Velvet, Mr Percy Fletcher with Ch. Shelfrect Sunlit Suzanne, Mrs Ann Barraclough with Ch. Pruneparks Jason Junior

Ch. Marnham Merry Maker (left) Born 1981, bred and owned by Mr and Mrs Brian Pollard, with her sire Ch. Willow Tarn Telstar (right) Born 1978 bred and owned by Mrs Ros Crossley.

Ch. Felthorn Beachcomber. Born 1972, by: Troubleshooter of Shemaur ex: Felthorn April Dancer, bred and owned by Mr and Mrs Dick Thornley.

Ch. Reubicia Orion. Born 1984, by: Ch. Pepperhill Naughty But Nice ex: Felthorn Star Appeal, bred and owned by Mrs Pat Jackman.

Ch. Felthorn Button Moon, born 1982 (left) and Ch. Felthorn Lady, born 1980 (right). Both by: Shelbrook Moonlighting ex: Felthorn Marionette, bred and owned by Mr and Mrs Dick Thornley.

Ch. Haytimer of Hanburyhill at Hartmere. Born 1977, by: Ch. Riverhill Ricotta ex: Hanburyhill Honeysuckle, bred by Mrs R. Archer and owned by Rev and Mrs Fred Hambrey and Mr and Mrs Malcolm Hart.

Ch. Ruscombe Silver Lining. Born 1981, by: Rockaround Sweeping Clouds ex: Ruscombe Crystal Cloud, bred and owned by Mrs Sandra Tinker.

Ch. Longdells Petrocelli. Born 1979, by: Ch. Salroyds Buzzer ex: Longdells Belle Fleur, bred by Mr and Mrs Michael Bray and owned by Miss G. Bray.

Ch. Francehill Goodwill. Born 1983, by: Ch. Glaysdale Buccaneer ex: Shelerts Sands of Time, bred by Mr Robin Searle and Mrs Margaret Norman and owned by Mrs Margaret Norman.

Ch. Pepperhill Blue Fizz. Born 1981, by: Solata Jet Set ex: Royal Sheena of Hilmisk, bred by Mr and Mrs Daniels and owned by Mrs Linda Sorockyj.
The Breed Record holder with 21 C.C.s

Ch. Rockaround Night Hawk. Born 1983, by: Forestland Poacher ex: Rockaround Bluetta, bred and owned by Mrs Jean Angell

Ch. Forestland Briar. Born 1977, by: Greenscrees Nobleman ex: Forestland Honeysuckle, bred and owned by Mrs Rosemary Marshall.

Left to right: Ch. Forestland Tassel. Born 1982, by: Snabswood Sandbagger ex: Forestland Honeysuckle, her daughter, Forestland Royal Bloom by: Ch. Monkreddan Royal Blend, her son, Ch. Forestland Farmers Boy, Born 1987, by: Scylla So Blessed at Felthorn. All bred and owned by Mrs Rosemary Marshall.

Ch. Shelderon Kiri. Born 1983, by: Ch. Salroyds Buzzer ex: Dunsinane Misty Memories, bred and owned by Mrs Sheila McIntosh.
The breed's current bitch Record holder with 14 C.C.s.

Ch. Listo Lullaby at Beckwith. Born 1985, by: Brantcliffe Bit of a Maestro at Beckwith ex: Listo Gold Charm, bred by Mrs P. Stokes and owned by Mr and Mrs Dave MacMillan.

that the bitch has given birth to another puppy, her preoccupation with cleaning up the first puppy being a distraction. Make a careful check that all is well from time to time.

With the maiden bitch it is wise to keep checking whether the first puppy has been born as she may have given birth and not know what to do next. It is not unusual for a Sheltie to do absolutely nothing with the first born. This is when help will be required. It is important that the sac is removed quickly. To do this simply pull the membrane apart with the fingers, wipe the nose and mouth with a clean towel and if necessary rub the puppy briskly until it is breathing. The bitch will then start to take an interest and she should be encouraged to take over. Her licking will stimulate the pup's breathing and clean any fluid from around the nostrils. If the puppy is not breathing then you will need to hold it in a towel and give it a fairly vigorous rub to stimulate the breathing, whilst continually wiping the nostrils and the mouth to clear the air passages. If this does not work then hold the puppy between your hands with its head by your fingertips and swing it vigorously to expel all fluid from the lungs.

Do not be afraid to be quite firm when handling new born puppies as they are very tough and pliable.

The afterbirth may not have come away at this stage but should follow. Do revive the puppy immediately. Do not wait for the bitch to deal with the afterbirth first.

Most bitches will sever the umbilical cord themselves but it will be necessary to watch that the bitch does not chew off the cord too close to the navel; it is very easy for her to become over enthusiastic and keep on chewing the cord until it is too short which could cause haemorrhaging or a hernia.

I prefer to sever the cord myself by pinching it between the finger and thumb nails, a good inch and a half from the puppy. Alternatively it can be cut with the sterilised scissors. Pinch the chord firmly to prevent haemorrhaging.

Make sure that there are the same number of afterbirths as puppies. It is perfectly natural for the bitch to eat the afterbirth which contains many nutrients and hormones which when eaten, stimulates the rest of the births and lets the milk down.

The time between each birth can vary but it is not unnatural for the bitch to take a rest and appear to have stopped. Do not be in a hurry to interfere. It is not unusual for a further puppy to appear some hours later.

The longest interval will be between the arrival of puppies from the first and those in the second horn of the uterus. This can be a good hour or more.

If the bitch is trampling over the new born pups before she has finished whelping place the pups in a box near by with Vetbed and a hot water bottle under the bedding, not too hot, and place a towel or piece of blanket loosely over the top to keep them warm.

When to call the Vet

If severe straining goes on for more than an hour and then stops a single dose of Caulophyllum tablet will help to start her contractions again. If you are worried then telephone your vet for advice and to forewarn him of the situation. If the vet needs to examine the bitch then it is better to meet him at the surgery because:
   a) it is quicker to meet there
   b) should there be a problem then you are on the spot for any treatment
   c) the car journey can have some astonishing results by jogging things along.

Examination of the bitch by the vet after a difficult birth can put the breeder's mind at rest. He will give an antibiotic and calcium injection to protect against infection and to bolster calcium reserves which will help to prevent eclampsia.

When you think that she has finished she will need to go out and spend a penny. You will need to take her outside on a lead as she will not want to leave the pups. If there is someone else around at the time they can be changing the bedding. Remove all the soiled paper and replace with several thicknesses of paper and a clean fleecy Vetbed. If the pups are strong and healthy and you wish to keep weights this is the time to weigh them, so as not to disturb the bitch.

Give the bitch a drink of milk with a beaten raw egg and glucose. Very often the acceptance of a drink is an indication that she has finished whelping.

When she has settled check each puppy for any deformaties such as cleft palate.

Check for rear dew claws which do occur occasionally and will need to be removed after three days by the vet.

Check tails for any kinks, any puppy that has a kinky tail should be disregarded as a show prospect, therefore being aware from the start saves any disappointment later.

Make sure that all puppies have a feed fairly soon as the first milk contains the colostrum which gives the puppies the maternal immunity. The colostrum is present for the first forty eight hours of lactation. After a few hours it will be obvious when the pups have had a good feed by the roundness of their tummies. Check regularly that all are feeding and are latched on for long enough and that the stronger ones don't knock off the weaker ones.

Three hours old, all feeding and content on their Vetbed

After twenty four hours it is very obvious if there is one that is not getting sufficient. This may be because the weaker pup gets pushed out by the stronger ones. If the weaker pup is not given a chance it can easily give up and not bother. So whilst the thriving, strong puppies are sleeping encourage the weaker one to suckle by drawing off a little milk, then open the pup's mouth and push the nipple into the back of the mouth. The smell of the milk will stimulate the natural instinct to suck.

It is not unusual for a maiden bitch not to want to clean up the puppies faeces. She will stimulate and clean up any urine by licking but will have a look of disgust on her face if you try to show her the messiness under the tail. A smear of margarine under the tail will encourage her to start cleaning but keep checking that she is continuing. After a while she will accept it.

From birth the puppies will require a constant background temperature whatever the weather. The good mother will give sufficient heat by curling her body round the puppies, provided she remains with them. Remember that central heating normally goes off at night. Nothing will kill off puppies quicker than cold.

An infra-red lamp securely fixed over part of the box will guarantee warmth. By having the heat over part of the box the bitch and the puppies have the option of moving under or away from the heat.

Test the temperature in the box as the bitch will be reluctant to stay with the puppies if she is too hot, the puppies will then spread themselves out to cool down. If they are cold and hungry they will cry continuously and the bitch will become distressed. Check that they are warm enough.

Shelties can be easy whelpers but slightly indifferent mothers. This does not imply that they are bad mothers, as they will do their duty, but after a few days the novelty can wear off and they will want to be doing all the things they would normally do, such as going for regular walks. It must be emphasised that the bitch should *not* leave the premises during the time that she is nursing the puppies for fear of bringing in infection.

The bitch who is restless for the first few days is best being closely confined to her box. A radio or music can block out any distracting noises which may upset her.

At three days old any dew claws that are present on the hind legs should be removed. This should only be done by a qualified veterinary surgeon.

If is *not* neccessary to have front dew claws removed. The trauma of the operation can affect the progress of a weak puppy.

After three or four days the nails of the puppies should be trimmed to prevent the bitch becoming scratched and raw as the pups fight to get to the milk 'bar'. Using nail nippers remove the hooked end of the nail. This should be repeated every few days or at least weekly. If the nails are not trimmed the bitch will become very sore which will make her reluctant to stay with them.

The dam should be given the same amount of good food she was having before the birth. If she has a good sized litter then she will need an increased amount to keep up with the demands of the growing pups. If there are only one or two puppies then the amount should be regulated accordingly after the first few days.

At around the third day after whelping careful checks should be made to see that the bitch does not have a build up of milk in the nipples that are not being used. This will be more acute when there is a small litter of two or three when only the easiest freer flowing nipples will be drawn from. Usually the unused ones will be either between her front legs or the ones nearest her back legs. If the bitch is flooding with milk and the build up becomes excessive the whole of the mammary gland will become hard and engorged. Immediate action will be required otherwise infection can set in, in the form of mastitis.

As a prevention, check the bitch every time she comes out of the box from the second day after the birth. At the slightest sign of hardness, give homoeopathic Urtica Urens (see page 219). Apply warm fermentations by standing the bitch over a bowl of warm water and with a sponge bathe

the affected part for a couple of minutes. Do not be afraid to use liberal amounts of water, the bitch will need to be dried off anyway, the more water the better. Repeat three times daily. After a couple of days the hardness will subside and the flow of milk will regulate itself. Do not try to draw off the milk.

Supplementary Feeding

When the bitch has little or no milk a single dose of Urtica Urens can help the flow (see page 210). Give her plenty of fluids, if in doubt have her checked by the vet.

The need to supplementary feed a weakly or small puppy can be due to a large litter or the bitch's lack of milk. There can be no substitute for the dam's milk which has a high fat and protein content and contains all the nutrients, calcium, phosphorous and antibodies needed. Goats milk or a proprietry dried milk formulated for the rearing of puppies can be fed from an eye dropper or, if the puppy will suck, a 'Belcroy' Premature Baby Feeder. Tube feeding is only for experts.

Keep the puppy warm, being with the other puppies and the dam is best but if it is being pushed out it will need to be placed in a separate cosy box, not too big, with a hot water bottle, suitably covered with Vetbed, so as not scald the puppy.

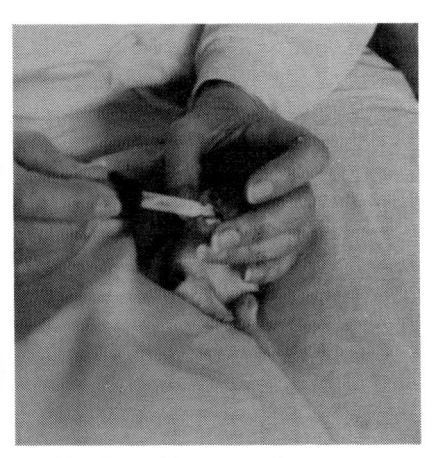

Feeding with an eye dropper

Feed little and often, at least every two hours, day and night. Normally the dam will lick the puppy to stimulate urination. If the puppy is not being attended by the dam there will be a need to massage the tummy gently with cotton wool. This must be done after every meal.

Occasionally there can be an intolerance to the substitute milk, Brands Chicken Essence diluted with equal parts of boiled water will provide an excellent alternative. It is most important that liquids are given regularly, in whatever form, to prevent dehydration. Glucose and water provides fluid and instant energy.

Hand rearing can be a very tiring business but can also have its rewards.

Eclampsia

The onset of eclampsia can be sudden and can occur at anytime, usually during the second week after whelping but has been known to be much later. The bitch cannot cope with the extra demands on her resources. Eclampsia can effect the bitch with a few whelps in the same way as the bitch with a large litter.

A strange expression, increased panting and muscular tremors are the first signs of eclampsia. As it progresses the bitch becomes excitable and her movements become unco-ordinated. In severe cases the legs will stiffen and convulsions occur. If not treated immediately the bitch will collapse and lose consciousness. Death can occur within a very short space of time.

At the first signs seek veterinary help as quickly as possible. The only way it can be treated is by the administration of calcium, intravenously.

Rearing the Litter

It is very important that each puppy is handled daily. The future temperament of the puppy can depend very much on the socialising from birth. Some puppies resent being picked up and can squeal as though they are being murdered, all the more reason why they should be handled. Puppies that are reared in the house have an advantage as they will be used to all the everyday noises that accompany any normal household. Puppies reared in a kennel away from noise and movement are at a disadvantage and this can have a great bearing on their future temperament.

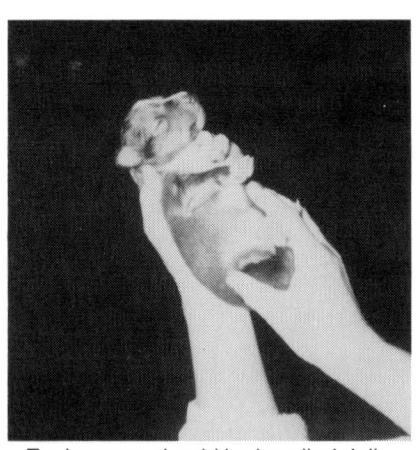

Each puppy should be handled daily

The eyes can start to open from ten days old but this is more likely at around fourteen days. There is a theory that the longer the eye takes to open the better the size of the eye. The larger, bolder eye will be open at ten days.

At the same time that the eyes open the ears will open, having been firmly closed from birth. Therefore the pups will become more aware of noises even if their ocular focus is not very acute at this age. Continue handling and talking to them daily. The radio and vacuum cleaner are all noises that they have to get used to at some stage or another, therefore the sooner the better.

When it comes to feeding they very soon learn the sound of your voice and will immediately rush out of their bed. This is helpful as the first thing they do after waking up is to spend a penny, therefore it is also the first stage of house training - not to foul the bed. The first staggering steps can be taken between two to three weeks and the dam will no doubt, being a Sheltie, want to spend more time away from them. Usually she will want to have access to them but also like to be able to see what else is going on. She will do her duty but will not want to miss anything! It is necessary at this stage that she is confined with them at night in her pen whereas at three to four weeks she may want a bed away from them. As the pups will want to follow her, two steps for her can be made out of firm cardboard boxes that are weighted inside and placed each side of the pen so that she can jump in and out without the puppies following. When the bitch is not sleeping with them a smaller bed can be used for the pups, replacing the larger whelping box. Again the faithful carboard box can be used with the side cut out and fleecy Vetbed bedding. As said before, having a smaller box discourages any fouling of the bed but if they do happen to wet on the Vetbed it will pass right through leaving the puppies dry. The puppies will keep warmer in a small, rather than large box.

Weaning

The time to start weaning the puppies will depend on the size of the litter and how well the bitch has been milking. The first meal can be introduced around three weeks of age. A good sized litter may need to start a few days before.

Milk can vary in its effect on digestions. Cow's milk does not always suit puppies as the fat content is balanced differently to bitches milk. Although diluted tinned evaporated milk can suit, goats milk is preferable and is more readily available these days. Unlike cow's milk goat's milk freezes well. It can be bought fresh from health food shops or direct from a farm. Make sure that it is really fresh, as it can go off very quickly. Divide into small portions to freeze.

A good recipe to start weaning four puppies is:

* milk - 4 teaspoons
* Greek yoghurt - 1 teaspoon
* Runny honey - ½ teaspoon.

Start by giving one small meal the first day and then two the next. Increase the amount as necessary. Use a heavy flat-bottomed dish that will not tip up. To start with the pups will paddle through the dish, uncontrollably spreading the contents. This will all be cleaned up by the bitch when she is returned to the pen. To encourage competition at the outset one can gently press a hand against a puppy who will then push against you thinking that another puppy is trying to gain an advantage.

After a day or so Weetabix or cereal can be added to the milky mixture and after another couple of days meat can be introduced as a third meal.

Finely minced or scraped raw beef has always been the traditional way to introduce meat but the modern method is to start directly with the specially formulated tinned Pedigree Chum Puppy Food. If given from the outset this food is consistent and few upsets will be encountered. Add soaked brown bread to start with; soaked puppy meal can be introduced later.

Some litters prefer to start on meat, being reluctant to take the milky meal first, especially if the mother is giving them an adequate amount. Others shun the meat, preferring the milk. It does not really matter which way round they are given or they can be mixed together. Putting milk onto meat may sound disgusting to us but puppies do not mind!

At four weeks of age four meals per day can be given, two milk meals and two meat meals.

* Breakfast - Weetabix or cereal soaked in milk, Greek yoghurt and runny honey
* Lunch - Puppy Chum and soaked brown bread or puppy meal
* Tea - as breakfast
* Supper - as lunch

Mash the Pedigree Chum Puppy Food with a fork to ensure that there are no lumps and soak the meal well in advance so that it is soft.

Keep the mother away from the pups well before each mealtime so that they do not feed from her before their meal. Allow her to go in after they have eaten to clean up the dishes and then they can top up from her.

The dam who eats her own food and then goes straight into her puppies and regurgitates it for them can be a nuisance as her meal may not be suitable in its content. It is a very difficult habit to break and measures should be taken to keep her away at the critical time. One can argue that it is a natural thing for her to do and wild dogs would do it for their whelps, the only difference being that we have domesticated our dogs to the extent that dietary needs are different.

Between five and seven weeks it is not unusual for puppies to have loose motions. This can be caused by a sudden intolerance to milk or a mild infection that their immune system has not met. Provided that the puppies appear to have nothing more than loose motions and are otherwise lively, not sickly, the first thing to do is:

* Cut out all milk
* Reduce the quantity of each meal
* Replace the biscuit-meal with boiled *brown* rice, not white rice and only flavour with a small amount of chicken or fish
* Give frequent doses of Arsen Alb - away from any food. Administer by crushing the tablet between two spoons and putting on the tongue. They will accept it quite readily as it is sweet to taste (see page 218)
* If you are in any doubt or the puppies do not improve after 24 hours seek the advice of your vet

Having sorted out any problem, or even if there has not been a problem, giving only a 'complete food diet' soaked well, is an excellent way of ensuring that the puppies are getting a fully balanced diet that can easily be followed when sold to their new homes. There are many excellent 'complete puppy diets' on the market. I have found that a 23%-24% protein content marketed for adult dogs is very adequate. For Shelties anything higher than 30% protein is undesirable. The diet will then consist of four meals of the same thing.

Worming

At four weeks the litter should be wormed using Antepar Elixir a children's worming syrup obtained from the chemist. Weigh each puppy and using a calibrated syringe, without the needle, give one ml. per 1816 grams (4lbs) body weight. Puppies that weigh less should be given only the appropriate amount for the weight.

Worming should be repeated every two weeks. The dam should be wormed at the same time.

Vaccinations

In order that the maximum amount of protection can be given to the very young puppy the use of homoeopathic vaccine or 'nosode' can be given as early as three weeks.

Whereas the normal time for vaccinations given by the vet is not until eight weeks this homoeopathic method can cover a critical time in-between when there could be doubt whether the puppy still retains any natural maternal immunity.

Distemper, hepatitis, leptospirosis, and parvovirus can all be given in one tablet.

Dosage is: One tablet morning and evening for three days then one per month until conventional vaccination can be given.

> * It must be emphasised that a formal vaccination programme should be carried out as soon as possible by the vet.

From five weeks the dam can be sleeping apart from the pups, without access. Her interest can wain quite quickly as they become more independent and self sufficient. Her own meals should be reduced in quantity as the demand for milk diminishes. Do not allow her to become grossly fat which will be difficult to reduce later, on the other hand do not decrease her meals too quickly so that she becomes poor and emaciated. Her coat will start to drop after weaning; the timing will depend on how much she has put into the rearing of the puppies. Some hold it until the puppies are eight or ten weeks old, others drop it after only four weeks.

It is quite natural for a bitch to lose all her coat after a litter. She will look simply dreadful for a while, resembling a Whippet with only a few wisps. This will be compensated by her next coat which will come through better than before.

Having mentioned the importance of early handling of the pups it is necessary to continue this. From six weeks of age each puppy develops a more individual personality and equal time should be given to each puppy. It is very easy to pick out the favoured one each time, ignoring the others. The pushy puppy will always be to the fore leaving the rest to flounder. Get as many people as possible to come and handle them. Do not let children pick them up as they can so easily wriggle and be dropped; make it a rule that the child always goes down to the puppies.

From four weeks old the litter become great fun and terrible time wasters! Give them the time. Play with them, cuddle them, talk to them, gently brush them, stand them on a table. Their future personality will be formed during this time.

Selling the Puppies

The accepted time for puppies to be sold is around eight weeks of age. Between six and eight weeks they learn so much and if in the right environment with plenty of attention can only benefit. It is a very impressionable age and they can learn both good and bad habits from their mother or any other dog that is around with whom they have contact. The bold outgoing dam will pass on her confidence to her offspring. The nervous, spooky bitch will teach her pups to be the same. In cases like that the sooner the bitch is out of contact the better.

If the puppy is to be sold before eight weeks then the breeder must be satisfied that the new owner is capable of giving the required amount of attention. Previous owners of Shelties are a safe bet as they will understand the breed. Obedience owners prefer to have their puppies around six weeks old to be able to bring them up their way, establish a rapport and routine.

The established breeder is more likely to have customers waiting for their stock. The pet owner with a litter will no doubt be assisted by the stud-dog owner who will pass on enquiries. If there is a need to advertise, try your local paper in the hope that the puppies will remain in the locality. It is always nice to be able to see the results of your efforts and hard work.

The pet owner may have to accept the fact that they may not get the same price as the well-known breeder.

Prospective customers should be asked:

* Why they want a Sheltie
* Is there someone at home most of the time
* Is the garden properly fenced

If the whole family is out at work for the majority of the day then their suitability is questionable.

When the new owners collect their puppy a pedigree should have been written out, a diet sheet given and any other details made clear. It may have been fifteen years since their last puppy and one does tend to forget.

Example Diet Sheet and Instructions

Instructions for your new Puppy

Sheltie puppies between 6 and 8 weeks need 4 meals per day.
The diet below is what the puppy has been having up to now. Keep to this diet until he has settled into his new home. If you wish to change the diet do it gradually so as not to upset him. Do not give excess milk as it can upset some Shelties. Keep to a specific diet, do not give too much variety, this will only make him fussy.

Breakfast: Weetabix, milk, Greek yogurt and a teaspoonful of runny honey. Or soaked Go-Dog.

Lunch: Soaked Go-Dog or Puppy Chum and soaked Small-Bite Mixer.

Tea: Soaked Go-Dog with milk.

Supper: As lunch.

If all the meal is not eaten then reduce the amount until the dish is cleaned.
Increase the amount accordingly as he grows. He needs to be well covered and rounded.
At 3 months stop one meal.
At 5-6 months reduce to 2 meals per day.
Worm in 2 weeks time and repeat every 2 weeks until 4 months.
Vaccinations. Enquire of your vet and be advised by him.

If you have any query, however trivial, do not hesitate to contact me.
Please keep in touch and give progress reports.
If for any reason you have to re-home your puppy please contact me first.

Make sure that the appropriate food has been obtained for their new puppy. If necessary give an amount of the food the puppy has been used to which will avoid any change.

Application should have been made to the Kennel Club to register the litter. Do not delay as it can get forgotten. Only the breeder can register the puppies. Remember that the form needs to be signed by the owner of the sire.

Applying for an Affix

Application for an affix or kennel name is made to The Kennel Club. There is an application fee then an annual maintenance fee. Once registered only the affix holder can use that name and all dogs will be identified with that person. Dogs that have been bred by the owner are registered with the affix before the dog's name, as a prefix. When a dog has been bred by someone else, then transferred, the affix is used as a suffix, after the dog's name.

Bringing up the Show Puppy

Picking the Potential Show Puppy

PRACTICALLY every breeder who is breeding for the show ring will be looking in each litter for that puppy that is better than anything else that they have ever bred.

One should have a 'gut' feeling about whether a puppy is right and worth running on. All other things being equal I am convinced that there is a certain attraction that draws one to the right puppy. Even the breeder of a one-off litter, if they are animal orientated, can pick out the right puppy.

Shelties are not the easiest of breeds in which to predict the outcome of the eight week old puppy. Any person who has bred another breed will admit that Shelties are more difficult to assess due to the great variation of size and type.

The novice breeder who is trying to breed a puppy to show should seek advice from an established breeder who, one hopes will guide them in the right direction. The breeder of your bitch will know what is behind her. The stud dog owner will no doubt have seen a number of puppies by their dog and will have some idea what to be looking for in his puppies. Some people have an eye for picking a puppy, others never will.

When there is really nothing in a litter worth keeping it is a great temptation to *try* to like a puppy; every excuse and reason can be found to justify running one on whilst knowing in one's heart of hearts, nothing is really good enough. I have done it myself and can fully understand other people doing the same.

When asked to give an opinion about a litter one tries to be forthright, on the other hand the decision must eventually lie with the owner. After all, it is only by experience that one will ever learn. One has, unfortunately, to learn the hard way.

Puppies of most breeds look similar at birth. There are some people who claim that they can pick a puppy when it is still wet. I am not convinced that one can predict the eventual outcome but one can pick out certain points at that stage that will remain.

The long tail at birth will end up as a long tail. The short stumpy tail at birth will appear to be long enough at eight weeks but will end up short.

The head of the new born puppy can resemble a Bull Terrier, being broad and thick with no evidence of a stop, and an underjaw that

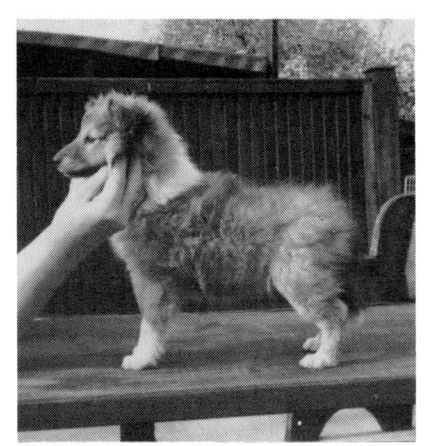

Bitch puppy at 6 weeks   Bitch puppy at 8 weeks

protrudes beyond the nostrils and equals the depth of the muzzle. This can be quite normal. A fine snipey muzzle with a distinct lack of underjaw will end up lacking in foreface and underjaw.

Where there has been a difficult birth the head can appear quite grotesque but alter to normality after a couple of days.

Size should have been assessed as far as possible, by the time the puppy has reached eight weeks of age (see pages 151-152).

The head should be well filled without being strong or too wide between the eyes. There should be a well defined stop and the muzzle and skull should be parallel when viewed from the side. The straight through head without a stop will end up lacking stop and possibly have a receding skull.

The set of the eye should be oblique and the shape and size should be evident. A sweet expression can be seen at this stage. The bold, round badly placed eye can easily be seen. The forward facing bold eye will often accompany a broad skull at maturity.

At eight weeks the puppy should look square, chunky or cobby with plenty of width between the front legs, which should not necessarily be absolutely straight, but the feet must face forward. As the puppy develops the slightly bowed legs will straighten. The shoulder placement and upper arm can be felt at this stage.

The hindquarters should be square with plenty of width, the stifle should be almost exaggerated and the angle of the hock positively defined with the hock very well let down. Straight stifles and cow hocks will not improve.

The tail that only just reaches the hock at eight weeks will end up short. It needs to be longer at this stage.

A good neck and head carriage at eight weeks will remain and will be an advantage in the show ring, giving the dog presence as well as being an indication of possible good showmanship. The short stuffy neck will always be stuffy.

The coat should be thick and almost felty, preferably with long guard hairs. The colour at eight weeks may not bear any relation to the colour at six months. The colour at birth may give more of an indication.

Beware the truly masculine, finished-looking dog puppy. You will not have been able to see anything else in the litter because he outshines them in every respect. He will, of course, be the most glamorous and definitely the most outgoing. Many Sheltie dog puppies can look quite magnificent at six months, but beware if he is well up to size and very 'finished' in the head. Remember that it is very unusual for a dog puppy *not* to grow on after the age of six months.

The very fine boned puppy with small feet, small nostrils and a face resembling a kitten will be too fine in foreface, probably be lacking in bone and will end up too small.

The heavily boned puppy that has a head that is ideal for the age may not grow as big as expected, the head being the indication of eventual size. The chunky bone on that sort of puppy can disappear by the age of nine months, ending up perfectly balanced throughout.

Check the teeth which should be a correct scissor bite with six incisors at the top and six at the bottom.

Always sell the obvious pets as soon as possible then the others will be easier to assess and observe without being overshadowed by the extreme puppy who may dominate one's eye.

If you are not sure whether or not you like anything from a litter then sell them all.

Before the litter is eight weeks old the litter should have been screened for Collie Eye Anomaly (see page 205). The result should influence any decision as to which puppies are to be run on. Anyone considering keeping a dog as a future stud dog has a moral responsibility to the breed, only to keep one that is clear.

One gratifying thing about C.E.A. is that the condition can be diagnosed at an early age before sentiment comes into the choice of puppy.

Have them tested early (before eight weeks) to get a true diagnosis. If tested later you will not know if it is a go-normal or not.

Conclusion

* Do not *try* to like a particular puppy. It should be an obvious choice.

Look for:

* Compactness
* Good underjaw
* Correct scissor bite
* Clean stop
* Well filled foreface
* Good head carriage
* Plenty of ear tip
* Well placed eye
* Feet pointing forward
* Reasonable width of chest
* Well laid shoulder
* Well bent stifle
* Well angulated and defined hock joint, well let down
* Plenty of width behind
* Good length of tail
* Dense coat with plenty of guard hairs
* Good temperament

Running on the Promising Puppy

'Running on' is a term used by breeders and is the period between the age of eight weeks and six months, during which time the breeder will be assessing and hoping that the favoured puppy will fulfil its early promise.

Running on a promising puppy can be one of the most interesting aspects of dog breeding, it can also be very disappointing. There are very few puppies, that one breeds, that turn out to be top winners. Those who have had a one-off high flyer usually find that it is not easy to repeat.

Months of anticipation can end in great satisfaction or in total disappointment and frustration.

Having 'picked' the puppy or puppies from the litter that are hopefuls it makes good sense to sell the rest as quickly as possible. There will then be more time to give to and observe the favoured ones.

If two puppies are to be run on they can be company for each other if they are kennelled. If they are to take their place as house dogs then the sooner a particular one is selected the better. This is because the individual is easier to train, settles to sleep more quickly and will learn from the adults in all aspects, such as house training. Unfortunately they can also pick up some of the bad habits from the older dogs. The shy dam can quickly transfer her odd quirks to her offspring, in which case they should be separated as early as possible.

The 'two peas in a pod' at eight weeks may well have sorted themselves out and be very different by the time they are twelve weeks. Often people will run two puppies on from a litter because they are convinced that the mating should have worked. It may be that the plan has not come out as expected. One spends hours watching and observing, trying to imagine the outcome.

Having ascertained which puppy is to be run on there will be the ensuing nail biting that will go on for the next four months. I have a rule, and that is that the puppy can stay for as long as he is not doing anything outrageous such as growing grossly overheight.

By twelve weeks the rounded cuddly puppy starts to get a bit longer in the leg and the head begins to 'pull out'. This means that the head will lengthen and the stop will not be so deep. The heavy headed, well filled foreface on a male puppy can often 'pull out' too much by the age of twelve weeks. The size of the head can often determine the eventual size of the dog. The majority of heads will lengthen after the age of six months. I measure the head at five months, from the tip of the nose to the occiput. Approximately 13cms (5½ inches) is about average for the age and will then grow at least another 2.5cms (1 inch) in length by the time the puppy is eight months old.

The very 'finished' head with a flat skull at six months will develop even more and become too strong and coarse with time. It is always worth remembering that the head shape can go on changing even over the age of twelve months.

By the time the puppy is five months old the body will have slimmed down. As the fat roly poly puppy grows up his body will take shape and

Jack Point of Janetstown at 3 months   Jack Point of Janetstown at 4 months

Jack Point of Janetstown at 5 months   Jack Point of Janetstown at 6 months

the legs will grow longer and the front become narrower. If he has sufficient width in front then this will allow for the front to settle. The correct looking front at twelve weeks will end up too narrow.

Five months can be the most ugly stage being all legs and no coat and no decision should be made at this time. Given another month he can grow more coat and body to look more respectable.

Jack Point of Janetstown a C.C. winner at 11 months

Do
* Worm regularly
* Vaccinate as soon as possible
* Screen for Collie Eye Anomaly before eight weeks
* Stand puppy on a table at least twice a week
* Brush regularly - even if there is no coat
* Put a small collar on at twelve weeks
* Take on small journeys in the car other than going to the vet
* Make sure that he has set, regular times for sleep, preferably on his own
* Check that teeth are coming in as they should
* Feed from the hand to encourage showmanship

Do Not
* Exercise too much
* Allow him to chase around all day
* Allow him to run up and down stairs
* Overdo the ringcraft class
* Bore him by over training
* 'Look' or make a decision at five months
* Allow your heart to rule your head

A bitch has usually finished growing by 9 months.
A dog can go on growing until over 12 months.

Size

From the breeder's point of view, size is one of the most difficult aspects of the breed. Trying to predict size can often be misleading and very disheartening.

Lines can vary at certain ages and for the breeder trying to make a judgement about which puppy to run on, keeping some records of the growth weights can be most interesting and useful.

Some breeders never bother to weigh or measure their puppies. Their experience and their eye will tell them which ones will be too big and which ones will be too small. These people are honest with themselves. The novice breeder who is desperate to breed something good often can not or will not see any problem.

The eight week old puppy can vary in weight, sometimes by pounds, this will not necessarily mean anything at all. There are some lines where a puppy of eight weeks would be expected to weigh around 4lbs (1816 grams). Others would wish to see them considerably more or less.

Dr. Karin Riemann from Germany has a method whereby each puppy of the litter is weighed weekly from five to eight weeks. They should be weighed at the same time of the day, preferably before breakfast, so that a true reading can be obtained.

At the end of this three week period the total amount of weight gained can be assessed. Generally the puppy that puts on a total of 33ozs (900 grams) or an average of 11ozs (300 grams) per week is more likely to end up the correct size, whether it is a dog or bitch.

I do like to weigh my puppies once per week, anyway. Not only as a matter of interest but also to check that there is a regular weight gain.

In spite of knowing in my heart of hearts roughly how a puppy will turn out, I do like to keep a record of weights and also measure height regularly.

It is good practise for a puppy to stand on the table to be measured.

Measuring

the height is measured from the withers, make sure that the dog is settled with his weight evenly distributed on an even surface.

No reliable guidelines can be given as to what height a puppy should be at what age but 22.5cms (9 inches) at 9 weeks is reasonable.

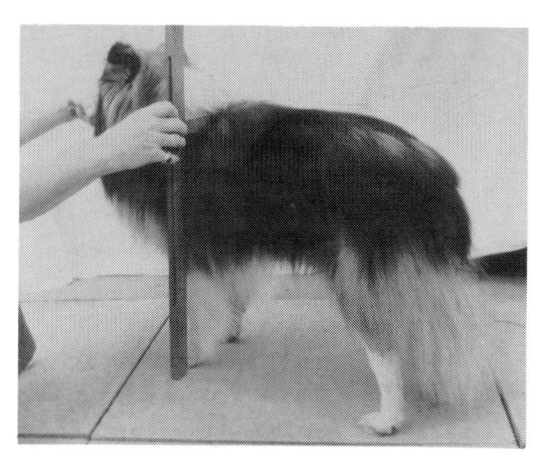

Measuring Height

Teething

Always make a point of checking a puppy's mouth as he develops. The show dog will be required to have his mouth handled when being shown but it is always useful for the pet owner to be able to handle his own dog's mouth. Start at the very earliest age by just lifting the lips to see the bite.

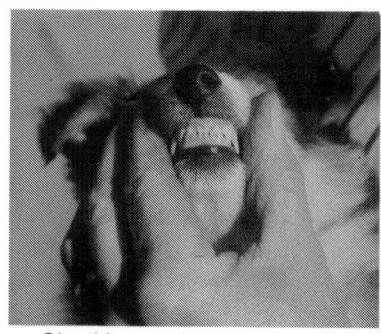

Checking teeth - a correct bite

Please do be careful. The puppy's mouth will be very sensitive and the potential show puppy can be ruined by over handling of the mouth. Be gentle but firm and positive.

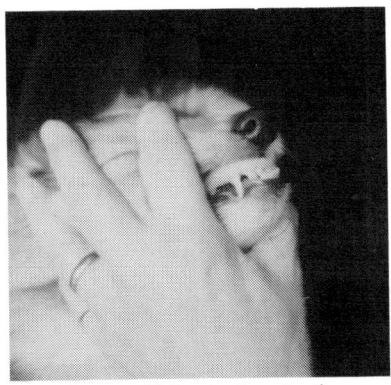

Incorrect bite - bottom teeth protrude in front of top teeth

The first premolars will start to come through from fourteen weeks. These are the first teeth behind the large canines and do *not* replace a baby tooth.

The next will not appear for about another four to six weeks i.e. four and a half months. These will be the incisors which will start coming out with the middle two, top and bottom - quickly followed by the ones either side. The outer incisors appear to take a bit longer. At around five months everything seems to happen at once. It seems that the canines are the last to appear but in actual fact the very back molars will be the last, but are not so evident.

If the baby canines do not drop out of their own accord and are distorting the new teeth then it is advisable for them to be removed by the vet.

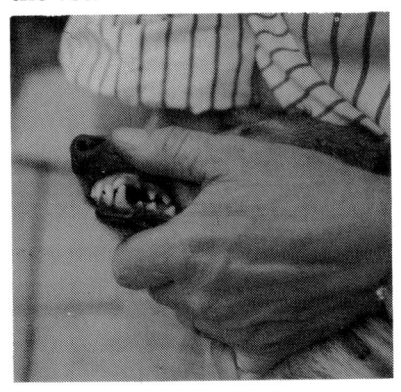

Misplaced Canine

Missing and misplaced teeth can be a problem in the breed and whereas this will not affect the pet Sheltie it should concern the breeder who intends breeding further generations. Bad mouths are a constructional fault and should be given the same consideration as any other fault.

One of the characteristics of a Sheltie when teething is the flying of his ears. It is at this time that the ears will most need treatment. Generally this is only temporary but immediate action should be taken to rectify the situation (see page 154).

Exercise and Food

Remember that a puppy grows at a very fast rate up to the age of eight months and will still be developing after that age. The male dog can go on growing up to the age of twelve months. Even if they are not actually growing upwards they are still developing.

This is a point grossly overlooked by many and not just the pet owner.

All youngsters, whether human or otherwise, have certain energy requirements for growth. They also need their rest. This cannot be emphasised enough. So many people will feed their puppies well but also expect them to take the same amount of exercise as an adult dog. All sorts of problems can stem from the overweight over exercised puppy. It is generally believed that a dog will end up more 'on the leg' if given too much exercise when growing.

Going up and down stairs or jumping out of the car can put a puppy's joints under great strain.

From the time you have your puppy make sure that he has his rests between meals. Many puppies may not do this voluntarily so he needs to be confined to ensure he will have his appropriate amount of sleep.

Try to create a sensible balance between the amount of food, the amount of sleep and the amount of exercise given. The four month puppy should not be taken for long walks as soon as he is clear of his vaccinations.

The adult dog in good coat, body and condition will not require as much food as the very out-of-coat teenager whose demands are much greater. Growing a new coat takes a lot out of any dog who also loses a considerable amount of body, and will therefore need to be fed accordingly.

Dealing with Difficult Ears

More often than not if a puppy's ears are going to go up and be pricked it will be at teething time, alternatively they go down like a Spaniel but this does not happen as frequently.

Ears are much better than when I first started in the breed when there was a major problem, even with show dogs, but I am glad to say that, through selective breeding and the advancement of the breed, ear size and shape are vastly improved.

The very small, thick leathered ear is usually pricked and no amount of treatment will rectify the problem.

The ears that appear to be perfectly tipped until teething can usually be won over with persistence. More often than not a little oil massaged into the fold with a touch of talcum powder will do the trick. Occasionally the problem could go on until the dog is nearly two years old but when the ears are settled with plenty of hair on them, they may never pose a future problem.

When the ear goes heavy this can be more of a problem than going up. If in doubt leave well alone. A little hair can be taken off the ear to lighten it but care should be taken as drastic removal of the hair can cause the ear to become pricked.

It is essential that the pricked ear is treated quickly and not allowed to remain up or there will be no possibility of ever getting it down.

If in doubt consult a breeder who will show you how to treat them. For those willing to try themselves a very good quality oil will be needed such as almond or jojoba oil, glycerine or cuticura. The use of leather softeners can be messy and difficult to remove from the show dog or can sometimes overheat the sensitive skin. Keep a piece of oil soaked sponge in a small dish so that it is handy to apply when needed. A little hand cream can sometimes be sufficient when the ear is not normally a problem.

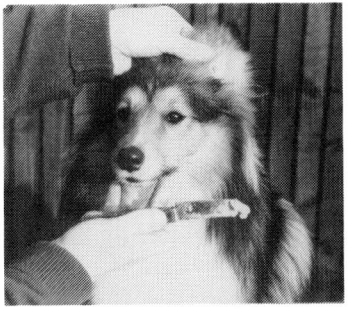

To treat liberally cover the top half of the inside of the ear. Massage well into the skin of the fold and the hair. Do be sure to apply PLENTY. One of the problems is when too little oil is applied which does not penetrate sufficiently. Having oiled the ear well there should be a considerable amount on the hair. A liberal amount of talcum powder dusted over the top of the ear will soak up any excess. Fold the ear over and gently massage at every opportunity.

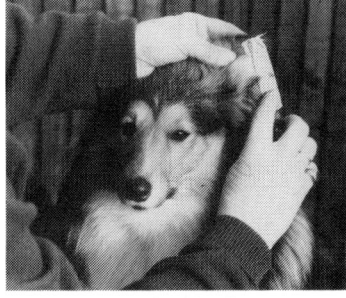

To weight the pricked ear use Kaolin Poultice

If the ear does not respond to the oil treatment more drastic measures will be needed. *Do not use chewing gum.* Once it is on it is permanent. When removed the hair comes off with the gum and the ear usually goes back up.

Kaolin poultice is the only thing that will have the desired effect. This is obtainable from a chemist and is quite expensive for what appears to be a small amount but will last for years.

Press the Kaolin well into the hair

Stir the contents but do not remove all of the oil as this helps the kaolin to penetrate the hair. Using the end of a teaspoon or small palate knife press a small amount into the hair on the inside tip of the ear. Do be sure that it has penetrated the hair otherwise it will come off too easily.

- on the tips of the ear

Having ensured that there is sufficient kaolin on the tip of the ear then press as

Keep powdering until firm

Tie ears weighted in correct position

much talcum into the kaolin as it will soak up. Keep powdering until firm. The warmth of the ear will soften the kaolin which will cause it to drip and if not blotted by the talcum, and the dog shakes his head, it will fly everywhere, up the walls and on the ceiling!

The kaolin will bring the ear down more than enough initially. Leave it to settle. A certain amount will come off but keep powdering to stop it dripping.

Oil the fold every other day and powder again. The oil will remove the kaolin if not powdered. If the ear is too low it is easy enough to remove a small amount but gradually the blob on the tip of the ear will wear off. Never wash the kaolin off with water before a show, it will make the ear go up. Gradually remove the kaolin, with the oil, over several days before the show. Use powder to soak up the oil and gently brush with a soft brush.

All too often one sees a Minor Puppy class where a number of dogs have their ears up. It can also happen to older dogs. The excitement of the show causes the adrenalin to flow and the otherwise natural ear to pop up.

The adult bitch will tend to 'lift' an ear prior to her coming in season which will be an indication that she is imminent.

The biggest problem for the pet Sheltie is that the dog will stand close to his owner looking up, causing the ears to flick backwards. The pet owner will not have the problem that breeders have whereby other dogs will lick anything off the ears. This is totally disastrous as the effects of licking, and the saliva, make the ears stick up more firmly like a board. The dogs that do the licking can become addicted to the taste of the kaolin or oil making the task more difficult. Separating the dogs is the only solution. Putting some foul tasting substance in with the powder can have some interesting results. A spice such as ginger can sometimes work. I suggested this to one person who had no ginger but thought that curry powder would suffice. The other dog loved the taste!

Showing

Making a Start

ANYONE who becomes involved in the showing and breeding of dogs can look forward to a varied career meeting people from all walks of life, making lots of friends, travelling to all parts of the country and a greatly increased phone bill!

Showing can be rewarding, frustrating, tiring and expensive but those who have been 'bitten by the bug' having won a few prizes will look forward to the next show with enthusiasm and anticipation. The preparation and work put into the dogs before the show is all part of the fun. Meeting all one's friends at the shows and discussing pedigrees, listening to other opinions and generally pooling experiences adds to the day.

Although the showing of dogs is reliant on the judge's opinion rather than the ability of the competitor the majority of judges are very genuine and will always give an honest opinion.

Information

Every exhibitor needs to be in contact with the show world therefore it is essential to take one of the weekly dog papers. 'Dog World' or 'Our Dogs' provide details of forthcoming shows, information and chat about each breed and results of the shows along with judge's critiques of winning dogs. Much can be learnt from a well written report.

The Kennel Club publish guidelines together with the Rules and Regulations. The monthly Kennel Gazette keeps in touch with the Kennel Club

The Shows

There are six categories of shows from which to choose:

Exemption Show

Open to pedigree and non-pedigree dogs, registered or unregistered. There are a maximum of five pedigree classes and any number of novelty classes for pedigree and non-pedigree dogs. Entries are made on the day.

Primary Show
Confined to members of the organising club. Entries are taken on the day. There are a maximum of eight classes, the highest being Maiden.

Sanction Show
A breed club or local club show often held in the local church hall with a maximum of twenty five classes up to and including Post Graduate. An ideal training ground for the novice exhibitor and for young puppies. Entries close prior to the show. Restricted to members but you may join when making your entry.

Limited Show
Similar to the Sanction show but will include Limit and Open classes. Champions and C.C. winners are not eligible.

Open Show
Can be an all-breed show or breed club show. Open to all including Champions and C.C. winners.

Championship Show
The highest level of show where Challenge Certificates (C.C.s) can be won which count towards Champion status. Wins in certain classes qualify the dog to enter at Crufts.

Crufts is the dog show that everyone has heard of and is a Championship show in the same way as any other Championship show with equivalant awards. Entry is by qualification and is open to any dog qualified for entry in the Kennel Club Stud Book or who has qualified in the appropriate class during the previous year.

In the past Crufts was open to all and everyone would keep their new puppies to 'bring out' at Crufts. Entries became so large that the show could not accommodate the numbers. The qualifications change from time to time.

Prize cards are awarded at all shows and the majority also have elaborate rosettes. Prize money is only occasionally awarded for class wins with the major sponsors providing money and perks to the few top winners at club shows, and Stakes classes at Championship shows.

The aim of everyone who is showing is to make up a Champion. to win that coverted green card is a thrill never to be forgotten. Along the way there are other awards to be won. Qualifying for Crufts is a satisfying win even if the dog in question is not in coat for the occasion and does not attend.

The Junior Warrant used to be a challenge but recent restrictions have made it virtually impossible to achieve. It used to be for points won between 6-18 months but it has been altered to discourage puppies being taken to too many shows. Now it is virtually impossible for Shelties as they tend to drop their coats during the qualifying time.

The Kennel Club Awards

Junior Warrant
Three points won for 1st prize at a Championship Show. One point for a 1st prize at an Open Show in the breed. A total of 25 points won between the ages of 12 and 18 months to qualify.

Kennel Club Stud Book Number
Entry into The Kennel Club Stud Book (KCSB) is achieved by winning 1st, 2nd or 3rd in the Limit or Open classes in the breed at a Championship show, and or, winning a Challenge Certificate (the C.C.) or Reserve Challenge Certificate (Reserve C.C.).

A Stud Book Number is allocated and replaces the original registration number for the purpose of registering progeny. Details of pedigree and the wins are listed in the Stud Book which is published annually.

A Stud Book number allows a dog to enter Crufts at any time without having to qualify during the preceeding year.

The Kennel Club automatically issue a certificate on the first occasion the dog qualifies.

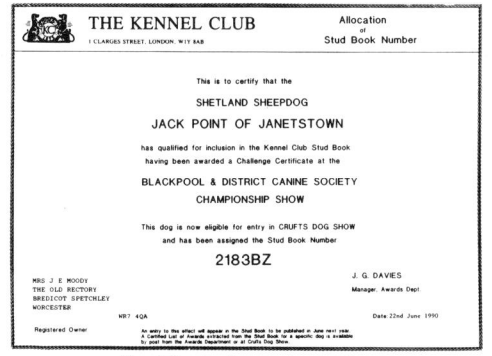

Certificate for entry in the Kennel Club Stud Book with KCSB number

Official Challenge Certificate sent by The Kennel Club

The Challenge Certificate
A Challenge Certificate (C.C.) is awarded to the best dog and the best bitch at a Championship show. A green

and white card is awarded in the ring at the show and an official Certificate is sent at a later date from the Kennel Club confirming the award.

C.C. awarded at the show

Reserve C.C. awarded at the show

Reserve Challenge Certificate

(Reserve C.C.) awarded in the ring to the runner-up to the C.C. winner.

Champion

A Champion (Ch.) is a dog or bitch that has won three Challenge Certificates (C.C.s) under three different judges. In the case of a puppy winning certificates one of the C.C.s must have been won over the age of 12 months to qualify as a Champion. A Champion Certificate is issued automatically by the Kennel Club.

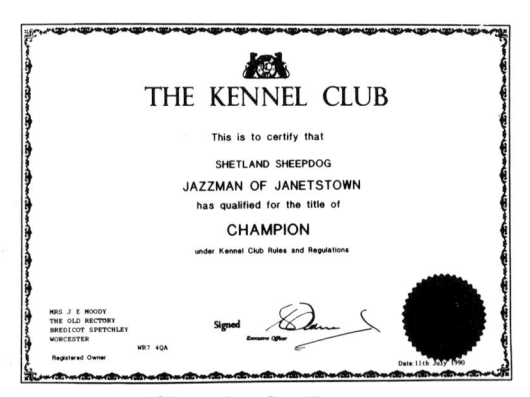

Champion Certificate

Breeders Diploma

A Breeders Diploma is issued to the breeder of a Champion, who may not necessarily be the owner, on application to the Kennel Club.

Entering the Show

All show entries have to be made on an official entry form and sent to the show secretary with the appropriate fee. Read the schedule and abbreviated Kennel Club rules and regulations which will all be relevant to the show you are entering. Classes are for age, qualification with regard to number of wins by the dog, 'special' classes which cover weight (not applicable in our breed) and colour, then the exhibitor qualification classes such as Special beginners where the owner has never won a C.C. in the breed.

The age classes are for those between 6 months and 2 and veteran for those over 7 years.

'Minor puppy' is for puppies between the ages of 6 and 9 months.

'Puppy' is 6 to 12 months.

'Junior' up to 18 months.

'Special Yearling' up to 2 years.

Thereafter the classes are defined by the number of awards won.

Read all the definitions of the classes, which are always listed in the schedule, before deciding which one to enter.

If you have a minor puppy then one class should be quite sufficient at a Championship show and perhaps two classes, puppy and novice, at an open show.

When you see the number of dogs that are entered in the classes for our breed you will understand that putting a puppy into all the classes is hardly fair. He will become tired and bored, and one cannot expect a youngster to compete against more mature dogs. Entering too many classes is a mistake that many novices make.

Make a note on the front of the schedule which dogs have been entered in which classes and the time judging starts. It is not unheard of for an exhibitor to arrive at the show with the wrong dog. Any alterations to time will be announced in the weekly dog papers just prior to the show.

When sending an entry by post it is always advisable to use a first class stamp and obtain a certificate of posting from the Post Office in case the entry goes astray. There is nothing worse than travelling a long distance to a show only to find that you are not in the catalogue and the show manager has not received your entry. You will be able to show but risk being disqualified by the Kennel Club later if adequate proof of posting cannot be supplied.

Ring Training

Informal Sheltie club matches and rallies are perfect for socialising youngsters where the relaxed atmosphere helps to make the outing enjoyable and fun. Experiences are exchanged and problems discussed. Nothing is too high powered and the dogs get to know and enjoy the regular get together. Do not over do it, keep the serious bit for the shows that are important, where most of the real training takes place. Club shows are the best start for a youngser who will be more relaxed with their own kind.

Once you begin to go to shows it is a grave mistake to go to too many. If you start off well and have some success it is easy to get bitten by the 'bug'. There is nothing like winning a few cards to adorn the mantlepiece to encourage you to enter whatever show there happens to be in the area or even further afield.

Give a thought to your young puppy who may have shown quite brilliantly at his first few shows only to become lethargic and bored by being dragged around the country week after week. Novices fall into the trap and then cannot understand why their superb dog who looks an absolute picture at home becomes an inanimate object as soon as he walks into the ring. Don't overdo it.

It can be appreciated that some dogs really do dislike shows, but with persistent socialising and making life fun they become accustomed to the routine. Once they have become used to going to shows and know that they are going to be the favoured one, having your undivided attention, they soon learn the pre-show procedure of bathing and packing of the show bag. They then expect to be the one to be going every time. They grow to enjoy the party and the accolade. Do remember that adult dogs as well as youngsters tire after a day at a show and can lose a considerable amount of body weight and will therefore need a day or two to recover.

So, spare a thought for your dog when making your entries. Think of the future when he has risen to the dizzy heights of the Open class. You will gain a great deal more pleasure from showing for several years with a happy dog on the end of the lead. Pick and choose the shows, spread them out then let puppies be puppies and enjoy themselves.

The essence of a good handler is to be able to accentuate the dogs virtues and disguise the failings.

The young puppy should be taught to:
* Walk on the left but occasionally on the right
* Stand on the table
* Be handled by strangers, men and women
* Move in a straight line
* Stand correctly and stay
* Listen to and watch the handler
* Use his ears for bait

Food or bait fed from the pocket will teach the dog to use his ears and keep his attention on the handlers. The reluctant showman can be fed his meals from the hand.

The handler should learn to:
* Walk in a straight line
* Not crowd their own dogs or others - standing or on the move
* Keep an eye on the judge as well as their dog

Preparation for the Show

Everything that is required for the show should be prepared beforehand. As most shows will require an early start it makes sense to have all bags packed and the dog suitably bathed and groomed the day before.

If the dog is entered for an important show and the coat is starting to moult do not groom until you get to the show. Drastic grooming and bathing will take all the coat out and it will go flat. Even the whites need to be done very carefully. When grooming at the show wait until just before entering the ring then really brush and comb thoroughly. This sounds an alarming step, but, if done too early the coat will flop. By waiting until the last minute the coat will stand off for sufficient time for the dog to be judged. The dog who is totally out of coat should be left at home and given time to grow a new jacket, without coat they can look dreadful appearing fine in bone, and can move very differently to when in fine fettle. They lose body as well as condition and can sometimes look drawn around the face.

The show bag should contain:
* The show schedule and passes
* Leather collar with identity tag and benching chain. It is a Kennel Club rule that every dog that is benched should be safely secured with the appropriate collar and chain
* Benching blanket
* Bowl and water. Water may not be easily available. Water from home is less likely to cause any upset
* Grooming kit
* Towel
* Kitchen roll. Most essential, has a variety of uses for both dog and owner
* Bait. Liver, chicken or a variety of types in case the dog takes a sudden dislike to the normally tasty morsel. Be sure to secure any bait during the journey, it is not unknown for the dog travelling in the rear of the car to push his way into the bag and consume all the food intended for both owner and dog!
* Ring number clip or safety pin
* Show leads
* Cage for on the bench, or at an unbenched open show with a piece of carpet on top the cage can double as a grooming table
* Food, drinks and any refreshments needed for the day. Food purchased at shows can be expensive
* A folding chair if you wish to be sure of having a ringside seat

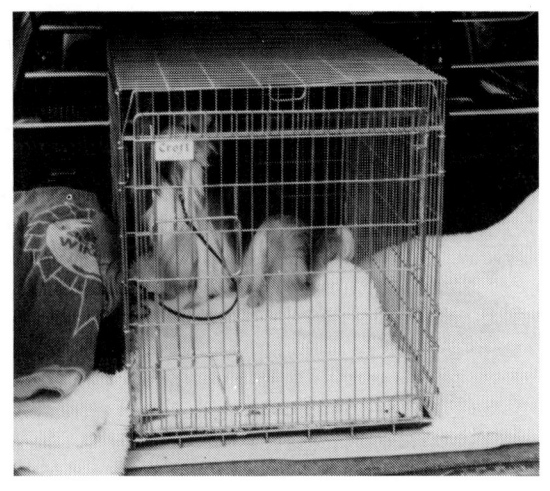

'Croft' folding mesh kennel for security when travelling

* Wet weather clothing. Wellingtons and raincoats should be taken to every show regardless of the weather forecast. Nature has a way of catching you out, particularly when the wellies are at home. It is good insurance to carry them at all times
* Sun cream for summer shows and ice pack and cool box for hot car journeys

The car should be filled with petrol and tyres and oil checked. A towel and kitchen roll should be standard equipment in the car for emergencies.

The day of the Show

Wear suitable clothing for all eventualities. It is easier to remove a layer of clothes than be cold and not have enough to keep you warm for the day. Shoes should be comfortable, non-slip and preferably without a heel. One garment should have a pocket for the bait.

Have a collar and identity tag on the dog for the duration of the journey.

Set off in good time to avoid traffic jams or having to rush. If only just enough time is left then you can guarantee there will be a hold up. If you are flustered then the dog will be unsettled and not give of his best in the ring.

Arrive at the show with enough time to accustom your dog to the atmosphere. A last minute rush at the entrance can panic a young puppy who is not accustomed to larger breeds. If the entrance to the show is congested carry the dogs in.

Exercise your dog so that he can relieve himself and be relaxed and comfortable in the ring. Make sure that any faeces are picked up and disposed of appropriately.

Walk your dog around so that he becomes familiar with the surroundings.

Check the catalogue to see that your entry is correct. Any discrepency should be checked immediately with the show secretary who will make sure your entry form corresponds with the catalogue.

The majority of grooming should have been done before the show leaving only a minimal amount to be done just prior to going in the ring. Make sure that you have a ring number clip ready. Your ring number may be on your bench or be given out in the ring. Check before you get to the ring to avoid having to do a quick dash back to the bench.

In the Ring

Grass rings are not always level so make sure that your dog does not stand in a hole thereby ruining his topline. Also, if the wind is blowing, do not face directly into the wind causing the dog's ears to fly.

Ring training before the show should have given you some idea of how to bring out the best in your dog. Try to relax, any tension will travel down the lead to the dog. If your dog has a tendency to be disinterested in any food, do not resort to rustling a crisp packet in your pocket as this will distract the dogs on either side of you. Squeaky toys can be equally annoying and distracting to others as can pieces of liver thrown indiscriminately across the floor.

When moving round the ring make a large circle and do not run into the back of the dog in front, putting him off. It is very common for this to happen. Sometimes it can be deliberate, or due to a total lack of concentration. Be considerate to fellow exhibitors and keep your distance. Keep an eye on the judge who will probably watch one side of the ring so have your dog stepping out in the right place.

When it is your dog's turn to be looked at, place him on the table whilst the previous dog is moving. The dog that is settled and feels safe on the table will give a better impression.

Ready to be judged on the table

Some dogs may need their head supporting when the judge stands back to assess the overall appearance; others will show for food. For a dog to be expected to use his ears on the table is hardly fair but there are some judges who seem to expect it. If that is the case, and the dog will not oblige, then being able to hold the ears up suitably can be an advantage.

Ears held in alert position

The exhibitor should never strike up a conversation with the judge but good manners should allow you to respond. Normally the only verbal contact will be when the judge asks the age of the dog, so be prepared to give the information.

After the judge has examined your dog on the table you will be asked to move him. Usually the judge will say 'triangle please' or 'straight up and down, please'.

Walk your dog at a sensible pace and in a straight line. Make each side of the triangle as long as possible and return the dog directly to the judge. Some people have difficulty walking in a straight line which could be misconstrued by the judge as trying to hide bad movement.

Some judges expect the dog to be 'set up' and show its ears at the conclusion of movement; others may only wish to see how the dog comes to a halt.

During the final appraisal your dog should be standing in a balanced way to show off his outline, neck and expression. By using tasty tit-bits one can normally hold the dog's attention. Make sure that his neck and, therefore, outline is not lost by holding your hand too high. The tip of his nose should be just lower than his skull to accentuate the neck and give the best expression. It is easy to

Handler standing too close - losing outline

give the dog a rounder eye by having him staring up at you. The dog with dicey ears will not be helped if his head is thrown back, making his ears go up.

The judge may pick out five or seven dogs if it is a large class, dismiss the rest of the dogs and then reappraise before making the final placings. Keep an eye on the judge at this stage as he may indicate to you that your dog is being placed.

Correct position of dog and handler showing neck and outline to advantage

Whether your dog has won or not give him lots of praise at the end of the class. He has been obliging and willing to please *you*. If you do not win never take it out on the dog, he never asked to go to the show and will not understand your attitude.

Accept the judges decision with a good grace. Sheltie exhibitors are generally very good sportsmen and congratulations are readily expressed. Bad sportsmanship, such as not accepting a prize card or a glowering look wll be quickly noted by other exhibitors.

Remember:
* Wear your correct ring number
* Position yourself in a suitable position in the ring
* Allow yourself plenty of room
* Do not crowd other exhibits particularly on the move
* Have your dog set up and settled on the table
* Remember the age of your dog if asked
* Move in a straight line
* Do not distract other dogs
* Be considerate to other exhibitors
* Be a good sport
* **Enjoy the day**

Judging

How to become a Judge

JUDGING is all about having an eye for a dog and experience. Some have a natural eye but experience takes time.

The novice exhibitor who has bred a couple of litters will, before too long, think they are sufficiently knowledgable about the breed and may want to judge. Wait to be asked, self promotion is very frowned upon.

The potential judge should serve their apprenticeship, progressing slowly by successful breeding and exhibiting. During this time, hopefully, recognition of breed type is established. The progression from handling and living with dogs to championship show judge can take years but all the time one is learning. The more dogs that are handled the better and advice from as many established breeders as possible will broaden the outlook. Different areas of the country will have different types of dogs, some excelling in one department and failing in others. Do not take as gospel one person's opinion, listen to everyone then make up your own mind. Knowledge gained will help with your own breeding plans at the same time as learning.

Your local breed club or ringcraft class provides excellent grounding for judges by either allowing you to go over the dogs or inviting you to judge a match.

Watching other breeds being judged can be helpful, particularly the short coated breeds as you can see the construction without having to actually handle the dog. You can see the reach of the forehand and the drive from behind without a long coat to disguise any faults.

Practice going over as many dogs as you can and develop a system in your mind which will become automatic after a while. Learn the breed Standard and *constantly* refer to it. Even the practiced and experienced all-rounder will read up the Standard prior to judging their own breed.

Breed club Training of Judges Schemes are helpful in that lectures are put on about the breed standard, conformation, stewarding, ring management and judging procedure. Anyone can attend whether they wish to judge or not. For the potential judge guidelines are issued emphasizing the necessity of 'hands on' experience, and private tuition is offered by top breeders and judges. An Assessment determines a candidate's ability and knowledge, success is compounded by inclusion in club judges lists. Even then there is always something to learn. Even

Assessors and Lecturers continue to learn through the teaching of others.

Stewarding

Stewarding is related to judging as it gives an insight into ring management and procedure which is all good experience for the future judge. The Kennel Club regulations (F(c)) "Instructions to the duties of Stewards" details what is required and is included as being significant. Show organisers will be pleased to hear from those willing to steward and the experienced Steward will be pleased to give guidance to newcomers.

Left: Stewarding - Alexandra Palace 1939, 'clearly marking the awards board'.

Instructions as to the Duties of Stewards

1. **Authority/Responsibilities**
    a. A Steward's responsibilities are at all times to assist the Judge in the course of his/her duties and to ensure the smooth and efficient running of the Ring.
    b. Stewards should always remember that the Judge is in overall control of the Ring and accordingly should follow the Judge's directives.
    c. Stewards are not authorised to allow any exhibit into the Ring unless it is entered in the class as recorded in the Judge's book and/or catalogue or unless a notice of transfer authority is provided by the Show Secretary/Manager.
    d. Steward are not authorised to transfer dogs from classes or allow unentered exhibits into classes without the necessary authority from the Show Secretary/Manager.

   Note: The Only Transfer Authority is - The Show Secretary/ Manager.

    e. Stewards are not authorised to instruct exhibitors concerning a dog's eligibility to compete in a class and should never prevent a dog which is entered in the class or has the necessary authority to be exhibited from competing even if it is considered that the dog is ineligible.

Note: The Only Authority to Disqualify is - The Committee of the Kennel Club.

2. Duties

a. Before Judging:
   (1) Ensure that all material has been provided in the Ring for the proper posting of awards and that all prize cards for each class are available.

Stewards Must be Aware of the Order in which Breeds are to be Judged in the Ring.

   (2) Take all reasonable steps to ensure exhibitors are aware judging is due to commence after which the responsibility for dogs being brought into the ring at the correct time for the classes entered, rests with the exhibitor.
   (3) Ensure each exhibitor has the correct ring number clearly displayed on entering the Ring.
   (4) Ensure that no dog is present in the Ring except those being judged: those persons allowed in the Ring are the Judge and Ring Stewards, no other person is allowed in the Ring without the authority of the Show Executive.
   (5) If so desired by the Judge, to place in the order of the previous awards the dogs coming forward from earlier classes and to stand new dogs by themselves.
   (6) Advise the Judge when all dogs are present in the Ring and then retire to a corner of the Ring and subsequently only converse with the Judge if requested to perform a specific duty.

b. During Judging
   (1) Ensure that dogs near or around the ringside do not interfere with exhibits being judged.
   (2) Ensure that photographers are not inside the Ring whilst judging is in progress.
   (3) Ensure that the attraction of exhibits from outside the Ring does not occur and that any persons so attracting are reported to the Judge.

Note: The Attraction of the exhibits' Attention from outside the Ring is Prohibited - it is not allowed even at the Judge's or Steward's discretion - Stewards must ensure that it is not done.

  c. After the class has been judged
- (1) Remind the Judge to place the dogs to be awarded prizes in the centre of the Ring in descending order from left to right before the Judge marks the Judging book.
- (2) When placed in order of Judge's awards - give out prizes.
- (3) Ensure, where Challenge Certificates are on offer that the Judge completes and signs the Challenge Certificates, Reserve Challenge Certificates, Best of Sex or Reserve Best of Sex cards and enters correct numbers of the winners in the Judging book.
- (4) Clearly mark awards on board provided in the Ring.
- (5) Where relevant, post correct award slips on board provided in the Ring and ensure other correctly marked and signed slips are sent to the Show Secretary/Manager's office.

The following has been included as being particularly relevent and covers all aspects of judging, and is reproduced by kind permission of The Kennel Club.

Guide to Judges

Introduction

This Guide explains what is expected from a judge of dogs at shows of all levels, including Championship Shows and should be read in conjunction with Kennel Club Show Regulations. Throughout the masculine also refers to the feminine.

Part 1
1. **Obligations of a Judge.** The essential ingredients of competent judging are:-
   - a. **Breed Knowledge** - The most important single aspect of judging is knowledge of the breed to be judged and its Standard. Judges must know the Standard of the breed, fully understand its implications and be able to apply this knowledge. They should also be able to recognised breed type and have a basic knowledge of canine anatomy.
   - b. **Integrity** - Judges must be honest and impartial, judging the dogs on merit.
   - c. **Temperament and stamina** - They should have a suitable

temperament to judge and sufficient stamina for what can be a physically demanding task.

d. **Procedures** - Judges should develop a sound and methodical ring procedure while conforming to Kennel Club Show Regulations. They should know the latter in relation to judging and be sufficiently well-organised to put the desired ring procedure into practice.

2. **The Invitation.** Soliciting appointments to judge cannot be condoned. Judges are usually first invited to officiate by becoming known as successful breeders and exhibitors of the breed concerned. Initially, invitations to judge are likely to be for small shows or club matches. Upon receiving an invitation a judge should:-
   a. Check that he will be available as invited and can comply with conditions imposed by the Show Committee.
   b. Ensure that the invitation is confirmed in writing by the Show Secretary.
   c. Confirm acceptance in writing, stating any fee or expenses required, and again ensure that an acknowledgement of the acceptance has been received. It must be appreciated that invitation and acceptance form the basis of a legally binding contract.
   d. Keep accurate records of appointments to avoid confusion and for future reference.

3. **Before the Show.** The Secretary of the Show will normally send a schedule to the judge. This will act as a reminder of the appointment and will also indicate the classes and breed(s) to be judged. The actual number of dogs entered may also have been noted. If, after agreeing to do so, the judge is unable to officiate every effort must be made to notify the Secretary as soon as possible. If shortly before the show this may have to be by telephone but, in any case, the withdrawal and the reason for it should be confirmed in writing.

4. **Arrival at The Show.** On the day of the show the judge should:-
   a. Arrive in good time. The usual requirement is at least 30 minutes before his judging is due to start.
   b. Report arrival to the show secretary and collect judging book, judge's badge and any other items the secretary may have for him.
   c. Enquire of the secretary whether there are any special instructions concerning the show of which he should be aware.

d. At the appropriate time, proceed to the judging ring to discuss intended ring procedures with the steward(s).
e. Start judging promptly at the scheduled time.

It should be noted that, apart from the exhibitors in the class, only the judge, steward(s) and those authorised by the Show Manager are allowed in the ring while judging is in progress. (Regulations F Annex C 2a(4).)

5. Judging The Dogs
a. Judges should acquaint themselves with the number of dogs to be judged, take into account the conditions and time available and pace their speed of judging accordingly.
b. Judges should not wait for exhibitors who are late reporting for their classes.
c. The eligibility of dogs entered in any class is not the concern of the judge.
d. Classes in each breed are to be judged in the order in which they are entered in the judge's book.
e. Judges should judge to the Kennel Club Breed Standard and conform to the recognised conventions of judging in the UK.
f. Judges must comply with the Regulations concerning the weighing and measuring of exhibits. (not applicable to Shetland Sheepdogs).
g. Judges should examine and move every dog in approximately the same systematic manner. Gentleness is most important. Many young dogs have been ruined by rough treatment.
h. Judges should dismiss from a class any dog which is of savage or vicious disposition and may excuse dogs which are lame.
i. Judges must not allow the attraction of exhibits from outside the ring whilst judging is in progress. If necessary, judging should be suspended until the practice has ceased. (Reg F17e).
j. After initial judging of all dogs in a class, several dogs may be "pulled out" for final selection.
k. Dogs awarded prizes must be placed in the centre of the ring in descending order of merit from the judge's left to right.
l. Judges should note they are empowered to withhold awards due to lack of merit and in such cases all the relevant slips in the judge's book must be marked accordingly. The Judge is not entitled to withhold an award for any other reason. When a Judge withholds a Third award, the subsequent awards in that class must also be withheld. (Reg F211).
m. The exhibit numbers of the dogs awarded prizes should be clearly marked in the judge's book and the slips signed. Equal awards are not allowed.

n. Judges must not comment publicly on exhibits whilst judging. (Reg F21r).
o. At Shows at which Best of Sex and Best of Breed are judged, the procedures for Championship shows given in part 2 paragraph 3 are to be followed.
p. On completion of judging, the judge should report back to the Secretary and check that everything is in order and that all judging slips have been removed from the judging book.

6. After The Show

a. It is expected, although not mandatory, that judges will write a critique on dogs which have been placed in the various classes for publication in the dog newspapers.
b. It is advisable to keep judging books and catalogues. These may be needed in order to complete a Kennel Club questionnaire at some time in the future should a judge be nominated to award Challenge Certificates at a Championship Show.

Part 2

Championship Shows

1. Approval. Once established at breed Open show level it is possible that a judge will be invited to award Challenge Certificates at a Championship Show. The mechanics of the invitation will be similar to that described in Part 1 except that, in addition, the judtge will be asked to complete a Kennel Club questionnaire on which his record of judging the breed and other judging experience must be listed together with further relevant information. On completion, the questionnaire is returned to the Secretary of the Show which issued the invitation. It is then considered by the Show Committee who may withdraw the invitation if it is felt that the judge's previous experience is insufficient to warrant its submission to the Kennel Club. Otherwise the questionnaire will be forwarded for consideration by the Committee of the Kennel Club and approval granted or refused. The Show Society is informed and, in turn, informs the judge. In making the decision, the Kennel Club Committee observes the following guidelines:

a. Length and depth of judging experience - Before the Committee will consider a first appointment to award Challenge Certificates, a minimum of five years judging experience of the breed before the date of the first proposed appointment would generally be expected.

b. The Open and Limited Shows judged - Details considered would include the type and number of shows, the number of classes and the number of dogs of the breed for which the nomination is made as well as the number of classes of other breeds and varieties judged.
c. Whether the proposed judge had judged a Breed Club Limited or Open Show for the breed concerned.
d. The number of dogs bred and/or owned by the proposed judge and included in the Kennel Club Stud Book.
e. Any other information which may be considered relevant.

2. **Number of Dogs to be Judged in One Day.** The maximum number of dogs one person should judge in one day is:-
One breed - not more than 250 dogs
Two breeds - not more than 200 dogs
Three breeds - not more than 175 dogs
Judges should not judge more than three breeds with Challenge Certificates in any one day regardless of the number of dogs entered.

3. **Challenge Certificates, Best of Sex and Best of Breed**
a. When the classes for a sex have been judged, in accordance with the procedure outlined in part 1, the judge must declare which of the exhibits is "Best of Sex" and "Reserve Best of Sex". He should ask for those exhibits he wishes to consider for these awards to be brought into the ring. They are normally selected unbeaten dogs although beaten dogs may also be considered. It is permissible for this judging to be deferred until the classes for both sexes have been judged and then to consider Best Dog and Best Bitch separately.
b. Where a Challenge Certificate is on offer it may only be awarded to the Best of Sex and then only if in the judge's opinion it is worthy of the title Champion. Similarly, the Reserve Challenge Certificate must be awarded to the Reserve Best of Sex which, equally, has to be worthy of the title of Champion as a subsequent disqualification might lead to the promotion of a Reserve to that of Challenge Certificate winner. If the Challenge Certificate is withheld then the Reserve Challenge Certificate must also be withheld but the Best of Sex and Reserve Best of Sex awards must still be made.
c. Subsequently, the judge (or the two judges jointly if there is a separate judge for each sex of the breed) must decide which of the two Best of Sex exhibits is Best of Breed. In the event of there being separate judges for each sex and they cannot

agree on the award then the appointed Referee shall decide which of the two Best of Sex exhibits shall be Best of Breed.
- d. Challenge Certifricates, Reserve Challenge Certificates and Best of Breed Card, must be completed and signed by the judge before final presentation to the exhibitors. (Reg F24g).
- e. Judges are reminded that where Challenge Certificates are on offer for the breed the awards of First, Second and Third in Limit and Open classes qualify a dog for entry in the Kennel Club Stud Book.
- f. The judge is responsible for the completion of the judge's book.

Part 3

Judges from Overseas

1. **Judges from overseas are expected to judge to the breed standards as published by the Kennel** Club. They are also expected to conform to the accepted conventions of judging in the UK and they should therefore familiarise themselves with the normal ring procedures of this country. They should note that grading is not part of that procedure and that no judging function may be delegated.
2. Overseas Judges will be assessed for approval in the United Kingdom in the same way as British Nationals. However, where a person is approved to judge a breed in his country of residence by a Ruling Body which has a Reciprocal Agreement with the Kennel Club and the breed approaches both in quality and quantity that in the United Kingdom then approval will usually be given for that person to award Challenge Certificates.

Part 4

Appearance and Behaviour

1. **Appearance** - It is important that judges maintain a proper appearance. They should not be the centre of attention through garish or outlandish dress or through bizarre behaviour.
2. **Smoking** - Judges must not smoke whilst judging.
3. **Drinks** - Alcoholic drinks are not to be taken into the ring.
4. **Hospitality** - Judges are at liberty to attend social functions organised by the Show Society before and after the show at which they judge.
5. **Conduct** - Ring etiquette and good behaviour are fundamental expectations in any judge.

The Day of the Show

Wear suitable clothing and comfortable shoes. Be sure that you leave home allowing sufficient time for the journey, to arrive at least half an hour to an hour before judging is due to start. The venue could be difficult to find or you could be stuck in a traffic jam only a few miles away. Traffic and weather conditions should be to be taken into consideration. Starting to judge when you are flustered and harassed does not instil confidence in the dogs or exhibitors. On arrival at the show find the secretary's office where you will be given a pack containing your judge's book listing all the numbers of the dogs entered in each class.

Meet your steward at the ring, preferably a good ten minutes before judging is due to start and go through the lay-out of your ring.

Position the table to suit *you* and place the mat whichever end of the table you prefer the dog to stand.

Agree with your steward where you would like the unseen, 'new' dogs to stand and which side the seen or 'old' dogs from previous classes should stand.

Indicate where and how you will want the dogs to move so that the steward can keep the area clear.

When the class is assembled the steward will need to indicate on his steward's card which dogs are present and the numbers of those that are absent should then be transferred to the judge's book under the section for absentees.

Judging

Walk round the ring and give each dog a brief appraisal. Moving them round will give a general feel of the overall quality of the class.

Giving a brief appraisal

As each dog is placed on the table for examination ask the handler the age of the dog, this can be relevant in puppy or veteran class or where a dog has been put in a higher class than it should. Go over each dog the same way, practice should have given you a system and procedure. An obvious system is to follow the order of the Breed Standard. Having started with the general appearance, the head would be next etc.

Be very positive in your approach, handling the dog firmly but gently.

Going over the dog

Remember to check the mouth, it will be noticed by others if you don't.

If, for some reason you have missed or are uncertain about a point then go back and check it again.

Having been over the dog ask the handler to move him, preferably in a triangle, this will enable you to assess all aspects of the dog's movement. If in doubt about a particular aspect then ask the handler to go again. The experienced eye will know in the first few strides of going and coming, how the dog can move. At the completion of the triangle having the dog come to halt in front of you can tell you how the dog puts it feet down and great deal about its construction. Waiting to see the dog set up and showing its ears at the end of moving can waste a great deal of time. You will be able to assess ears and outline later.

Clever and crafty handlers will naturally try and disguise any fault in their dog. One such ploy is to not move in a straight line or not move the dog directly towards the judge, which would prevent the judge seeing doubtful front movement, although some people do find it impossible to walk in a straight line!

After all the dogs in the class having been seen, walk round and refresh your memory, check on the expression and ear carriage. Stand back view the dog as a whole; its outline, its balance and type. Weigh up the assets at the same time as being aware of the faults.

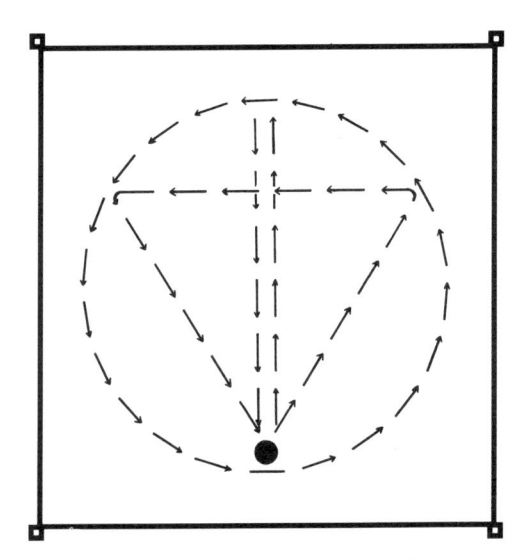

Dogs can be moved in a triangle, straight up and down, or around the ring

If it is a large class pick out a short list of five, seven or more dogs you know you will be placing or that are of interest. Do not pick out six dogs if there are only five prizes or ten dogs if there are twelve in the class.

When short listing indicate positively that you are not actually placing the dog.

Politely dismiss the rest of the class and ask the remaining dogs to reassemble at the side of the ring for reappraisal. Move a dog again if neccessary and be absolutely sure before you indicate your final placings. Line up the winners from left to right, facing the judge and preferably the audience.

The judge's book must be filled in, by the judge, with the winning numbers. When you have finished taking down the numbers the steward can give out the prize cards. Make sure he does not try to give them out before you have completed the judge's book as the handlers may disappear.

Avoid making any excuse to an exhibitor as to why their dog has not been placed higher, it could be embarrassing.

The Winner of the class

Line-up of The Best Bitch (also Best of Breed) and the Best Dog, with the Judge. Norwegian Shetland Sheepdog Club Show, 1990

Reporting

Writing a report can be the most arduous task but it has been tradition that the results, and judges report on the winnintg dogs, is published in the dog papers. Exhibitors, and those who did not attend the show, look forward to seeing the results and opinion of the judge in print.

For your report you will need to make brief abreviated notes or use a personal tape recorder. If a tape recorder is to be used check the batteries beforehand, one hears of whole reports never materialising due to a flat battery or failure to switch on, testing beforehand is therefore eseential. The use of the tape recorder does enable you to say a great deal more and makes vvery intersting listening!

Miss Beryl Herbert with Shelerts of all colours - 1988. The Cavalier is not a Shelert!

Crufts 1977. Left to right, Mrs Margaret Searle with Ch. Francehill Beach Boy, Mrs Audrey Britten with Ch. Loughrigg Kings Minstrel, Mrs Rose Wilbraham with Ch. Midnitesun Justin Time.

Miss Margaret Osborne judging at Birmingham in 1982. Feeling for shoulder angulation.

Janetstown Jaybird C.D. ex: Born 1977, by: Ch. Jefsfire Freelancer ex: Janetstown Jodhpurs, bred by Mrs Jan Moody and owned by Mrs Verity Turrell seen here clearing a long jump of 7ft 6in.

Charlotte Laughton enjoying agility with Janetstown Jingles.

In the Norwegian mountains 1977. Left to right, N. Ch. Sumburgh Witch Hazel by: Ch. Sumburgh Tesoro Zhivago ex: Sumburgh Queen Kristina, Int. N. Ch. Sumburgh Lulubelle by: Ch. Sumburgh Tesoro Zhivago ex: Sumburgh June Rose, N. and S. Ch. Ellington Endow by: Ellington Elliston ex: Remlaw Reward. Cover Girl. Int. Nor. Ch. Riverhill Ring of Bells bred and owned by Aud Jorun and Helge Lie.

N. Ch. Leeland Ringflower, N and S Ch. Leeland Golden Moss, Leeland Ring in Topaz, Int. N. and S. Ch. Leeland Ring-Around-A-Rosy.

Int. and Nor. Ch. Mondurle's Bannock. Born 1979, G.B. Ch. Francehill Andy Pandy ex: Stationhill Yolanda. Sire of 50 C.C. winners in Norway, Sweden and Finland owned by Jorun and Helge Lie.

Tooniehill Funny Face. Born 1988, by: Int. Nor. Ch. Eastdale Classic Clown ex: Shemaur Dawn Chorus bred and owned by Ingrid and Frode MykleBostad.

Norwegian Shetland Sheepdog Club Championship Show 1990. Best in Show and Best Bitch Kari Schulstad's N. Ch. Blenmerrow Magic Moment by G.B. Ch. Lythwood Sky Master ex: Priesthouse a Touch of Magic at Blenmerrow. Judge: Mrs Jan Moody. Best Dog Anna Uthorn's S. and N. Ch. Shelgate Scallywag by: Shelgate Lucky Devil ex: S. and N. Ch. Rockaround Sky Blue.

Australian Ch. Felthorn Harvest Moon. Born 1982, by: Shelbrook Moonlighting ex: Felthorn Marionette, bred by Mr and Mrs Dick Thornley and owned by Mrs Leslie Tanks.

Int. and Nor. Ch. Merrymaid Moonlight - Madonna (centre) with her daughters Swed. Ch. Starbele Soft Samona (left) and Swed. Ch. Stargbelle Serene Solitude. All owned by Mrs Madeleine Lund.

Finnish Ch. Glensanda Gadabout by: G.B. Ch. Haytimer of Hanburyhill at Hartmere ex: Glensanda Unique Gem, bred by Mrs Sheila Powell and owned by Raija Perala.

Int. and Nor. Ch. Rhinog The Guardian. Born 1976, by: Ch. Rhinog The Black Watch ex: Such A Myth at Shelert, bred by Miss Diana Blount and owned by Birgitta and Per Svarstad.

Training

THE Sheltie who has something to think about and something to do is a happy dog, and this is why so many people gain so much enjoyment from training their dogs. An intelligent breed such as ours thrives on the attention, apart from which a well trained obedient dog is a pleasure to own and will be welcomed anywhere.

As a breed Shelties are very easy to train and willing to please, which is why they are so popular with Obedience enthusiasts everywhere. In the UK. Shelties are the third most popular breed used in competition, after Border Collies and German Shepherd Dogs.

Because of the Shelties' enthusiasm when working many owners become addicted to training and derive a great deal of pleasure when persevering with the higher tests. This may be at the weekly class or at one of the many obedience shows held each year.

The interest may not just be in obedience, there are other forms of activities which are becoming very popular. Working trials have a definite following and recently there has been an overwhelming increase in Agility tests, which have now become more formalised and are under the jurisdiction of the Kennel Club. Fly Ball is a new competition recently introduced.

Pat-Dogs

Pat-Dog has become a very popular activity with many Sheltie owners. This marvellous and worthwhile way of communicating with the elderly, the sick or handicapped has only in recent years been recognised and accepted as a therapy in hospitals and institutions.

Club Activities

The English Shetland Sheepdog Club has a very thriving Obedience, Agility and Working Trials section, holding training days regularly where problems can be sorted out. There are obedience classes, restricted to Shelties, at two of the Club shows each year and the enthusiasm is tremendous. Other regional Sheltie Clubs also incorporate obedience.

News of Shelties working in obedience is welcomed by breeders as their stock may be involved. A representative of the breed can usually be seen working at Crufts each year.

Obedience Competitions

There are a wide variety of competitions at different levels with a range of shows and classes catering for all levels of proficiency. Club matches and Exemption shows are not too high powered and can be entered on the day. Sanction and Limited shows can include a Pre-Beginners class which does not require the retrieve. Open and Championship shows allow dogs to win into higher classes.

Shelties regularly work in the Class C competitions, which is the class, at Championship level, where the coveted Obedience Challenge Certificate is awarded. Winners of Obedience C.C.s are eligible to compete at Crufts.

Shows are advertised in 'Dog World', 'Our Dogs' and 'Dog Training Weekly'. Details of classes are published in the schedules.

Obedience Clubs

The Kennel Club provide a list of obedience Clubs throughout the country and there is sure to be one locally. Many popular Clubs have a waiting list for their beginners classes. These classes are designed for the pet owner who may never have owned a dog before or may have a particular problem that they are unable to overcome.

Because of the variation of approaches to obedience training I would suggest that having found the local class, the first visit should be without your dog. Observe the format of the class and talk to the trainers, explaining that you have a Sheltie. You will then gain some idea of their attitude to the breed. Too many Shelties have been ruined by a trainer who is totally unfamiliar with our breed.

If you are tempted to take the dog with you, then do not join in on the first occasion. Sensible trainers who are sympathetic to the breed will suggest that both you and your dog watch for the first time. You will learn from watching the other dogs and their handlers. If the club is not orientated to Shelties then find one that is. Other Sheltie obedience enthusiasts in the area will guide you in the right direction, it is not unusual for handlers to travel many miles to attend the right class.

Trainers must never be heavy handed with a Sheltie, in the way that can be seen with big dogs, which may reduce a Sheltie to a gibbering heap. Encouragement and praise is the essence and the whole thing should be fun. Reward can also work wonders as the greedy Sheltie will sell his soul for a tit bit! One word of warning, tit bits are not allowed in the competition ring. However they are excellent for training when all else fails. Naturally it would be preferable to have an instant response to a command without having to resort to bribery, but that's Shelties!

When to Start

Very basic commands should be given to the puppy from a very young age. The commands to *come, stay, no* and *good boy* should be started from day one and continued. This will set the pattern for the future. Do not try to overtrain the puppy. Let him be a puppy, let him enjoy his puppyhood and take in all the other aspects of life. There is so much for a puppy to learn in a relatively short space of time. Many obedience Clubs will not accept puppies under six months old.

The Class

The beginners class at the obedience club will concentrate on basic heel work, sit stays, recall and down stays. The objective of these classes will be to teach the *owner* how to train his dog to be an acceptable part of the family.

The first competition will be a progress test to encourage handlers to persevere in achieving a particular standard.

The next class up will concentrate on tidier heel work, straighter sits, longer stays and may touch on the retrieve, a test that does not come naturally to the Sheltie.

As one progresses to the world of obedience competitions the most suitable class may not be the nearest. The more proficient handlers may train at home, but it is necessary to do a certain amount in the environment of a class.

Sit, stays - at the ESSC Obedience Sheltie Camp, 1990

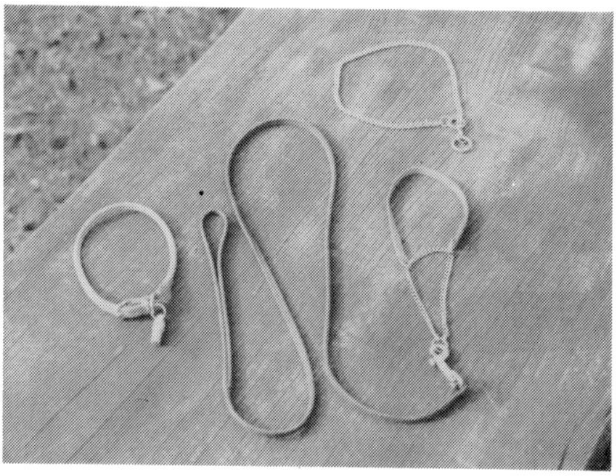

Equipment

A choke chain, or check chain is required when training. There are two sorts, the continuous chain that has a ring at each end and the double choke that is popular with many Sheltie handlers. A fine rolled leather collar with identity tube and a fine leather lead should also be part of the equipment.

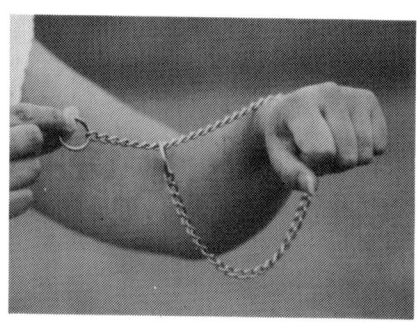

The choke chain can literally choke if wrongly used.

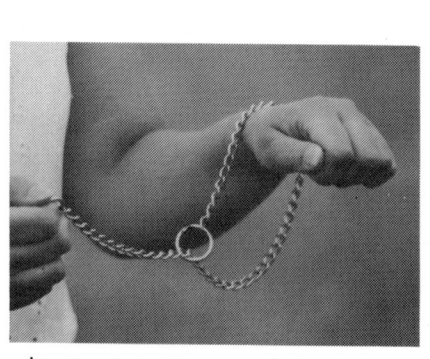

Choke chain, double choke, rolled leather collar and lead

The correct way to use a choke chain - the ring underneath, will slacken when the lead is relaxed

Incorrect way to use a choke chain - will remain tight when the lead is relaxed

Choke chain correctly fitted on the dog

Basic Training Exercises

All commands should be consistent so that you always say the same thing. It is no good saying *stay* or *come* one day and *wait* or *here* the next. A short single word command is also preferable to *stay there* or *come here*. The tone of the voice is all important. Again if you are consistent and vary the tone to each specific command the dog will anticipate the command by the tone of your voice.

The basic commands should be started as soon as the puppy has taken his place in his new home, but nothing too high powered should be attempted before he is six months old, in the mean time he can learn the ground rules such as *stay* or *come,* particularly in relation to an every day occurrence such as whether or not he should go through a door.

Your tone of voice is all important to the youngster as he will learn very quickly whether he has done right or wrong. Remember to praise him when he is right, it is very easy to only chastise when he has done wrong. Everything needs to be fun.

When lead training has been achieved always walk the dog on your left, if he knows which side he should be on he will never trip you up. All obedience exercises are conducted from that position although agility requires the ability to work from both sides.

Never let your puppy lean on a tight lead. Have enough slack so as not to put any pressure on his neck, but short enough to be able to check him without too much movement of your arm. Precede each command with the dog's name.

Heel

With the dog sitting by your left side and the lead in your right hand

Always walk the dog on your left - Correct length of lead

With the dog sitting on your left side, gain his attention

gain his attention and in a bright and cheerful voice give the command *'Shep heel'*, at the same time step off with your left foot.

If he deviates from your side check him firmly, but be encouraging in tone of voice if he lags, or mildly chastising if he goes ahead. When he is walking correctly give him plenty of encouragement by telling him *good boy*. Try to keep his attention for several yards before changing direction. A different command should be given for each turn so that he knows whether you are going to do a right turn, left turn, about turn or left about-turn. At the same time as giving the command you can pat your thigh to indicate that a command is being given.

Step off with your left foot

A few minutes daily, gradually increasing in time, will perfect.

Sit

Having taught *Shep* to move correctly by your side you can teach him how to sit when you come to a halt. Give the command *Shep sit* a split

Indicate with your left hand

Hold the lead tightly across your body and above his head

second before you come to a halt, giving him time to anticipate you stopping. If he does not know how to sit hold the lead across your body with your lead hand above his head. Indicate initially with your left hand, the lead should be tight so as to hold his head up, then press down gently but firmly on his hindquarters. Give plenty of praise, pause for a moment before proceeding with the heel work.

Continue to press down on his hindquarters each time you come to a halt until he sits automatically on the command.

Press down gently but firmly on his hindquarters

Note: Do not teach the show dog to sit before he knows the command to *stand* and *stay*.

Stay

With the dog at the sit position give the command *wait* or *stay*, at the same time giving a signal with the whole of the hand. Still holding the lead move away from the dog. When he learns not to move, gradually move further away or even move all around him. When you are confident that he will stay then drop the lead and move further away each time. Do not leave him too long before returning.

If he should break then take him back every time to exactly the same spot and repeat. If you can anticipate that he is going to get up give the command to *stay*. Do not say anything to him if you have to take him back except give a firmer command to *stay* the next time.

When you return to him at the end of each exercise return to the original position, with the dog on your left hand side, pause for a second or two before giving him plenty of praise. Fuss him whilst he is still in the sitting position otherwise he may get up before the end of the exercise.

Recall

The command *Shep stay* should be in a firm voice together with a hand signal in front of his face - not too close. When you are sure that he is settled move forward to the extent of the lead and face him. Wait a few seconds and then call him in a happy voice. *Shep come*. Take a few steps backwards and at the same time pull in the lead towards you using your hands to guide him in front of you. When he reaches your legs give him the command to *sit*. To finish, with the lead in the right hand, take a step back with the right foot, taking the lead behind your back into the left hand, all the time guiding the dog round. Bring your right foot back and the dog into the heel position.

Right: Give the command to *Stay* together with a hand signal

Below: At the extent of the lead - face the dog

Second right: Take a step backwards as you call the dog

Bottom left: When he reaches your legs give him the command to sit

Bottom middle: To finish, take the lead behind your back

Bottom right: Bring him back into heel position

188

The Down

With the left hand exert a little pressure on the dog's left shoulder at the same time as giving the command *down*. Lift the right front leg whilst still pressing on the shoulder until he is lying on his side. Then slowly stand up, giving the command to *stay*, using the hand to back up the command and keep his attention. Remember to give him plenty of praise at the end of the exercise.

A little pressure on the left shoulder

Lift the right front leg

Lying down on his side

Stand up giving a signal and the command to *stay*

Retrieve

Begin with your dog, on his lead beside you. Gently open his mouth and place the dumb-bell just behind his canine teeth, commanding him to *hold*. Close his mouth onto the article and praise him. After a few moments, take the article from him using the command *give*. Practise until your dog voluntarily opens his mouth to take the article from you.

Ideally, training should be done several times a day in short sessions of five or ten minutes.

Gradually hold the dumb-bell nearer and nearer to the floor encouraging your Sheltie to reach for it. With patience and perseverance he will eventually pick his retrieve article up from the ground. Once this has been achieved, place the dumb-bell at arm's length and, with your

Place the dumb-bell in his mouth

Close his mouth onto the article

Gradually hold the dumb-bell nearer to the floor

Lavishly praise every achievement

Sheltie still on his lead, run him up to the article, encourage him to pick it up, then take a pace or two backwards before taking the article from him. Gradually increase the distance until you have a full length retrieve.

Keep all training lessons short and happy and lavishly praise every achievement. Repetition on the lead will instil the habit of correct retrieving.

When you are certain he will obey all commands and that he thoroughly understands what is required of him, take him off the lead and allow him to retrieve on his own. Do be prepared to encounter problems and set-

The retrieve - bringing back the article

Holding the article    Taking the article

backs, this is quite normal and can usually be solved by going back to basics.

However, do seek the advice of an experienced trainer if you come across a problem you cannot solve by yourself.

Agility

An increasingly popular activity which only started at Crufts 1978 with a demonstration. Considered to be something of a *fun* competition it is proving a great sport for dog and handler as well as fast becoming a spectator sport through the media of television.

Its popularity has grown so quickly that the rules and regulations are changing all the time. Recently introduced is Mini Agility, creating a second height category with the break height at 15ins. This can be rather hard on Shelties because, as a breed, the dogs can be legitimately above or below the 15ins. The breed Standard states that the 'Ideal height at the withers: Dogs 37cms (14$^1/_2$ins): Bitches 35.5cms (14ins). More than 2.5cms (1in) above or below these heights highly undesirable'. Therefore, dogs that are just above the 15in limit have to clear the same obstacles as dogs that stand 25ins at the shoulder. However, Shelties do have great jumping ability and the majority do cope with the extra height. Hopefully an intermediate height for jumps will be introduced before too long.

The attraction of agility is that it is not as exacting and precise as obedience tests, is more exciting and stimulating for both dog and handler, and Shelties enjoy it. There is not the retrieve to master, which is a requirement in competitive classes of obedience, and defeats so many otherwise excellent working Shelties, or rather their handlers!

No dog will be accepted at an Agility training class or can enter an Agility competition until eighteen months of age. This is because any excessive jumping can over-strain the joints of a developing dog, particularly the shoulders when landing. Dogs should be physically sound and fit, should not be fat but be in lean hard condition before any concentrated training programme is undertaken. A check-up by a veterinary surgeon is advised prior to starting any jumping. Dogs suffering from Hip Dysplasia would have the condition aggravated by early jumping. Hip Dysplasia has been diagnosed in our breed and regrettably seems to come to light in young dogs in training who, one would suspect, have been encouraged to over-exert themselves before they are fully developed. (see page 211).

It is, however, necessary to do some fairly comprehensive ground work before embarking on any sort of jumping. One must be in control at all times, therefore basic training is essential otherwise you will not be able to guide the dog around the course. He must learn to listen to commands, watch his handler and stop when necessary. It does not take much to get a Sheltie over-excited, particularly when he is enjoying himself.

Basic obedience exercises should be mastered such as the *sit, stay, come when called* and *heel-work*. Having the dog go forward needs great encouragement at the same time as curbing over-enthusiasm.

Being able to work the dog on both sides is an advantage especially if the handler cannot run, it allows short cuts and saves time. Be sure to use a different command when the dog is working on the right.

When training a leather collar with lead can be worn, a choke chain should never be worn as it can interfere with the dog or catch on an obstacle. Collars must not be worn in competition.

Bribery with food works wonders with the greedy Sheltie, but in moderation as they learn to concentrate more on the food than the job in hand.

Notices and advertisements for Agility Tests can be found in 'Dog Training Weekly', 'Agility Voice', or through Clubs who organise events for members and hold inter-club competitions.

Only official Kennel Club licensed Agility Tests should be entered, unofficial tests can be dangerous.

Schedules should be read closely as definitions of classes, heights of the jumps and method of marking can vary from club to club.

In an Agility Test there are a minimum of 10 obstacles but no more than 20. These can be a combination of jumps or hurdles, tunnels, ramps, see-saws and a table.

The hurdle

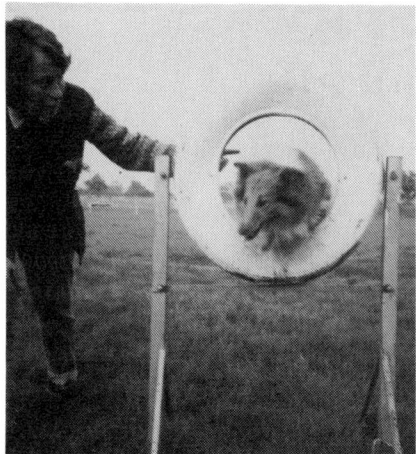

Hurdle

A maximum height of 2ft 6ins, can be any type of fence and poles should easily dislodge to avoid injury. There may be just a single pole or even a brush fence with a pole across.

Hoop

Usually a car tyre that is suspended on a frame and has been filled in to prevent legs becoming caught in the gap where the inner tube would normally be. The aperture diameter should be 1ft 3in minimum with the centre of the aperture 3ft from the ground.

The hoop

Table

A table that is a minimum of 3ft square and 3ft high with a non-slip surface such as a piece of carpet. Once on the table the dog should be at the down position for a minimum of 5 seconds.

Long Jump

Three to five low units that combine to make a long jump with a *maximum* length of 5ft.

The Long jump

Collapsible tunnel

Pipe tunnel

Collapsible Tunnel
A diameter of 2ft-2ft 6ins and a length of 10ft with a rigid entrance and a canvas material tunnel that the dog pushes himself through.

Pipe Tunnel
A rigid tunnel that is a minimum of 2ft in diameter and a minimum of 10ft long.

Weaving Poles
Five to ten poles, 2ft 6ins high, set 1ft 6ins - 2ft apart. The dog weaves between each pole starting with the first pole to the left of the dog.

A-Ramp
Two 9ft ramps hinged at the top and 6ft 3ins from the ground, 3ft wide with anti-slip slats set across the boards 3ft 6ins from the bottom of each ramp is a painted *contact area* which the dog should touch at each end of the obstacle. This is so that the dog does not jump on and off, he must cover the whole of the area.

Weaving poles

See-Saw
Literally a see-saw with 3ft *contact points* at each end. 12-14ft long, 8ins wide.

Dog Walk
A 12ft-14ft plank 4ft 6ins high with a ramp at each end, each ramp 12ft-14ft long and 8ins-12ins wide with anti-slip slats at intervals and a 3ft *contact point* at the bottom of each ramp.

A-Ramp

These are some of the more usual obstacles seen at Agility training and competitions.

Mini Agility

For dogs not exceeding 15ins at the withers. The same equipment is used as for the larger dogs except the heights are reduced.

Hurdles and Jumps - Maximum height of 15ins
Hoop - (Tyre) - Height at centre of aperture maximum of 20ins from the ground.
Long Jump - Maximum length 3ft with the height adjusted in relation to the size of the dog.
Weaving Poles - Maximum distance of 2ft apart.
    The A-frame is the same height as for the larger dogs but is presently under review.

The classes or tests are defined with regard to the number of wins. For example, the Elementary class is for owners, handlers or dogs which have not gained a third prize or above in a licensed competition. Starters is for *dogs* not having won a 1st prize in Starters, Novice or Intermediate.

Marking
    By doing a clear round the score is 0. Faults are in units of 5.
    a) Table/Pause - faulted at the judges discretion.
    b) Weaving poles - Incorrect entry 5 faults. Failure to complete 5
        faults or disqualification depending on the class. Total 10 faults.
    c) All other obstacles - 5 faults if failed to negotiate correctly.
    d) Refusal/Runout - 5 faults for each refusal or runout.
    e) Out of control - elimination.
    f) Contact area - 5 faults for failure to make contact.
    g) Course time - Standard timing is 2 to 5 yards per second.

Time faults are added to any faults accumulated by failure to negotiate obstacles. One time fault per second over the time allowed.

Working Trials

A combination of obedience and agility including nose work and tracking.
    The attraction of trials work is that the control work is not as exacting as the usual obedience tests but the dog has to use his own initiative in the search or tracking. To qualify for a title a certain standard has to be achieved rather than having to win the class.
    Shelties enjoy the work but those that just exceed 15ins (37cms) at the shoulder are sometimes thwarted by the 6ft scale.

Companion Dog (C.D.) Stake is the first grade which is the one usually worked by Shelties. Utility Dog (U.D.) is only occasionally attempted and achieved.

The jumps and scale for C.D. and U.D. Stakes are relative to the height of the dog:

Clear Jump
Dogs not exceeding 15in at shoulder	2ft
Dogs exceeding 15in at shoulder	3ft

Long Jump
Dogs not exceeding 15in at shoulder	6ft
Dogs exceeding 15in at shoulder	9ft

Scale
Dogs not exceeding 15in at shoulder	4ft
Dogs exceeding 15in at shoulder	6ft

Exercises and Points

Companion Dog (C.D.) Stake

	Maximum Marks	Group Total	Minimum Group Qualifying Mark
Group I. Control			
1. Heel on Leash	5		
2. Heel Free	10		
3. Recall to Handler	5		
4. Sending the dog away	10	30	21
Group II. Stays			
5. Sit (2 Minutes)	10		
6. Down (10 Minutes)	10	20	14
Group III. Agility			
7. Clear Jump	5		
8. Long Jump	5		
9. Scale (3) Stay (2) Recall (5)	10	20	14
Group IV. Retrieving and Nosework			
10. Retrieve a dumb-bell	10		
11. Elementary Search	20	30	21
Totals	**100**	**100**	**70**

Utility Dog (U.D.) Stake

	Maximum Marks	Group Total	Minimum Group Qualifying Mark
Group I. Control			
1. Heel Free	5		
2. Sending the dog away	10		
3. Retrieve a dumb-bell	5		
4. Down (10 Minutes)	10		
5. Steadiness to Gunshot	5	35	25
Group II. Agility			
6. Clear Jump	5		
7. Long Jump	5	20	14
8. Scale (3) Stay (2) Recall (5)	10		
Group III. Nosework			
9. Search	35		
10. Track (95) Article (15)	110	145	102
Totals	**200**	**200**	**141**

A dog that qualifies with 70% in a Championship Stake is entitled to add C.D. or U.D. its dog's name. If 80% or more is achieved 'ex' (excellent) is added after, thus C.D. ex. or U.D. ex.

Those interested should join a club specialising in Working Trials, for proper guidance. The English Shetland Sheepdog Club incorporate a section for Working Trials.

Flyball

A new team event which was first demonstrated at Crufts 1990 and has become very popular, with the first actual competition at Crufts 1991.

It is a relay race with four dogs to each team. The first dog jumps a series of hurdles after which he lands his front paws on a step, or pedal of a box which activates a mechanism which brings the ball to the top of the box or throws it into the air. The dog catches the ball and returns over the hurdles to his handler. The next dog in the team repeats the exercise until all four dogs have completed the course.

The height of the jumps is relative to the smallest dog in the team.

Flyball

Pat-Dogs

The Pat-Dog has become a very popular activity with obedience enthusiasts or anyone who has a dog and is interested in charity work. This marvellous way of communicating with the elderly, the sick or handicapped has only in recent years been recognised and accepted as a therapy in hospitals and residential homes. Anyone who has seen the reaction of people, who have otherwise lost interest in life, when they are with the dogs will understand why the owners so enjoy their visiting. Faces light up and stories of pets, long gone, are told. Doctors and hospital staff now readily accept the benefits of Pat-Dog visits as a therapy.

To enrol your dog as a Pat-Dog one has to be a member of Pro-Dogs who then organise a temperament test. Registration as a Pat-Dog is done through the Pro-Dogs organisation who circularise places that may be interested in having a Pat-Dog visit. Pat-Dog owners can approach hospitals or homes for the elderly with the offer of visiting.

Each registered Pat-Dog owner is issued with an identity card and badge to be worn on official visits.

Membership of Pro-Dogs and Pat-Dogs includes third party insurance cover in case of accidents or injury.

General Health

Going to the Vet

It is very important to have a vet who is orientated to small animals, having one who is particularly interested in Shelties is a bonus. My own vet has always taken a great deal of interest in the breed which is very gratifying. Nothing is too much trouble and having had the experience with our breed, can be relied upon to diagnose and treat the problems sometimes peculiar to Shelties.

Having the right approach to the Sheltie is all important, the heavy handed vet can unnerve a dog for life making him apprehensive of men.

A dog is not able to explain how he feels, therefore, it is up to the owner to observe any change in general behaviour, a change in eating habits and the type of faeces, all things that can help the vet give a diagnosis.

* If you are ever in doubt about the health of your dog then do seek the advice of your vet.

Never allow a condition to progressively get worse before seeking advice. Some conditions should not be left untreated.

Never sit in the vet's waiting room with uninoculated puppies or if you suspect that your dog has something that is contagious such as Kennel Cough or Parvovirus. The puppy is vulnerable and could pick up something from another dog whose owner has been inconsiderate enough to sit with it in the waiting room knowing that the dog is sick. Leave the puppy or dog in the car then carry it into the surgery when called. Keep the puppy in your arms all the time.

Diarrhoea

The breed has a reputation for a sensitive stomach which is made all too evident by the accompanying dirty petticoats.

The most frequent cause of diarrhoea in the Sheltie is due to a change in diet. This may be deliberate on the part of the owner who thinks that their dog would like a change in his diet, and is tempted to give the newly advertised product a try. If a dog is doing well on a particular diet - leave well alone.

Shelties can have an intolerance to milk, particularly after weaning and even into adulthood (see page 92).

The amazing thing is that they can eat the rotting leftovers of the cat's previous meal without any ill effects, yet the odd unfamiliar tit-bit can cause instantaneous looseness.

Over excitement can cause diarrhoea but will be only temporary. Where there is bacterial infection starvation is the first course of action.

Do not be tempted to give 'just a little bit of something'. Give water only for a period of 24 hours before giving a small bland meal such as boiled brown rice flavoured with a little fish or egg. Keep to the small meals until the faeces are formed before gradually re-introducing the normal diet.

If the diarrhoea persists after 24 hours seek the advice of your vet.

If antibiotics have been given a course of vitamin B tablets will help recreate the flora in the stomach.

Where there is mild looseness homoeopathic Arsen. Alb. can be most effective and is readily and easily administered. (See Homoeopathy).

Parvovirus

A deadly virus requiring *immediate* veterinary attention. Takes five days to incubate, is transmitted via the faeces of affected dogs or can be carried on clothes and shoes. Can remain viable for one year in the premises where there has been an infected dog. It can be endemic in boarding kennels. Vaccination is essential as early as possible and boosters should be kept up.

Symptoms are obvious pain, depression, diarrhoea and vomiting with a considerable amount of blood.

The virus destroys the lining of the intestines thus preventing absorption of vital fluids. An intravenous drip will need to be administered by the vet to prevent dehydration, which is the main cause of death.

Puppies are the most vulnerable, the majority of deaths occurring during the first year. Where a puppy has supposedly recovered there could be a heart problem which may not manifest itself until later when they suddenly collapse and die.

Breeding bitches should be well up to date with vaccinations to be able to pass on antibodies to the puppies.

Owners should refrain from contact with other dogs for six weeks after any contagious disease. Shows should *not* be attended, the declaration signed on the entry form states that dogs who have been exposed to any contagious disease, should not attend a show for six weeks after the last contact.

Kennel Cough

Highly contagious, spread through airborne viruses usually when there are a number of dogs together such as dog shows or boarding kennels. For this reason usually more prevalent during the summer.

After waking or exercise the dog wretches and chokes, as though he has something stuck in his throat. Veterinary advice should be sought to prevent side effects particularly in a puppy or elderly dog. Relief can be gained through giving cough mixture, honey, or homoeopathic Bryonia (see page 218/9).

Metritis

Inflammation of the womb. This can occur after whelping especially if the whelping has been difficult and there is some retained placenta which can set up an infection. This may not become apparent until some days after whelping. If left untreated it can develop into Pyometra.

Pyometra: (A hormone related problem)

When chronic Metritis causes the womb to become filled with pus. Pyometra is not always readily apparent. When Metritis has occurred, usually without any signs, it can remain dormant for some weeks after an apparently normal season. As the cervix has closed up after the season the uterus becomes full of pus, and can occur whether the bitch has been mated or not. If the bitch has been mated the slightly enlarged look of the bitch's abdomen can lead one into believing that she is in whelp. The critical time for a bitch to develop Pyometra is approximately four weeks after her season.

The bitch who has never had a litter is more susceptible to Pyometra but one should not be complacent as it can also occur in a brood bitch. Any deviation from the norm should be taken into account.

The biggest problem with Shelties and this condition is that they rarely display the outward and visual symptoms of excessive drinking, reduced appetite and lethargy that are usually associated with the condition. This has caught out many a vet with the consequence that one often hears of disasters. I have, over the years, had calls from people totally unknown to me, telling me the symptoms displayed by their bitch. I have told them what I thought but the vet who is unfamiliar with the breed often makes the decision to spay too late. My advice is: If you are in doubt do not wait too long. A second opinion may help with the decision.

Eczema

In Shelties wet eczema can often be seen around the root of the tail. Care should be taken to keep the area clean and combed through so that undercoat is not matted. Homoeopathic Sulphur or Merc. Sol. can be effective as can bathing the area with a solution of Hypercal. Zemol Antiseptic powder or cream is most effective and soothing for any skin problem.

Bob Grass's Skin Cure is an old fashioned remedy to keep as a stand by.

Vaccinations

Every puppy should be fully vaccinated as soon as possible and annual boosters should not be missed. The consequences of failure to vaccinate regularly can be disastrous. Anyone who has been through the terrible experience of a dog with any of the killer diseases will never forego a vaccination programme, including boosters.

Each veterinary surgeon will have their own ideas with regard to a vaccination programme. Regardless of what advice you are given by others always be guided by your vet.

Every year there are outbreaks of Parvovirus or Distemper, these could be a new strain that can affect the unvaccinated or unboostered dog. Regular boosters will include any new strains, hence the importance of being up to date.

The Pharmaceutical companies are progressing and updating all the time with new vaccines to safeguard our pets. One cannot be too specific about when a puppy should start his programme of vaccinations, one can only be advised by the vet and the breeder about the present day courses.

Natural Immunity

Every puppy will have inherited some natural immunity from the mother. As the puppy is weaned that maternal immunity will diminish. Without regular blood testing there is no way that one can tell if there are antibodies present. With Parvovirus it makes sense to vaccinate at the earliest possible age as the maternal immunity could have gone by the time the puppy is six weeks. On the other hand it may remain until the age of five or six months and can vary from breed to breed and puppy to puppy.

If a vaccine is given whilst there is still a maternal immunity then the vaccine will be cancelled out by the antibodies. Hence the necessity to give a second or third dose later to cover the possibility that the earlier ones may have been ineffective due to the presence of maternal immunity.

Present day vaccination programmes can start between eight and twelve weeks with Hepatitis, Leptospirosis and Parvovirus. (H.L.P.). The Parvovirus will be given at each injection finishing with just a Parvovirus at sixteen weeks plus, depending on the vaccine. The Distemper vaccine will be given at twelve weeks as it is pretty well guaranteed that the maternal immunity will have disappeared by that age. This will be given as a combination injection, (H.D.L.P.) against all of the four diseases. There must be at least two weeks between vaccinations.

Kennel Cough vaccination is beneficial and most good boarding kennels insist that kennel cough be included in all the vaccinations required before entry into the kennels.

Worming

Roundworm

The roundworm inhabits the intestines of puppies. The bitch who carries the roundworm larvae will pass them to the foetus through the placenta. The dam may have no outward and visible sign of infestation therefore all puppies should be wormed as a matter of course.

As there is evidence that the larvae of roundworms can cause health problems in humans it is the responsibility of the breeder to ensure that puppies are wormed by the breeder at least twice if not three times before sale at eight weeks. Due to the concern, vets now recommend worming fortnightly until four months of age. This is an instruction that I will pass on to new owners.

Thereafter worming should be carried out every six months. Follow the instructions which will tell you to dose again after two weeks. This is to ensure that any eggs that hatch in that time will be dealt with before another cycle commences.

Puppies can be started on a worming programme from four weeks of age. This should be done carefully and each puppy weighed. Some worming preparations can have the most alarming effect on Shelties but one of the most effective and safe preparations is for children. It is called Antepar Elixir and is a basic piperazine in a syrup base which can be easily administered orally with a calibrated syringe. The dosage is 1ml per 4lbs (1818 grams) body weight. Dosing should be repeated every two weeks until 4 months of age. By the time the puppy is 10 weeks other forms of worming preparation can be given. Panacur can be used when there is a resistance to piperazine.

Tapeworm

Infestation of tapeworm can be seen when white segments resembling a cucumber seed are shed and stick to the petticoats under the tail. Internally the worm is usually very long and can sometimes be difficult to remove. If tapeworm is suspected the vet should be consulted.

Steps should be taken to remove the intermediate host to the tapeworm - the flea.

Fleas and Lice

Regular spraying with one of the proprietary sprays, such as Nuvan Top, obtainable from your vet, will keep your dog free from parasites. Use Nuvan Staykil for bedding and kennels, at the same time as keeping bedding regularly washed.

Evidence of flea infestation can be detected at your Sheltie's regular grooming time. Groups of little black specks of dried flea dirt around the head, neck and ears should prompt immediate treatment. Comb through the hair on the head for further evidence.

Care should be taken if young puppies are infested, read instructions carefully whatever the product.

Inherited Problems

Collie Eye Anomaly (C.E.A.)

Collie Eye Anomaly affects only Rough Collies, Smooth Collies, Shetland Sheepdogs and Border Collies. Being congenital it should be easier to control as it can be diagnosed at a much earlier age than Progressive Retinal Atrophy. The condition is visually apparent as soon as the eye is big enough to see into with an ophthalmoscope. All the puppies in a litter can be checked as early as six weeks of age.

The advantage in being able to test puppies at six weeks is that one can sort out a litter and any decision about keeping a puppy can be made at this early age, unlike other hereditary eye diseases, such as P.R.A. which does not manifest itself until the dog is older. There can be less heartache by eliminating even the mildly affected dog from any future breeding programme, earlier rather than later. He can quite easily go as a pet without there being any problem to himself or his owner.

Although it is recommended that puppies are tested before they are twelve weeks old it is more desirable that they are tested between six and eight weeks, due to the fact that it is easier to see into the eye when the puppy is younger as they will behave better. As a litter will be dispersed at eight weeks it makes sense to have the whole litter tested before they go to their new homes. If only part of a litter are tested there will not be an accurate record for future reference.

What is Collie Eye Anomaly?

C.E.A. is an inherited disease affecting the fibrous and vascular layers of the eye, the sclera and choroid. It has two main features - Choroidal hypoplasia and Coloboma which may be complicated by Retinal Detachment and Intraocular haemorrhage. The number of animals with defective vision is small and blindness caused by Retinal Detachment or Intraocular Haemorrhage is rarely bilateral.

Choroidal Hypoplasia can vary from very mild to quite severe depending on the pigment and the blood vessels.

The blue merle eye has a complete lack of tapetal tissue and retinal and choroidal pigmentation. Thus mildly affected cases with lack of retinal and choroidal pigmentation in the absence of choroidal blood vessel abnormalities cannot be detected.

There are five categories of Collie Eye Anomaly which concern the breeder.
* Blind
* Affected
* Go-normal
* Clear
* Genetically clear

Blind

It is unfortunate, but a fact, that there can be Shelties that are blind. This can be from birth or the dog can go blind when older. Hence the importance of early testing.

For any breeder to produce a totally blind puppy from birth is very disturbing. Those breeders who have experienced the trauma of having to have an otherwise healthy puppy put down are for evermore anxious about their future breeding policy. This will include using only 'clear' or 'genetically clear' dogs in the future. The possible 'go-normal' stud dog will not be acceptable.

The quiet, not very forthcoming puppy could be found to be blind in one eye. The over anxious, restless mother who fusses around her puppies may well know that there is a problem. When the offending puppy has been identified and removed the mother will settle.

It should be the responsibility of the breeder to have any totally blind puppy put down immediately.

Blindness is due either to Retinal detachment or Intraocular haemorrhage from unsupported blood vessels associated with a coloboma, or vessels in areas of Choroidal hypoplasia. The condition could be painful if it became glaucomatous resulting in the necessity to remove the eye.

Affected

Those who are visually affected will always be affected and the condition may never alter throughout their lives.

There is no reason why a mildly affected puppy should not be sold as a pet and never give any problem.

The badly affected dog could be blind before he is twelve months old even though he could see as a puppy. This could be due to a detached retina seen as a presumed congenital defect or an early complication of the disease that would appear to develop in the first two or three years of life.

I personally would never keep a dog at stud if it had not been tested and cleared before the age of eight weeks. I am certainly not condemning anyone for keeping and showing a male dog that is affected.

There are many excellent dogs winning well and giving their owners a great deal of pleasure even though affected. These dogs can make their contribution in terms of temperament or conformation if mated to a clear or even genetically clear bitch. The responsible owner should make it clear to any one wishing to use their dog at stud that he is affected. It is then the decision of the bitch's owner, being aware of the situation whether to use that dog or not.

Go-normal

The 'go-normals' are those that are borderline cases, having the very slight abnormality of the reduction in the amount or absence of pigment in the retinal pigment epitheliun and are not passed when tested between six and twelve weeks. When submitted for retesting from three months onwards, these can be passed, there being no apparent abnormality. These cases are called 'go-normal' or 'go-clear'.

Unfortunately there are some who regard the 'clear' eye certificate as more important than anything else. The failure, as a puppy of eight weeks, is tested again at six months and is then passed. The owner of the known 'go-normal' stud dog with a 'clear' certificate is deceiving those who come to use him. Perhaps the stud fees are the pull! When the dog is examined the owner or representative signs the certificate and should state whether the dog has been examined before and with what result. Unfortunately this tends to be ignored.

Bitch owners should enquire as to what age the dog was first tested and what age the certificate was given.

Clear

To be visually or clinically 'clear' means clear on ophthalmoscope examination before the age of twelve weeks. If either of the parents is affected then the offspring will be carriers.

There are a healthy number of stud dogs available who are 'clear' but not 'genetically clear'. Knowing some of the history behind both the prospective parents can be very helpful but not everyone has that information to hand. Putting a 'clear' dog to a 'clear' bitch can produce any combination of 'clear', 'affected' or perhaps a 'genetically clear'.

Genetically clear

With the high incidence of Collie Eye Anomaly in the breed it is very difficult to find a 'genetically clear' stud dog that is available and within a reasonable distance.

For a stud dog to be proved 'genetically clear' he should have sired a number of litters where the whole litter have been tested and cleared.

There is more opportunity for a dog to be proved 'genetically clear' if he is being used regularly at stud and *all* progeny are tested around the age of eight weeks and no later than twelve weeks.

Test mating to several affected bitches can prove categorically that a dog is 'genetically clear' although there would have to be a representative number in the litter and some puppies may be affected if he were a carrier. Every puppy must be tested.

Equally there is every opportunity for a bitch to be 'genetically clear'. Unfortunately it can take some years for this to become apparent, and then only by test mating. The bitch who is 'genetically clear' can only be proved as such if mated to an affected dog, have several litters with a representative number in each litter. Naturally, all her offspring should prove to be visually 'clear' on early examination.

The stud dog that is 'genetically clear' will always produce 'clear' puppies regardless of the condition of the bitch's eyes. If the bitch is affected or 'go-normal' then all the puppies will be visually 'clear' but will be carriers. If the bitch is visually clear then there is a good opportunity for there to be genetically clear puppies.

B.V.A./K.C. Eye Testing Scheme

The British Veterinary Association in conjunction with the Kennel Club have an eye testing Scheme. There is a panel of highly trained specialists who are qualified to examine for all eye diseases, in all breeds.

To have an individual dog tested within the Scheme can be quite expensive. There is a scale of charges drawn up by the K.C. and B.V.A. dependent on the number of dogs. Societies and Clubs organise eye testing sessions whereby the cost is dramatically reduced when there are more than a certain number of dogs being tested. Notice of these sessions are advertised in the dog press.

The panelist issues a certificate at every examination as to whether it is a pass or a fail. If it is a pass then the panellist signs to the effect that there is *no* abnormality to be seen. Where there is a doubt a second opinion can be sought at no extra cost. This should be taken up before the puppy is twelve weeks old otherwise he could become a 'go-normal'.

At each examination the Kennel Club registration certificate should be stamped with the date and result. Where there is not a registration certificate i.e. at six to eight weeks, a litter certificate is given. This will show the breeding and details of the puppies with as much identification as possible. It is also proof that the puppies were tested at the critical time.

Those dogs who have a certificate clearing them of any visual abnormality will have their names published in the Kennel Club's official publications, the Kennel Gazette and Breed Records Supplement. If the certificate is submitted to certain breed Clubs then it will also be published by them. This is the case with the English Shetland Sheepdog Club who regard the problem seriously and collate a list which is issued in their bi-annual publication, The Nutshell. This is invaluable as a reference and can help members when they are trying to choose a stud dog.

The fact that a certificate has been issued allows the owner to advertise that the dog is clear. 'Tested' does not mean 'clear'.

A very valid comment was made many years ago by a leading eye specialist. He said that we should all be very much aware of the problem in the breed, which was about 80% affected at the time. He went on to say that although we, as breeders, should be very aware of the problem we should keep the whole thing in perspective. He also said: "There would be no point in having a dog with perfect eyes if it was walking on its elbows". A very sensible statement.

The last reported survey had reduced the number of affected dogs to 70%. It is felt that some progress is being made and the numbers are improving.

As a matter of principle I have all my litters of puppies checked at six to eight weeks and will encourage others who use my stud dogs to do the same.

Those who are totally honest and open about any problems have the breed at heart. Those who bury their heads in the sand do not help to overcome the problem.

Unfortunately there are still kennels that never have their dogs tested. This is regrettable but there is no legislation compelling anyone to test.

The Eye Examination

Examination, which is painless, is by a qualified eye specialist, using an ophthalmoscope. Sometimes the specialist will put drops into the eyes to dilate the pupil. This enables the eye to be seen into more easily, the pupils remain dilated for some time and the dog will find bright light distressing. He will keep his eyes closed until the effects have worn off. Keeping him quiet in a dark room will alleviate any anxiety.

The Importance of Early Testing

The most important aspect, more recently proved, is the testing of puppies before they are eight weeks old. This is because the back of the eye has not developed the amount of pigment which can otherwise mask the problem. Puppies tested and failed under the age of eight weeks can be cleared by the time they are three months old. This is because the eye has developed to the extent that the real problem has been shielded within the eye. Owners will tell me that the vet was 'not sure' or that it was a 'borderline' case at eight weeks. They will then go and have the dog tested again at three or six months of age only to be passed. The certificate is then published and advertised as a 'clear'.

How is Collie Eye Inherited?
The condition is supposedly a simple recessive but there have been a few instances which dispute this. However, the fact still remains that it is an hereditary problem and should be regarded as such. There has been reference to the fact that there are more instances where there is a smaller eye. This has not been proved.

There is still a long way to go with regard to its inheritance but we are lucky in having some proved, 'genetically clear' dogs and the number is increasing. Not enough work has been done to date to identify any particular mode of inheritance but some work is being done with the co-operation of data gained from interested breeders.

Inheritance of Recessive Genes

Code:
C = Clear,
a = affected

CC = Genetically clear
Ca = Visually clear carrier
aa = Affected

CC x CC
CC CC CC CC
All genetically clear

CC x Ca
CC Ca CC Ca
Two genetically clear
Two visually clear carriers

Ca x Ca
CC Ca Ca aa
One genetically clear
Two visually clear
One affected

Ca x aa
Ca Ca aa aa
Two visually clear carriers
Two affected

CC x aa
Ca Ca Ca Ca
All visually clear carriers

aa x aa
aa aa aa aa
All affected

The Pet Sheltie and Collie Eye Anomaly
My advice to the prospective pet owner is to ask the breeder about Collie Eye Anomaly and whether the puppies have been tested. A puppy that is mildly affected will not show any outward and visible signs of any problem and will therefore make an excellent pet.

If you ever intend breeding then consult a responsible breeder who will guide you in the right direction.

Progressive Retinal Atrophy

Progressive Retinal Atrophy (P.R.A.) is an inherited disease which affects many breeds including Shetland Sheepdogs. As the name implies it is progressive but may not become apparent until the dog is eighteen months old. One does not hear about much P.R.A. in the breed these days but it does still crop up. As it is thought to be a simple recessive it means that both parents carry the gene although not displaying the disease themselves.

The unfortunate aspect of the disease is that it may not manifest itself until later in life by which time an affected popular stud dog may have been used extensively. Annual screening by an ophthalmic specialist ensures that all breeding stock are clear and any problem can be picked up before it is evident to the owner. There is no treatment and affected stock should not be used for breeding.

The disease takes the form of a progressive destruction of the photoreceptors, the rods and cones. The pupils are slow to react to light and as the disease progresses the pupil will remain dilated and there will be a distinct reflection from the tapetum at the back of the eye.

The first indication of P.R.A. is an inability to see at night, hence the so-called 'Night Blindness'. The dog will bump into objects or furniture that have been moved to a different position. In the later stages the eye becomes staring and bulbous due to the dilated pupil which is trying to gain enough light as the blood vessels to the retina have diminished.

The British Veterinary Association and the Kennel Club operate a joint scheme for the screening of the disease. This is incorporated with screening for other eye defects.

It is important that dogs are tested annually for P.R.A. as it can be overlooked due to the fact that the screening for Collie Eye Anomaly can be completed by the time the puppy is twelve weeks.

Hip Dysplasia

Although it has never been recognised as one of the major problems of the breed there are an increasing number of cases of Hip Dysplasia reported in the breed each year. The disease is associated more with the big heavy breeds but Sheltie breeders should not bury their heads in the sand as it is primarily hereditary. There are certain factors such as poor rearing, over exercising and over-weight during the maximum growth period that can aggravate the situation causing the disease to progress.

The dog that is carrying the H.D. genes may not necessarily display the symptoms if carefully reared. The genes do not affect the skeleton primarily but rather the cartilage, supporting the connective tissue and muscles. It is therefore dependent on not only the actual hip joint but the surrounding tissues and muscle mass. The disease is preventable if normal growth is maintained without undue stress to the developing tissue.

Care should be taken to balance the correct amount of exercise in relation to the amount of food given at the time that a puppy is growing.

Breeders should be careful to only breed from well constructed sound dogs who can move freely and easily.

Monorchids

A male dog that is 'entire' means that he has two normal sized testicles descended in the scrotum.

Unfortunately not all dogs are blessed with both their testicles and this seems to be a failing in Shetland Sheepdogs as well as other breeds.

When there is only one testicle descended this is called a 'monorchid' or to be technically correct, a 'unilateral cryptorchid'.

When there are no testicles at all that is known as a 'bilateral cryptorchid'.

It is not uncommon for Shelties to have no apparent sign of testicles as a puppy. The experienced breeder will have checked all the males in a litter and will have some idea as to which ones will eventually become entire.

Experience has told me that if I cannot feel both testicles by the time the puppy is eight weeks old I would not consider keeping him to run on as a possible show dog. I have had too many disappointments and have seen the same thing happen to other people and feel that it is not worth the heartache. You can always guarantee that the one that is not entire will be quite superb in every other respect.

If both of the testicles have been positively felt before the age of eight weeks there can be every chance that they can 'disappear', which can cause a few heartstopping moments, then reappear at any time up to two years of age. Very often they will reappear when the puppy has finished teething, around six months old, and then have the infuriating habit of disappearing when taken to a show. This may be only temporary.

It has been known for an eighteen month or two year old dog to become entire after he has been rehomed. A stay in boarding kennels can have a similar effect.

Breeding and Fertility

The monorchid can be fertile and be capable of producing puppies whereas the cryptorchid will be infertile due to the fact that the temperature of the testes is too high.

Cryptorchidism is an occurance that can happen all too frequently and there does not seem to be any conclusive evidence to determine its mode of inheritence. Assuming that the gene is recessive one should not knowingly use a 'monorchid' at stud. It is a major fault that should be taken into serious consideration when breeding and judging.

Showing and Cryptorchidism

The standard for every breed states that two apparently normal testicles must be descended in the scrotom. It should therefore be considered a major fault if a dog is not entire. Judges will not, and should not, consider a dog that is not entire if he is over twelve months old. Occasionally a judge will give a puppy that is not entire the benefit of the doubt, as it is not unknown for Shelties to become entire after the age of twelve months. Also a puppy can 'pull up' one testicle due to the excitement of the show.

There was a time when all dogs were examined by a vet on entry to every show. Any male that was not entire was not allowed to compete. After nine years this was abandoned and it then became the responsibility of the judge to decide on the severity of the fault.

In the past there were many well known dogs, to whom the breed owes a great deal, that were monorchids, notably, Ch. Helensdale Ace, Ch. Orpheus of Callart and Ch. Francis of Merrion.

These dogs would not be Champions today and the breed would have been denied all the dogs that are descended from them.

The Cryptorchid Pet Sheltie

The pet Sheltie that has an undescended testicle can live his whole life quite happily without any problems.

Some vets will advise owners of young puppies to have them castrated because that vet has been unable to feel both the testicles. Do not be hasty about having any retained testicle removed. Due to the fact that Shelties can become entire at such a late stage it is advisable to defer any surgical operation until the dog is well over two years old.

Castration of a male is not necessarily a bad thing for the pet Sheltie as it will not affect his intelligence, affection and natural guarding instincts. It will, however, stop any sexual and dominant tendencies.

Alternative Treatments

Homoeopathy

Homoeopathy is a subject which I find absolutely fascinating and first came to use it through having had an illness to which modern day drugs tended to have rather unpleasant side effects. I consulted a homoeopathic specialist who whilst treating me said that he was also trying to teach me how to treat myself. I must say that my initial attitude was somewhat cynical but my understanding was enhanced by the results.

People give me very funny looks when I try to explain homoeopathy, which can take a bit of absorbing because of its different approach. Visions of cauldrons obviously flash through their minds and comments about placebos means they know nothing of the basis of this form of treatment. Remarks like 'of course, you have to believe in it for it to work' are nonsense. Animals do not know what or why we give them their 'sweeties' so there is no 'having to believe' for it to work for them. Similar comments are made about other alternative medicine such as chiropractors.

The body is a healer and the method of homoeopathy is to give a small dose of a particular substance which stimulates the body's natural responses of recovery. If for instance you cut yourself then your body will react to heal the wound, what homoeopathy will do is to prompt the body to react more quickly.

What is homoeopathy? The word is derived from the Greek word *homoios* which means *like*. Homoeopathy means treating *like with like*. Dr. Samuel Hahnemann a 17th century physician was responsible for the present day method of homoeopathy even though the use of vegetable, mineral and animal substances had been known since the time of Hippocrates, the Greek founder of medicine around the time 450 B.C. It was Hahnemann who discovered that if you were to give a substance it created the symptoms of a disease. In his initial trials this was with conchina bark. When this was given to patients suffering from malaria they would be cured. He discovered that the more the substance was diluted the more effective it became.

Homoeopathic remedies are available over the counter at the present moment so no prescription is required. They are safe to use, and have no adverse effects even if a child was to eat the whole bottlefull. Apart from the tablets there are mother tinctures and creams. The tablets are easy to take and pleasant tasting being a small white sucrose based tablet. When treating oneself you take the recommended number of tablets at certain intervals. Contrary to the instructions that are given with modern medicines, whereby you should complete the course, if you do forget to take a tablet then you are probably better. Very often with homoeopathy a small number of doses are best and then wait a while to see what results. In the case of Sulphur, which can be used as a very effective remedy for skin problems, a three day course will probably be sufficient but the result may not become apparent for a further few days, after which a single dose will be sufficient if necessary.

There are many books written on the subject and I have an intriguing selection covering both humans and animals which are based on the same principle and all use the same remedies. You can therefore have a joint medicine box of remedies which will be suitable for both humans and dogs. I read all of these books when I am trying to find the right remedy for a particular complaint and through that usually arrive at some sort of conclusion. However for the purpose of every day application I shall try to keep things relatively simple.

There are varying degrees of strengths available and for use in dogs a potency of 6c or 30c is adequate for our needs. 30c is more dilute than 6c but could in some cases be more effective. As many of the substances that are used are poisonous it does seem strange that they can be effective but given in these very dilute doses they become totally harmless in relation to their original form. The gratifying thing about the whole use of the method is that whatever you take, or how much you take, it cannot do you any harm. The side effects are nil and in the main can be given alongside conventional medicines without interfering with their function. Although I am a great advocate of the whole aspect of homoepathy, and use it frequently, I still appreciate that there are many instances where modern medicines must play their part.

One can build up a number of remedies to have in stock, none of which should deteriorate if kept in the right conditions.

* Keep in a cool dark place *away from strong smells*
* Do not handle the tablets
* Use the lid to select the tablet from the bottle

The whole nature of the substances are such that they should not come in contact with powerful aromas or food as this will render them useless. It is for this reason that when administering a dose it should be given *away* from food and strong flavours. When receiving brief instructions from the pharmacist you will be told to avoid food for up to half an hour before or after a dose. This confuses many people as it is contrary to the usual instructions given with conventional medicines when one is sometimes categorically told to take the dose with food or drink.

The reason for having a clean palate is not just that you do not want to destroy the potency of the remedy but the substance is absorbed quickly into the system through the sensitive membranes of the mouth, hence the reason for the recommendations that the tablet should be chewed or sucked. In the case of dogs this is quite easy as they like the sweet taste of the sucrose base and will accept them readily and chew them, obviously thinking that it is a treat.

If, however, they will not accept it the best method is to crush the tablet between two spoons and place the powder onto the tongue. This is the best way to administer when the dog is recovering from an anaesthetic as it allows immediate treatment when it is most needed. Very often the results can be seen quickly, as in the case of shock, which includes the effects of anaesthesia.

Homoeopathy is a complex subject and one can certainly obtain good results. However, if you are at any time in doubt seek the advice of a qualified homoeopathic veterinary surgeon.

In the event of an emergency do not hesitate to go to your veterinary surgeon, whether homoeopathic or not.

There are certain basic remedies which I suggest everyone should have to hand and are easily obtained. A potency of 6c is recommended for home use and are more readily available.

Dosage:
In the case of acute conditions more frequent doses may be required, one dose hourly for three to four hours. In less severe cases one dose two to three times daily. In severe, chronic conditions one dose twice daily then once per week.

Mother Tinctures

These are useful for external applications such as eye drops and the bathing of wounds. Dilute one drop of mother tincture to one tablespoonful of cooled boiled water. Never use mother tinctures in their undiluted form.

Euphrasia Eye Drops - See under Euphrasia.

Hypercal - (Hypericum and Calendula) obtainable in cream or lotion or mother tincture. For the treatment of wounds, burns.

Tablets

Aconite - (Aconitum Napellus or Monkshood).
In cases of shock such as accidents, fights or recovery from anaesthesia. Dose immediately, prior to giving Arnica.

Apis. Mel - (Apis Mellifica - The Honey-bee).
For stings and insect bites. Inflammation of the eyes such as conjunctivitis. Incontinence and cystitis. Arthritis.

Arnica - (Arnica Montana - Leopard's Bane).
One of the most useful remedies, it is 'the healer'. Essential after any accident, injury, strain or surgery. Reduces bruising, helps recovery after whelping. For stiffness after over-exercise. Arthritis. Dose immediately and frequently.
In tablet form, lotion or cream. With dogs the lotion is easier to apply to the affected area. Apply frequently.

Arsen Alb - (Arsenicum album - Arsenic trioxide).
For any upset with diarrhoea, sickness, loss of appetite. Eczema and dandruff conditions. Restlessness.

Bryonia - (Wild Hops).
For arthritis and rheumatism which is worse for moving. Respiratory conditions such as coughs. Kennel cough. Nose bleeds. Helps reduce inflammation of the mammary glands caused by a build-up of milk two to three days after whelping.

Carbo Veg - (Carbo Animalis - Vegetable charcoal).
Flatulence, passing of wind. Collapse. Give one dose one hour before a meal if there is a tendency to flatulence.

Caulophyllum - (Blue Cohosh or Squaw root).
The root was chewed by the Indians when they went into labour. I have proved this to be a most effective remedy for any bitch in whelp or at the time of whelping. It will stimulate the uterus and help the birth process. Where inertia is apparent this can often start things along. A single dose per day from five weeks will ensure a toned uterus. Give a single dose at the onset of labour.

Euphrasia - (Euphrasia officinalis - Eyebright).
To use as an eye wash dilute one drop of mother tincture to one tablespoonful of cooled boiled water. Ideal to flush out congested eyes. Soothes tired eyes and stimulates all eye structures.
Use tables 6c or 30c in conjunction with the lotion. Particularly effective for allergies such as hay fever.

Hammamelis - (Witch Hazel).
A well-known lotion known to most as helping to reduce bruising. Use as a lotion or in tablet form, 6c or 30c.

Hypericum
Helps reduce pain. Post operative. Bites.

Merc Sol - (Mercurius Solubilus - Quicksilver).
For sore gums and mouths, bad breath. Sore throat. Acute and chronic kidney problems. Wet eczema.

Nux Vom - (Stychnos nux vomica - Poison nut).
Chronic forms of colic, constipation, flatulance, bad breath, loss of appetite, hiccups, hepatitis and jaundice.

Pulsatilla - (Pulsatilla nigricans - Meadow anemone, pasque flower or windflower).
False pregnancy, agalactia (shortage of milk) in the bitch. Given at whelping time can help the birth. Incontinence, liver complaints. Threatened pyometra.
At the start of parturition give every thirty to forty minutes throughout the birth.

Rhus Tox - (Rhus toxicondendron - Poison Ivy or Poison Oak).
Arthritis, rheumatism and muscular disorders. Sprains and strains. Skin conditions, chronic eczema.

Sulphur - (Sulphur sublimatum - Flowers of Sulphur).
One of the oldest remedies and excellent for skin conditions. Eczema, dermatitis, dandruff, mange, conjunctivitis, chronic diarrhoea, fever, incontinence, rheumatism.
Sulphur produces the best results when used sparingly. Give one tablet twice daily for two to five days then wait for a week to see any results.

Symphytum - (Symphytum officinale - common comfrey - 'Boneset').
Give after the treatment of any fracture. One tablet three times daily for ten to fourteen days.

Urtica - (Urtica Urens - The small stinging nettle).
For urticaria (nettle rash) and other allergies affecting the skin. Agalactia (lack of milk).

The Nosodes
The nosodes are used as a vaccine and are available for any of the diseases, Distemper, Hepatitis, Leptospirosis and Parvovirus and can be obtained as a combination or separately. Kennel Cough comes separately. Nosodes can also be made up to treat allergies. Nosodes of Mixed grasses,

pollens, horse dander and house dust are regularly used and available. Anything can be made up specially if the ground around one's house becomes 'dog-sick', a nosode can be made up from a sample from the soil.

Nosodes can be made up from bacterias such as Staphylococcus, Streptococcus and E.coli and can be used for the treatment of skin infections or neonatal septicaemia.

Chiropractic

The Chiropractic method can be applied to dogs in the same way that it is applied to humans. I have had personal experience for myself as well as with dogs and horses, hence my recommendation. The following is a brief explanation.

What is Chiropractic?

Chiropractic is a method of maintaining and restoring health by means of manipulation or adjustment of the bones of the spinal column and other joints of the body.

Since the whole of the body is controlled by the nervous system and most of the body's nerve supply passes through the spine, it follows that if the spine is maintained in its proper alignment, nerve impulses travel freely and without interference. When there is interference with, or impingement on, the nerves with subsequent nervous dysfunction, the body loses its ability to regenerate, with resultant disease. When there is no interference, natural self healing maintains health.

This is the philosophy on which Chiropractic is based: no cell or organ of the body can function properly without its correct supply of nerve impulses. The body's chemical processes can also be altered by a change in the functioning of the nervous system. So Chiropractic manipulation is a valuable healing technique for all conditions and is as important in a general preventative role as it is in treating specific conditions.

Who started Chiropractic?

Manipulative techniques have been used throughout the history of man, but it was Daniel D. Palmer of Davenport, USA who, in 1895, first used the word chiropractic to mean manipulation by hand.

What does a Chiropractor do?

Chiropractic means 'done by hand', being derived from the Greek words *cheir* meaning hand and *praktikos* meaning 'done by'.

A Chiropractor uses his hands to analyse the spinal column and other joints of the body for subluxations (slight displacements). Some Chiropractors also use X-rays to assist in their analysis.

A Chiropractor is trained to use his finger tips in a particularly sensitive way so as to perceive the most subtle misalignments. He will then manipulate the bones accordingly.

What is the difference between Chiropractic and Osteopathy?

An osteopath mostly treats the affected bones indirectly, by twisting the body, whereas a Chiropractor treats individual bones separately with specific thrusts applied directly to the misaligned bone.

How do subluxations arise?

Subluxations arise from strains, stresses and accidents, however trivial. Symptoms may take years to develop and Chiropractors believe that much ill health in adults may originate from accidents in early life.

What does the treatment do?

Having carefully analysed the misalignment the Chiropractor applies a specific thrust to the subluxated bone (this is called an adjustment) assisting the displaced bones to return to their correct position and thereby allowing the process of healing to commence. It is important to understand that healing is a process not an event, therefore healing can take time! Some only need one treatment depending on the length of time between injury and treatment.

The McTimoney Chiropractic whole Body Technique

The McTimoney technique is a particularly effective and comfortable treatment. It obtains its results by examination of the whole spine and other joints of the body at every consultation, adjusting those parts that need attention each time.

Examinations and adjustments are carried out entirely with the hands. McTimoney Chiropractors are trained to use their fingertips in a particular way. Having detected any misalignment the Chiropractor will manipulate with a very precise, deft and very quick movement resulting in the minimum amount of discomfort.

When can it help?

In humans great benefit can be derived from the treatment when there is pain in the back or major joints. Others seek help for migraine, headaches, neuralgia and finger numbness, sports injuries or arthritis.

Animals can suffer with back problems in the same way as humans. Lameness is a classic example.

From my own personal experience many an animal has been relieved of pain and restored to soundness after treatment from a Chiropractor. The first time I was in contact with a Chiropractor was when my sister's successful working hunter pony went lame. His near hind leg became wasted after months of inactivity. Every possible horse vet had seen him and were unable to help. The final verdict was to have him destroyed. Somebody suggested that he should be seen by Ronnie Longford who is a Chiropractor working mainly with horses. His diagnosis was immediate and after manipulation of his pelvis and a few other adjustments the pony was sound. That pony lived for another twenty years, working regularly until a couple of months before he died. He was probably suffering from sciatica, a trapped nerve, causing pain in the hip and down the leg when he tried to put his foot to the floor.

When it was obvious that there was something wrong with one of my own dogs, the vet, who was slightly baffled, thought that he had had a stroke. After a few days, when he was clearly in pain I thought of Ronnie Longford. The diagnosis was the same as the pony. After one treatment he became sound.

When the owner of a ten month old puppy phoned me to say that a vet said that her lame dog had probably got hip dysplasia. I put her in touch with the Chiropractor. After one treatment the dog became sound. It was not hip displasia but a trapped nerve causing him to favour one leg.

Chiropractors will work in conjunction with Doctors and Veterinary surgeons. Professional etiquette requires you to inform your veterinary surgeon that you are taking the patient to see a Chiropractor. With humans there is no need for there to be a referral by the doctor.

A directory of McTimoney Chiropractors can be obtained from The Institute of Pure Chiropractic. PO Box 127, Oxford, OX2 8RH. This will cover both humans and animals.

Useful Addresses

The Kennel Club
1 Clarges Street, Piccadilly, London W1Y 8AB
Telephone 071 493 6651.

English Shetland Sheepdog Club
Mr R. D. Thornley,
Pie Hatch, Brettenham Road, Buxhall, Stowmarket, Suffolk IP14 3DZ
Telephone 0449 737729.

English Shetland Sheepdog Club (Obedience).
Mrs C. Graham, Timber Gates, Westbeams Road, Sway, Nr Lymington, Hants.
Telephone 0590 683246.

Mid-Western Shetland Sheepdog Club.
Mrs M. M. Dobson, Tavistock, Clifton Village, Nr Preston, Lancs PR4 0ZA.
Telephone 0772 683505.

Northern Counties Shetland Sheepdog Club.
Miss M. G. Gatheral, Sockburn Hall, Neasham, Darlington, Co. Durham DL2 1PH.
Telephone 060 981 293.

Scottish Shetland Sheepdog Club.
Mrs M. Anderson, Vaila, Ayr Road, Irvine, Ayrshire.
Telephone 0294 311447.

Shetland Sheepdog Club of Wales.
Mrs V. Dyer, Waterend Cottage, Hayes End, Longney, Nr Gloucester GL2 6SW.
Telephone 0452 720594.

Shetland Sheepdog Club of Northern Ireland.
Mrs I. McGucken, 20 Station Road, Carnalea, Bangor, Co. Down.
Telephone 0247 452678.

Shetland Sheepdog Club of North Wales.
Mr B. Kenny, 4 Higher Road, Harmer Hill, Nr Shrewsbury, Shropshire SY4 3EQ.
Telephone 0939 290082.

Yorkshire Shetland Sheepdog Club.
Mrs B. Butler, 8 Drake Close, Burncross, Sheffield S30 4TB.
Telephone 0742 462291.

Pro-Dogs.
4 New Road, Ditton, Maidstone, Kent ME20 6AD.

Dog Training Weekly.
Penrhiw Cilau, Letterston, Haverfordwest, Dyfed SA62 5XB.

Agility Voice.
Keba Cottage, 100 Bedford Road, Barton-le-Clay, Beds MK45 4LR.

Bell and Croydon (Belcroy feeder).
50 Wigmore Street, London W1.

General Index

Affix 115, 144
Agility 181, 192-193
    marks 196
    mini 192, 196
    obstacles 194-195
Agility Voice 193, 222
Appearance 57, 70
Barking 58, 88, 89
Bathing 112-113
BB Line 7, 8, 16-31
Bed 81, 82-83, 87, 113, 139
Bedding 83, 113, 134, 139
Belcroy Feeder 137, 222
Bitch 77, 119-123
Boarding 89, 91, 203, 212
Body 65-66
Breed Record Holders 11, 21, 25, 28, 33, 42
Breed Record Supplement 208
Breeding 78, 115-126
    colour 116-117
    terms 45, 47, 78
Buying, adult 88
    puppy 77-80
Cage 87, 163, 164
Car Training 86-87, 151
Cars 87, 89, 90-91, 164
Charts 10, 15, 16, 18, 31, 33, 35, 36, 45, 118
CHE Line 16, 31-36
Chiropractic 219-221
Coat 57, 63, 66, 70-71, 80, 97-114, 142
Coat dressing 99, 102, 104
Collar, leather 85, 89, 90, 151, 163, 164
Collie Eye Anomaly 31, 36, 80, 115, 124, 147, 151, 205-210, 211
Colour 71-74, 78, 79, 80

Conformation 10, 64, 168
Crufts 158, 159, 181, 192, 198
Cryptorchid 212-213
Cystitis 84
Dew claws 111, 134, 136
Diarrhoea 85, 200-201
Diet 81-82, 85, 92-93, 128, 200
Diet Sheet 81, 143
Dog Training Weekly 193, 222
Dog World 157
Ears 22, 24, 62-63
    difficult 154-156
    grooming 106
    trimming 100, 109-110
Eclampsia 134, 138
Eczema 97, 202
English Shetland Sheepdog Club 5, 6, 10, 15, 18, 50, 52, 53, 118, 181, 208, 222
Exercise 86, 89, 93, 123, 127, 151, 153-154, 164, 211-212
Expression 22, 58, 59, 62, 63, 74, 146, 166
Eyes 62 (see Collie Eye Anomaly)
Families 15-16, 37-48, 118
Faults 49, 56, 75
Feeding, adults 92-96
    in whelp 128
    lactation 136, 142
    puppies 80, 81-82, 139-141, 143-144, 154
    veteran 93
Feet 67-68
Fleas 97, 123, 204-205
Flyball 181, 198
Forequarters 63-65
Foundation bitch 12, 35, 39, 42, 43, 44, 45, 115, 116

Front 63-65
Gait 68-70
Garden 19, 77, 85, 89, 90, 143
Genetically clear 31, 36, 124, 207, 210
Genetics, C.E.A. 210
Gestation 127
Grooming 89, 97-114, 165
    bathing 112-113
    brushing 103-105
    combing 105-106
    equipment 97-101, 163
    moulting 102-103
    puppy 101-102
    routine 97
    teeth 114
    trimming 107-111
Hand Rearing 137
Handbooks 10, 15, 36, 52
Head and Skull 58-60
Health 79-80, 200-221
Heat Lamp 131, 135
Hindquarters 66-67
Hip Dysplasia 192, 211-212
Homoeopathy 121, 129-130, 134, 136, 137, 141-142, 201, 202, 214-219,
House Training 84, 85, 139, 148
In-breeding 8, 25, 117-118
Insurance 91, 199
Judging   49, 67, 75, 168-180, 213
    K.C. guide 171-176
    procedure 177-179
    report 49, 64, 180
Junior Warrant 158-159
Kennel Club 5, 6, 7, 13, 53, 56, 57, 77, 81, 99, 144, 157, 158, 159, 160, 161, 163, 181, 193, 208, 211, 222
Kennel Cough 201-202, 203
Kennel Gazette 5, 6, 157, 208
Labour 132-133
Lead Training 85-86
Lice 204-205
Line breeding 25, 29, 31, 116, 118

Lines 15-36, 118
Markings 73-74
Mastitis 136-137
Mating   125-126
    timing 120, 122-123
Measuring 152
Metritis 121, 202
Mid-Western Shetland Sheepdog Club 222
Mismark 74, 117
Monorchid 212-213
Mouth 60-61
Movement 68-70
Nail Clippers 101, 111, 136
Neck 63
Neutering 78, 121-122, 213
Northern Counties Shetland Sheepdog Club 53, 222
Obedience 143, 181-183
    Agility & Working Trials 181, 222
    equipment 184
    exercises 185-192
Obesity 92, 93, 121, 122
Oestrus cycle 120
Origins 1
Our Dogs 157
Outcross 31, 118
Parvovirus 201, 203
Pat-Dogs 181, 199
Pedigrees 10, 15-48, 77, 81, 115, 116, 122, 124, 143
Pooper Scoopers 90
Pregnancy 127-131
    diagnosis 130
    phantom 120-121
    resorption 121, 130-131
Pro-Dogs 199, 222
Progressive Retinal Atrophy 205, 211
Protein 93, 128, 137
Puppy Pen 82, 85, 129, 131, 139
Puppy,   buying 77-80
    development 149-150
    diet sheet 143-144

Puppy, exercise 153-154
  feeding 81-82, 139-141
  grooming 101-102
  house training 84-85
  new 81-87
  picking 145-148
  rearing 134-144
  rest 81, 82, 151
  running on 148-156
  selling 142-143
  size 151-152
  weaning 139-141, 143-144
Pyometra 121, 202

Rearing puppies 134-144
Registration Certificate 81
Registrations 10, 11, 13
Responsibility 78, 89-91
Ring Training 151, 161-162, 165, 168
Rough Collie 1, 7, 8, 9, 49, 50, 56, 57, 58, 74

Scissors 71, 100, 107, 110
Scottish Shetland Collie Club 5
Scottish Shetland Sheepdog Club 50, 53, 222
Season 78, 85, 115, 119-120, 121, 122, 123, 125, 156
Shetland Collie 3, 5, 7
Shetland Collie Club 5
Shetland Islands 1-6
Shetland Sheepdog Club 49, 50
Shetland Sheepdog Club of North Wales 222
Shetland Sheepdog Club of Northern Ireland 222
Shetland Sheepdog Club of Wales 222
Show Puppy 145-156
Showing 157-167
  arrival 164-165
  entering 160-161
  in the ring 165-167
  preparations 163-164
  training 161-162
Shows 7, 10
  awards 159-160, 171, 175

Shows, classes 161, 182
  types 157-158
Size 3, 4, 5, 7, 8, 49, 50, 52, 74-75, 79, 80, 116, 118, 124, 146, 151-152, 192, 196-197
Spaying 121-122
Standard 7, 49-75, 171, 173
Standard, explanation 57-75
Standard, interpretation 49
Stewarding 168, 169
Stewarding, K.C. guide 169-171
Stools 82, 92, 93
Stud Book 5, 158, 159
Stud Dog 15, 116, 122, 123, 124-126, 147, 209
Supplementary Feeding 137
Supplements 94-96, 129

Talc and chalk, 99-100, 154-156
Teeth 60-61, 93, 114, 147, 151, 153
Teething 61, 83, 152-153, 154
Temperament 4, 58, 77, 78, 79, 116, 124, 148
Temperature 132, 135-136
Testicles 75, 212-213
Training 181-199
Training of Judges Schemes 168
Travel Sickness 86, 87
Trimming 71, 107-111
  nails 111
Type 9, 49, 58, 77, 79, 118, 124, 171

Vaccination 80, 81, 89, 141-142, 151, 201, 203
Vet. 134, 200-204, 216
Vetbed 83, 134, 137, 139
Vitamins and Minerals 93-96, 129, 201

Water 81, 82, 128, 163, 201
Weaning 139-141
Whelping 131-134
  box 129, 131, 132, 139
  equipment 131
  Vet. 134
Working Trials 181, 196-198
Worming 80, 89, 141, 151, 204
Yorkshire Shetland Sheepdog Club 222